T0345731

JAKUB DRÁPAL

DEFENDING NAZIS IN POSTWAR CZECHOSLOVAKIA

THE LIFE OF K. RESLER,
DEFENCE COUNSEL
EX OFFICIO OF K. H. FRANK

TRANSLATED BY ANNA BARTON

KAROLINUM PRESS
PRAGUE 2017

KAROLINUM PRESS
Karolinum Press is a publishing department of Charles University
Ovocný trh 560/5, 116 36 Prague 1, Czech Republic
www.karolinum.cz
© Karolinum Press, 2017
© Jakub Drápal, 2017
© This English edition is a revised version of *Poslušen zákonů své země a svého stavu* (Auditorium, Prague 2014), translated from the Czech by Anna Barton.
Photography © Archival fonds of Prague City Archives; National Museum; and Václav Trojan and Eliška Trojanová (heirs)
Layout by Jan Šerých
Set and printed in the Czech Republic by Karolinum Press
First English edition

A catalogue record for this book is available from the National Library of the Czech Republic.

This book is published with the support of Foundation Hugo Grotius, Law firm VKS Legal and Czech Bar Association. The publication of this book was also supported by the Ministry of Education, Youth and Sports – Institutional Support for Longterm Development of Research Organizations – Charles University, Faculty of Law, PROGRES Q05.

ISBN 978-80-246-3730-3
ISBN 978-80-246-3731-0 (pdf)

CONTENTS

ACKNOWLEDGEMENTS

In Spring 2012 I asked Prof. Jan Kuklík, professor of legal history and dean of the Law Faculty at Charles University, to give a short talk about post-war society before a screening of the film *Ex offo*. He kindly agreed, and was delighted with my interest in Kamill Resler.

The matter didn't end there – subsequent discussions with him led me to decide to write this book, and Prof. Kuklík was extremely supportive in helping me to access the archive materials relevant for my research, discussing the book with me, and providing me with some materials he had in his collections that related to the K. H. Frank trial. There is little a student could want more than that his teacher welcome his ideas, support him in them, discuss them with him, and eventually help him to bring them to the wider world. My heartfelt thanks therefore go to Prof. Kuklík. Without him, this book might never have been possible; certainly, it would not have taken shape so soon.

Many thanks are also due to the VKŠ law firm, in particular to Dr. Buzková and Dr. Tyll, to the Hugo Grotius Foundation and to the Czech Bar Association and its president JUDr. Martin Vychopeň, whose generosity enabled this book to be translated into English. Annie Barton translated it splendidly and the publisher Karolínum helped me to further improve its structure.

I wish to extend my thanks, too, to my Czech language and literature teacher at secondary school, Eva Podzimková, for having awoken my interest in literature and history, over the five years that she taught me, together with a desire to interpret literary texts and apply literary characters' experiences to real-life situations. If she had studied law, I believe that with her enthusiasm for work, literature and ethics she could well have resembled a modern-day Kamill Resler. Instead, as a teacher she has succeeded in inspiring hundreds and thousands of students to pursue their projects, of which this book is one.

While working for barrister Pavel Čižinský for eighteen months I learned what great things a barrister can achieve, and that even today there are barristers who dedicate themselves to pursuing justice even when that means defying public opinion and the national authorities. Interesting though it was to observe Čižinský defend a murderer, what really caught my attention were the small, everyday cases at which he defended foreigners, often enabling them to stay in the country and giving them – sometimes for the first time in their life – an understanding of what justice is. This book is therefore dedicated to Pavel.

I am grateful to the staff of the Literary Archive at the Museum of Czech Literature, The Prague City Archives, the Archives of the National Museum and of the National Museum Library, the Archive of Charles University, the East Bohemian Museum in Pardubice, the Central Military Archive and the Archives of the Czech Bar Association, for their exceptional willingness to assist me. Furthermore, my thanks go to Pavel Muchka, who wrote a bachelors dissertation on Kamill Resler, for his kind help.

Last but not least I am grateful to my parents, who encouraged me to write this book, and in particular my mother, who read and commented on my manuscript at many stages.

Jakub Drápal

PREFACE

It is a great pleasure indeed to contribute this foreword to the English edition of "Poslušen zákonů své země a svého stavu: Kamill Resler – obhájce K. H. Franka", a book written by one of our faculty's promising graduates, Jakub Drápal, that looks at the life and work of the eminent Czech defence lawyer Kamill Resler.

I would like to make use of this foreword to introduce new readers to this book that they have just opened, in a few words. The first thing worth noting is how it came into existence. It is certainly not a common occurrence that a master's student should write such a highly acclaimed book that the university publishing house decides not only to publish it in the Czech original, but subsequently also to publish it in English translation. I am delighted that this has happened to a student of the law faculty and I am pleased to have been able to contribute to the book's progress and watch it take shape right from the beginning. I first met Jakub to discuss his academic writing essays and our paths crossed again at a screening of the film *Ex Offo*, which brought Kamill Resler's story to the screen back in 1998. Jakub impressed me not only with his stylish writing, but in particular with his desire to see K. H. Frank's defence counsel in a broader context and on several levels. Resler's life interested him sufficiently that he was willing to give up most of his free time to undertake detailed research using the relevant literature and archival materials. The results of this research were turned first into his dissertation and subsequently into a stand-alone book – the first complete book-length biography of Resler, which was not only favourably reviewed in the legal press, but was also praised by the Rector of Charles University as one of the best academic monographs written by researchers from Charles University in year 2014.

The second thing to note concerns the chosen topic and the character of Kamill Resler in particular. He is not particularly well known in Czech circles, and very little known in the wider world. When he is mentioned, it is usually as defence counsel to K. H. Frank in his trial before the Extraordinary People's Court in spring 1946: part of the so-called post-war retributional trials, which took place at a time when overblown nationalist passions were still rife. Resler was a well-respected Prague barrister with high moral credit, who had been involved in the home resistance movement during the Second

World War. He became an enemy to the Czech State literally overnight when he became (not through his own decision but as an ex officio allocated defence counsel) the legal representative to K. H. Frank, "executioner of the Czech nation," the man responsible for the Lidice extermination and a symbol of the break-up of the Czechoslovak state in 1938 and its occupation during the Second World War. Jakub Drápal also takes this powerful motif as the starting point for his book, but he is not only interested in the historical context of the war crime trials, but also in the right of any defendant to a fair trial, and the principle of a thorough defence even in cases when the public is convinced of the defendant's guilt and extends its negative attitude to the defendant's legal representative. Similarly, Jakub Drápal looks at barristers' professional ethics, examining how Resler carried out the defence as his professional honour dictated, even in the case of a war criminal, and how this paradoxically led to him being hated by his fellow citizens, damaged his reputation forever, lost him several friends and even caused problems within his own family. Resler himself put it thus: "A barrister must forget his own feelings and attitudes, give up his own character and, however hard it might be, carry out his duty thoroughly." All this is, moreover, intensified by the fact that K. H. Frank and Kamill Resler stood on opposite sides during the war, and, had his anti-German activities been revealed, Resler could well have been arrested and tried for them and thus the two men's roles would have been reversed. What is more, Resler's engagement in the post-war retribution was by no means over with K. H. Frank; as a barrister he was involved in several other no less sensitive cases involving political collaboration that were heard before the National Court.

Although these post-war retributional cases are no doubt among the most interesting for the reader, Jakub Drápal looks beyond these at the other aspects of Resler's life and work. Resler is, after all, connected with the eventful fate of the independent Czechoslovak state in the first half of the twentieth century. He was active at the time of its establishment and as a leading lawyer became involved in the legal, political and artistic life in Prague. He represented both left-wing intellectuals and, in 1935, German banker Kiesewetter, who was accused under the law on the protection of the Republic of plots against the Republic (i.e. treason) and acquitted thanks to Resler's excellent defence. As you will read later in this book, Resler was already called a traitor to the Czech nation as a result of this trial, and it eventually led to him ending his long-term involvement in the Czech national sporting association Sokol.

Personally, I think that Resler's attempt to prevent the anti-Jewish measures from being implemented at the Czech bar shows his great determination, and is nowadays rather forgotten. The Munich agreement of 1938, which not only led to the forced cession of the borderlands and their minority German population to Germany but also put an end to the liberal parliamentary democracy of the inter-war period, affected Resler deeply; this is evident, too, from the fact that he put together a book of poems related to Munich (which was published only after the war). The undemocratic post-Munich regime known as the Second Czechoslovak Republic was marked by a growing wave of antisemitism and anti-Jewish measures, introduced following the German example but well before the Nazi occupation began. It was at this time that the Bohemian Bar Association, together with the Medical Chamber, took it upon themselves to prevent Jews from practising their professions, and it was none other than Kamill Resler who stood up against this oppression and defended his Jewish colleagues. He even proposed openly suing the group of so-called Aryan barristers for their anti-Jewish attacks, and pursued this even after 15th March 1939, when the Germans made what remained of Czechoslovakia into the Protectorate of Bohemia and Moravia. Under the Protectorate, Resler continued to represent a number of Jewish clients and besides his resistance activities fearlessly took on the defence of more than 60 Czech patriots who had been sentenced to death by German courts, including courts established under martial law.

Resler's strength of character is further demonstrated by the fact that, after the Communist Party of Czechoslovakia came to power in February 1948, he did not hesitate in suing two editors of the party's newspaper *Rudé právo* and successfully demanding his name be cleared of the defamation published in their articles.

Kamill Resler was an interesting character for many other reasons, too: he wrote poetry, had his own private publishing house, and collected books. This book, then, is one that you should not miss if you are interested in twentieth century central European history or legal history. Even small countries in central Europe have their great heroes, albeit underappreciated and rather forgotten ones.

Jan Kuklík

FOREWORD

A hunched figure, sitting smoking a cigarette in a dim room, pondering impending difficulties; yet someone of immense inner strength and courage. Those were my first impressions of Kamill Resler – as portrayed in the excellent film *Ex offo* produced by Czech Television.

After seeing the film, I immediately wanted to know more about Resler, and so I read Ladislav Tunys' fine book *K. H. Frank – Noc před popravou* (K. H. Frank – the Night before the Execution), part of which describes Resler's character. From the references in the book it was evident to me that there must be more material on Resler than had so far been processed. And so it was that I decided to go to the archives and research Resler's life academically, in greater detail.

Studying Resler's legacy led me into the lesser known aspects of his life, and many of the documents I found positively surprised and even touched me – in particular the final letters Resler received from those condemned to death during the Second World War and passed on to their families, and his descriptions of some of the circumstances of his relations with K. H. Frank. It gradually became clear to me that Kamill Resler was not only an extremely active and able man, but also very modest. He did not boast about his successes, and never expected recognition for them. In some cases he received the recognition he deserved only after his death.

Every profession, in any era, needs people who serve it as examples, perhaps even heroes, even though they are not perfect; it is constantly on the lookout for such figures, and consciously or subconsciously appreciates them. Kamill Resler could serve many as an example to the legal profession, in the way he understood justice and worked to achieve it, in the meaning that the barrister's profession had for him, and in the fact that he was able to find happiness elsewhere once he ceased practice in the profession.

Before I begin to describe Resler's life in detail, I would like to warn my readers of one thing: Resler once mentioned that as a barrister he always stood on the defendant's side, whether he liked it or not. In the course of writing about a defence lawyer whom I consider a role model and perhaps even a hero, I naturally tend to see things from the defence side more than that of the prosecution, however hard I attempt to give a neutral and objective account of the facts. I trust that my readers will forgive me, therefore, if I have inadvertently not remained entirely unbiased in my account.

Jakub Drápal
Prague, 12 November 2016

INTRODUCTION:
THE FINAL HOURS BEFORE THE EXECUTION[1]

Just three hours passed between the pronouncement of the verdict and the execution itself. Karl Hermann Frank, the highest ranking Nazi in the Protectorate of Bohemia and Moravia during the Second World War, spent almost all of that time with lawyer Kamill Resler and his assistant Drahoslav Kroupa.[2]

It was 1946 and the Czechoslovak retributional courts had just passed sentence in their most important case. They had judged a man who was hated by all the Czechs – including the judges, the prosecution and even his own defence lawyer. Despite that, the trial was carried out fairly and the quality of the defence was particularly remarkable. Despite his distaste at having to defend Frank, defence lawyer Kamill Resler managed to bring himself to provide his client with both legal and personal support, in particular during Frank's final hours.

Once the full sentence had been pronounced, Frank was taken to the photographer and Resler then went to meet him in his cell. He took up the guardian role that he had to play for the following three hours even before he had reached the cell: a group of women accosted him and asked him to find out some details from Frank about a certain case. He promised them that he would pass their request on to Frank, adding that he did not want to bother him in the final hours of his life.

Frank was taken to cell A I 52 at Pankrác prison in Prague, where Czechs had awaited execution during the war – which was right opposite the "Pankrác Guillotinery." Female prisoners walked along the corridors around the cell, as it was in the women's section of the prison. Everyone who passed by

---

1   This section is based on the following sources: AHMP 15, Drahoslav Kroupa. "Poslední chvíle K. H. Franka" [Kroupa's account of Frank's last hours](for abbreviations used to refer to archival sources please see page); AHMP 15, Doslovný přepis rukopisného záznamu JUDr. Kamilla Reslera o poznatcích, diskuzích a pocitech při posledním setkání s K. H. F. [Resler's handwritten records of his last meeting with Frank]; AHMP 16 and KNM 3, NM 214/168, Lecture *Zaniknutí K. H. Franka* [On the demise of K. H. Frank]; Kroupa Drahoslav. *Poslední dny a chvíle K. H. Franka* [K. H. Frank's last days and final moments], *Almanach VIII. B, maturitního ročníku 1942 Reálného gymnázia v Třebíči* [Class VIII B final year almanach, 1942, Reálné gymnazium in Třebíč], 1997.

2   Kroupa wrote a record of events in the cell. Later, Resler also wrote an account of this time for his own personal records, and described his feelings while waiting for the execution in his lecture *Zaniknutí K. H. Franka* [The demise of K. H. Frank] (hereafter "Demise").

In the cell where Frank waited to be taken to court each day. (AHMP)

looked into the cell out of curiosity. Resler was not sure how best to start the conversation – he offered Frank and his prison officers cigarettes, and they smoked. "I thought about how to make the dismal wait through the three final hours of his life easier both for Frank and for me," he recalled later. The only interruption they could expect was a response to the mercy plea – Resler did not have the slightest hope that mercy would be granted, although he did expect the negative decision to be delivered.

He realised that he must move on to another topic, both for Frank's sanity and for his own, and so he cautiously mentioned the request the women had made outside the prison. Frank jumped at this with delight, as it enabled him to think of other things, and wrote down several lines about the case as a statement for the court.

A prison officer came to ask whether Frank had any final wishes, and Resler translated this to him as a question about whether he would like anything to eat or drink, attempting to put it to Frank in a way that avoided directly mentioning the execution. At first, Frank replied that he did not want anything, but on Resler's insistence he accepted some bread with butter and salami, although only after checking that he would not throw up the food when he was executed. In the end Resler also persuaded him to ask for eggs with salami – but he did not eat the sardines that Resler had requested in addition. To top it off, he ordered a cognac.

Frank decided to write down a few final wishes, but Resler talked him into writing down a complete legally binding will instead. In his will, Frank remembered his wife and children, to whom he left his ideals, and concluded with thoughts about Germany. He read out some of his wording to Resler, who commented on it. Some time later, after his pen had got stuck several times, Resler's assistant Kroupa lent him his own pen – he later kept that pen in Frank's memory. As there were only seats in the cell for Frank and Resler, Kroupa was sat on the closed toilet.

While Frank was writing his will the priest Monsignor Tylínek arrived, whom Resler had previously met before another post-war execution. As before, even in his approach to the priest, Frank's wish not to offend anyone was evident. Although he did not want to speak to him, he wanted to thank him for having stopped by, and after a short conversation wished him a good day. He ended with the words: "I believe in 'god'. (...) I want to die in the spirit of the German legend."

After the priest had left, Frank finished writing his will. Suddenly, he paused and asked: "I hope it works – the thing, (...) the hanging, (...) without an ordeal." Resler nodded in agreement, convincingly and knowledgeably: "Even for a thick-skinned lawyer it is sometimes strangely emotionally difficult to do a simple thing like nodding one's head," he later wrote. Frank also wanted to remember his barrister in his will; Resler agreed to this so as not to upset him. He did not want to accept anything of material value and so made various excuses in order to refuse his watch and similar items, but asked him to leave him a button from his uniform. In the end Frank symbolically left him his personal copy of *Men and Gods* by E. G. Kolbenheyer to remember him by, although Resler knew that he would probably never receive the book since Frank's house had already changed ownership a number of times; indeed, he never did.

Frank was also interested in what would happen to his body. Resler explained to him straightforwardly that it would be taken to the anatomy institute and then to the Ďáblice cemetery. When he saw how well Frank was distracted by writing his will, he suggested that they make a copy. Frank did not want to, and asked why. Resler came up with the explanation that he would like to give a copy to Frank's family, as he could see that while writing Frank had forgotten where he was and that these were the last hours of his life.

At the end of his last will, Frank wanted to add a political testament, but he did not know if this was possible – and so turned to Resler, who confirmed that he could do so. He therefore concluded with the words "Germany must live, even if we must die! Long live the German nation! Long live the German spirit!" Resler understood this to be very significant – after two months of debate with Frank he recognised that it was an "expression of Frank's total departure from Nazism, even a direct and solemn renunciation of Nazism

Frank with his guard, Resler and Resler's son Jiří (bottom), who assisted him during the first days of the trial. (AHMP)

and its political programme. Only Germany, only the German – not Nazi – spirit. Frank here wished something that no-one, not even the Great Powers, who are now in charge there, would wish to deny Germany."[3]

Frank wanted to give his calendar to one of his guards, Sergeant Major Jankovský, as he had promised to do so, but Resler encouraged him to copy it out and to keep the original for his family. Frank thought this a good idea, and so began to carefully copy it out line by line. Resler was impressed that he was able to work so meticulously in the last minutes of his life so as to pay a courtesy to the prison warden who had looked after him. When he then handed it over, Frank told Jankovský that he hoped his daughter, to whom he wanted to give the calendar, would grow into a good, pretty girl.

---

3   It remains unclear to what extent Frank renounced Nazism – it is unclear, for example, whether Frank had, with this declaration, also renounced the ideas of the German Reich and the annexation of the Sudetenland to Germany. See also Andrej Tóth, Lukáš Novotný, and Michal Stehlík. *Národnostní menšiny v Československu 1918–1938: od státu národního ke státu národnostnímu.* [National minorities in Czechoslovakia 1918–1938: From a national state to an ethnic state]. Prague: Univerzita Karlova v Praze, Filozofická fakulta a TOGGA, 2012; and Milan Sládek. *Němci v Čechách. Německá menšina v Českých zemích a Československu 1848–1946.* [Germans in the Czech lands. The German minority in the Czech lands and Czechoslovakia 1848–1946]. Prague: PRAGMA, 2002.

Resler left the cell briefly to ask presiding judge Kozák whether a response to the mercy plea had arrived. Since it hadn't, the conversation then turned once again to that topic. Resler told Frank that he had prepared a request for the hanging to be changed to execution by firing squad, and that he could have it sent within five minutes. Frank replied that he had considered it, but that he believed the final rite should be carried out according to Czechoslovak customs. Resler then asked him whether he wouldn't like to write a final letter to his wife – like those that Resler had frequently passed on to his executed clients' relatives during the war. He popped out once more to ask whether a reply to the mercy plea had come, but did not manage to reach anyone, and so instead went to look at the gallows in their final stages of preparation.

At 12:11 on 22 May 1946, Frank sent his last letter to his wife, in which he wrote that despite everything the two of them remained respectful and clean people and that he was depending on her to continue their good Frank family tradition.

When Resler returned to the cell, Frank asked him about the fate of his gold and platinum teeth. "I am a horrible person," replied Resler. "I had already thought of that." Frank laughed at this, with what sounded like natural amusement. The last food was then brought, and as Resler later recalled, "t[T]he last snack one hour before death makes those present feel rather sombre." Frank remarked to Resler that he had had the public up to his neck during his life, and gestured to that effect; Resler reflected that the fact that he was about to be hanged in public had perhaps not even occurred to him at that moment.

A little while afterwards, crews started to film from the corridor, and when Frank and Resler objected to this the cameramen responded that they had permission to film. Once Resler had established that they had only been given permission to film the execution itself, he ordered them to leave, and shut the cell doors. Not long afterwards they came into the cell again and this time it was Frank who stood up and went to shut the door.

A few minutes before being taken to the execution, in his most grave moment, Frank took out a leather pouch containing family portraits and with great affliction and a stricken look on his face gave them to Resler. "At that moment K. H. Frank parted with the thing most dear to him, and in so doing began to part with life. I did not take the pouch straight away. I put down my pen, stood up, leaned a little towards K. H. Frank, and then took the pouch with both hands from him and held it there for a moment or two, in the hopes that this ceremonial handover silently indicated that I had solemnly received his most treasured keepsake, that I would keep it safe for his family, and that I would thus fulfil the last wish he had of me."

Angry and upset, Frank threw down his wedding ring on the table, took a sip of brandy (even though he had asked for cognac) and smoked his last cigarette. He asked whether he would be handcuffed. He would be, as there were no exceptions to this practice, but even so, Resler said that he would try to arrange for him not to be. He left the cell, found one of the judges, and asked him to convey the condemned's final wishes to the presiding judge. He quickly returned to the cell to bid Frank farewell: "Mr Frank, the time has come for us to part. I must leave you. There is no other option, you must die. Die like a man!" – "Mr Doctor, I thank you very much, thank you!" replied Frank warmly, and shook Resler's hand, which Resler clasped with the words "It was my duty!" and quickly left. On his way out, all he heard was the question whether Frank had to be handcuffed. When he reached the corridor and heard that the presiding judge had agreed to Frank's final wish, despite the hangman being strongly against it, Resler returned to the cell once more and told this to Frank. Resler was himself pleased that the judge had decided thus – "far from taking the pernickety and easy approach, he took great responsibility and defended his decision strongly." Only later did he learn that the judge had had to stand up for his decision against the hangman and a representative of the Ministry of Justice. When he told Frank, he responded gratefully: "You succeeded. Thank you, I thank you very much. I am very glad. I am most grateful to you," while all the time clasping Resler's hand. Resler left the cell once more, and with that his duties for Frank were almost over.

Presiding Judge Kozák reads the sentence before the execution, prosecutor Drábek stands at his side. Resler observes from the first row (with his briefcase), next to him stands prosecutor Gemrich. Guard Beneš stands next to Frank. (AHMP)

He joined the crowds and went out into the courtyard of the Pankrác prison, where he first of all had to suffer a further twenty-five minute reading of the sentence, ending with the pronouncement that the plea for mercy had received no response. The plea did not have suspensory effect, and so the sentence was to be executed.

Karl Hermann Frank died at 13:35. His lawyer's tasks did not end at that, however, as Resler had set himself the duty of taking care of Frank's dentures. He had to wait the allotted hour while Frank hung on the gallows, during which he watched journalist E. E. Kisch counting how many times saliva dripped from the corpse's mouth, and autographed entrance tickets for a number of onlookers. Once the body had been taken down he followed to the morgue, where it was laid out together with two women who had been executed for informing. Frank's gold teeth and false eye were taken out and collected in a sock, so that Resler could take them to the prison building to hand them over. There, he wrote an inventory of Frank's property and with that his duties as defence lawyer ended.

While Resler's assistant Kroupa concluded his account with the words "Causa Frank finita," Resler's own fifty-page description of the proceedings ends with a sentence that looks to the future – he knew that this was not the end. "In cell A I 19 next door, former Deputy Reichsprotektor Kurt Daluege continued to await his trial."

Not even Resler knew where Frank was buried. However, information from gravedigger Mr Hubný at Prague's Ďáblice cemetery, which was published in *My* magazine in 1947, indicated that Frank's body had been thrown into a three metre wide, two metre deep, common grave. The bodies of Kurt Daluege, Vladimír Krychtálek, Karel Werner and others were buried in the same grave. Emanuel Moravec and two other Germans had been buried in a large casket a few metres away.[4]

The rope with which K. H. Frank was hanged was apparently one of few not to survive, because the hangman drank it away in the pub.

---

4   Kurt Daluege was deputy *Reichsprotektor* in 1942–1943, Krychtálek and Werner were journalists executed after the war. Emanuel Moravec was a protectorate politician who committed suicide on 5 May 1945. Jindra Suchý. *Ďáblický hřbitov zrádců národa. Viděl jsem hrob K. H. Franka. Původní zpráva Jindry Suchého.* [The *Ďáblice cemetery of national traitors. I saw K. H. Frank's grave. Original message from Jindra Suchý*]. My 45, 21 June 1947, vol. 21, published by *Mladá Fronta.*

PHOTOGRAPHS OF FRANK'S FAMILY[5]

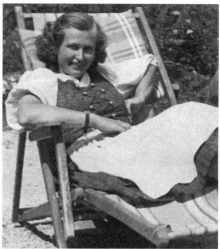

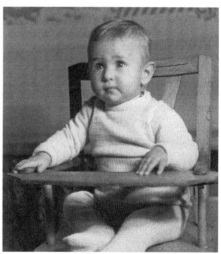

Frank's wife and children from his second marriage. (AHMP)

Resler's personal relationship with Frank is evident from the fact that, during the last few hours of Frank's life, Resler accepted his pouch containing four photographs of his second wife and their three children. Because he realised how important it was to Frank that these last memories of his family should not be lost, the pouch was the only item that he did not include on the inventory of Frank's property, and therefore

---

5   AHMP 11, Pouch with photographs and pages.

did not have to surrender to the court. The pouch survived, and is to be found today in the Prague City Archives.[6] Behind the photo of Karola Franková, Frank's second wife, is a lock of her hair with the dedication: "13. 8. 1945. For my dear Lola, from the prison courtyard, arms bound, with much love and pained with longing, K. H." On the reverse side of the children's photos are Frank's handwritten notes from prison. The later ones read: 14. 3. cell inspection, 15.3. charges brought, 22. 3. trial began, 26. 4. death sentence proposed (intervening time five weeks), 25. 4. heater removed! 21. 5. death penalty!" This very last note dated 21 May 1946 is composed of just two words: "Todesstrafe! ö!" On another calendar he had made, he had pre-drawn boxes as far ahead as 3 July. On 21 May he had written: "Todesurteil. ö." And on 22 May simply: "Schlüss".[7]

The prudence of Resler's decision not to include Frank's most treasured possession in the inventory of his property was to become apparent only later, when he requested that the Ministry of Justice release Frank's possessions to his family. He also sent a similar request to the Extraordinary People's Court. Although he knew that all Frank's belongings had been forfeited to the Czechoslovak state, he had believed, as had Frank, that the Czechoslovak state would have the dignity to leave a few worthless items to Frank's relatives. Resler added to his request a recollection that when Czechs had been executed during the Second World War, the Germans had returned their possessions to their families. Resler was convinced that the Czechoslovak state would behave more respectably than the Reich. He wrote that Frank's possessions were items that had no museum value and whose exhibition "would only have the look of a freak show, serving to satisfy a few peoples' exceptional sensationalism." Characteristically, Resler did not forget to add specifically that he had himself provided Frank with a comb and hairbrush, and that these items should therefore be returned to him. Despite this, the Ministry of Justice did not release any of Frank's possessions to Resler, and instead gave them all to the Museum of Nazi Barbarism in Liberec.

---

6   AHMP 11, Pouch with photographs and pages.
7   The three German phrases translate as: "Death penalty! Oh!"; "Death sentence. Oh."; "The End."

1. THE FIRST REPUBLIC

Defending K. H. Frank was the biggest case in Kamill Resler's legal career. Although it wasn't the most time-consuming or the most complicated case he handled, from a legal perspective, and it did nothing to secure him financially, but rather cost him a lot of money, it was exceptional in terms of the energy he had to put into it, and the effort it took to overcome his own and others' distate. Kamill Resler had to defend a man who had been responsible for the death of his own relatives and acquaintances, a man whom he deeply detested. This is what makes Resler's defence of K. H. Frank so interesting.

There is, however, far more to Resler and his life, than his defence of Frank. Prior to the notable Frank trial, Resler's career and character had been formed over many interesting years. Examples of aspects of Resler's life and work that are well worth a look at include his defence of politically and ethnically troublesome individuals during the First Republic, his assistance to his Jewish colleagues during the Second Republic, and the part he played in the resistance movement during the war. These events were certainly not just a prelude or prequel to the Frank defence, although it is clear that Resler's character was shaped by these situations and that his stance in the Frank trial reflected his previous experience. Rather, it is worth seeing these events separately from their relationship with the later Frank trial. Several of Resler's actions, such as the disciplinary suit Resler brought against Aryan lawyers on the day Bohemia and Moravia were occupied by the German army, arguably demanded greater courage and had a greater influence on the lives of others than his more famous defence of K. H. Frank. Therefore, while focusing on the Frank trial as the most interesting and significant of Resler's career for the Czech nation, we will also look in detail at the rest of Resler's life, which is necessary to give a fair and full picture of who Resler really was, and what he experienced as a lawyer. Kamill Resler's legal career began at the time of the First Czechoslovak Republic, a time when Czechoslovakia was an island of democracy in Central Europe.[8]

---

8   For more on the history of Czechoslovakia see Hugh Agnew. *The Czechs and the Lands of the Bohemian Crown*, Stanford: Hoover Press, 2004, chapter 11.

DEFENCE OF ANTONÍN KIESEWETTER IN A TREASON CASE[9]

Three years before the start of the Second World War, Kamill Resler defended a client in a case that served as a model for the Frank trial. His client was a Czech German who was accused of treason, and the public therefore did not look positively on his defence lawyer. This was Resler's most high profile pre-war case.

His client was arrested under the law on the protection of the Republic. This led to criminal proceedings in defence of the basic constitutional ideas and institutions of the state. Antonín Kiesewetter, general manager of the bank Kreditanstalt der Deutschen (KdD),[10] was accused in 1935 of his bank having financed the subversive magazine *Der Weg*, and been complicit in other subversive acts.[11] The accusation was connected with a charge brought against Dr. Patscheider, a professor from Opava who had moved to Silesia from the Tyrol before the First World War, and had allegedly led a group that were preparing to annex German populations from the Silesia, North Moravia and North-Western Bohemia regions to the German Reich. This case was particularly fiery in the tense period leading up to the Second World War.[12]

For example, unsubstantiated threats were made that the court files would be stolen while being transferred from Opava to Ostrava (resulting in them having a police escort), and that certain imprisoned individuals would be forcibly freed. None of this in fact took place, and Resler was quite used to these sorts of threats; in one of his previous cases, similar messages had been sent by personal enemies of the accused himself, in order to make his time in custody more difficult.

In a later letter about the trial, Resler wrote: "the entire proceedings were dominated by strong-mindedness and rigorousness, which is rare for our courts; I recall only the decision, whereby all anonymous reports and statements were dismissed, which is and will long remain unique, and was sufficient on its own to inspire respect. Indeed, the way they handled personal contact with the defendant was also refined."

Resler had at first been reluctant to take on the defence of a German accused of disloyalty to the Republic, and the only reason why he agreed to do so in the end was that a Czech colleague of his asked him to, personally

---

9   PNP 33, This section is based on the following sources: Dopisy, podání a přání [various correspondence], unless stated otherwise.

10   See also e.g.: Kreditanstalt der Deutschen. [online]. [accessed 2017-11-28]. Available at: http://www.cnb.cz/cs/o_cnb/archiv_cnb/fondy/kredit_deutschen.html.

11   NM, Transcript of the programme *Advokát, který měl rád knížky* [A barrister who liked books], produced by Pavel Kosatík, Český rozhlas Vltava, broadcast on 18 June 1995 at 8:00 pm, p. 13.

12   For a more detailed presentation of Czech-German relations in Czechoslovakia, see Chad Bryant. *Prague in Black. Nazi Rule and Czech Nationalism*, Cambridge: Harvard University Press, 2007, chapter I.

vouching for Kiesewetter, and assuring Resler that he had not been part of any treacherous plots. Resler was also somewhat attracted by the opportunity the case offered for him to see how the Germans did things.[13] And it was for this very reason that Kiesewetter had chosen him: it was important for him that someone should look at his case from the Czech perspective and be persuaded that he had not committed any wrongdoing.

After the year 1926, when Kiesewetter had resigned from a prominent position in the German National party and gone into banking, he had not been at all involved in politics. The magazine *Der Weg* had indeed been funded by the KdD bank, which he represented, but its purpose was to give a positive picture of contemporary political, cultural and social events – and not to promote subversive acts, as Resler argued in his submission to the Regional Criminal Court.

Resler worked on the defence together with Ostrava-based barrister JUDr. Rudolf Prchal, whom he had known for many years. They made sure they left out certain details from their written communication, however, for fear that third parties might intercept and misuse their letters. This applied in particular to their dealings with officers of the Ostrava court: they were trying to have the case assigned to judge Dr. Hahn, not so that he would in any way favour them, but because he was considered a very objective judge. They kept this strictly to themselves. In the end, the case was presided over by chief counsel Emil Kämpf, who Resler reported did a very good job of it.[14]

Resler's opinion of the public prosecutor's handling of the case, on the other hand, was somewhat different. He considered the prosecutor's speech in court to have been weak, of little legal value, and of a style more fitting to a political speech in parliament or at a gathering.[15] The presiding judge managed to quell the defence's discomfort with the speech, but did so in such a way that it was clear to Resler that he could not hold it against the defendant. Ironically, Resler observed during the main hearing that the prosecutor's speech was the most persuasive defence that could have been made.

Resler reported that the trial was very tiring and tense. The defence lawyers were extremely good, and so it was not easy even for Resler to compare favourably with them. Resler succeeded, however, despite the newspapers misnaming him as Rössler (an occurrence he had become familiar with).

Resler gave the last of the defence's closing speeches, and therefore had a task somewhat harder than the others, since, as he claimed, he had "therefore not only to close the defence of his own client but the whole case." In his speech he pointed out that according to the Code of Criminal Procedure, the

---

13   AHMP 14, Request for print corrections in the *Lidové noviny*.
14   PNP 38, Undated letter to the chief counsel.
15   NM, Letter from Resler to Erna Jánská on 3 March 1936 (sic).

final speech in a trial is the most compelling, and it was therefore not undig-nified for him to speak last. He was the only defence counsel to give his clos-ing speech in Czech, which a number of newspapers reported as a surprise, especially as he was known to speak perfect German. List *Národní politika* reported that "the gallery was full to bursting for his speech. (...) As the last speaker, he then appealed to the court to uphold its reputation as a demo-cratic court by making a fair judgement that both Czechs and Germans would recognize as good work. Defender Dr. Resler concluded by proclaiming the honour of the Czechoslovak process."[16] Resler's words were: "It is my wish that of the verdict that will here be made every person, whether Czech or German, might be able to say: 'That is work worthy of credit'."[17] In his clos-ing speech he also praised the careful handling of the trial, and mentioned that the state prosecutor Chalupa was an extremely fine gentleman, whom one could not but respect. He did not mention his legal abilities, however, for which he had little respect.

The last of the public prosecutor's tasks, which followed the closing speeches and preceded the verdict, was to withdraw the charges brought against Resler's client on 12 March 1936. Resler himself did not have much confidence in this, as can be seen from the fact that he changed his mind at the last minute and rather than requesting that the criminal proceed-ings against his client be terminated, he asked in his closing speech that his client be entirely absolved. The public prosecutor in the end declared that "he accepts Resler's evidence and is persuaded that the evidence brought against general manager Kiesewetter is insufficient for a verdict to be made."[18] This success was unexpected – of some twenty accused, Kiesewet-ter was the only one acquitted before the verdict was brought. Many of Re-sler's acquaintances wrote to congratulate him on this success, including his father and his cousin.

As this was Resler's most medialized case, Resler was interested in know-ing what the newspapers were writing about it, and decided to order cuttings from the *Spektator* company from both foreign and Czechoslovak news, re-lated to his part in the trial. There were hundreds of articles, largely in Czech and German.

This case in Ostrava was also one of Resler's longest, as far as the main hearing was concerned. Resler spent a total of 60 days in court for it, from 9 December 1935 until 12 March 1936. On about a third of these days the case was heard in both the morning and afternoon sessions, on the rest only in

---

16   *Národní politika*, no. 73, 13 March 1936, p. 4.
17   PNP 54, Handwritten closing speech.
18   *Národní osvobození*, no. 62, 13 March 1936, p. 3.

the morning.[19] It was not only Resler's longest case, though – *Národní listy* reported that the case was the longest and most politically important in the history of the Czechoslovak Republic.

On 24 March 1936, 13 of the 17 accused in the case were sentenced, and four were acquitted. The heaviest sentence was handed to Dr. Richard Patscheidr – four years of hard labour and the loss of his civil rights for five years. The others received lighter punishments.[20] A number of those involved avoided imprisonment by escaping to Germany.[21] But not Kiesewetter, with whom Resler remained in contact after the end of the trial, even once the disputes over newspaper corrections were past. For Christmas 1937 he sent him a book as a gift, and received a reply from the Kiesewetters in Czech.[22] They remained in touch until Resler's death.

CHILDHOOD AND EDUCATION

Kamill Karel František Resler had not always wanted to be a lawyer. As his father's job often required him to move, the family moved with him, and Resler went to a different school with each move. He attended the first year of school in Chlum (near Hlinsko), the second in Pardubice, the third in Nový Bydžov, the fourth in Kostelec nad Černými lesy and the fifth in the Pankrác area of Prague, as his father had been appointed Director of the tax office there.

After leaving primary school Resler attended a humanities-focused secondary school (*gymnázium*) in Vinohrady. On completing his secondary schooling, he attended a year-long course at the Business Academy on Resslová street in Prague. After this, during what turned out to be the last year before the war, he worked as an accountant (or rather an accounts auditor) in Pavel Zuna's audit office in Nusle.

Unexpectedly, Resler found his way into the legal profession by way of his military service. He read for a degree at Charles University's Law Faculty in Prague between 1917 and 1920, during his military service after he was hospitalized. Researcher Pavel Muchka reports that it was JUDr. Josef Scheiner,

---

19   PNP 38, Main hearing time sheet.

20   *Slezští zrádci odsouzeni.* [Silesian Traitors Sentenced]. Národní listy. 24 March 1936, vol. 76, no. 83. Available at: kramerius.nkp.cz.

21   During the war, Patscheider worked in occupied Krakow, and after the war he was one of the organisaters of the Sudeten-German Compatriots Association. For more on Patscheider see: Mirek Němec. *Erziehung zum Staatsbürger? Deutsche Sekundarschulen in der Tschechoslowakei 1918–1938.* Essen: Klartext Verlag, 2010.

22   PNP 38, Letter to Resler on 7 January 1938.

Resler as a child (AHMP) and as an adolescent. (NM)

president of the Czech Sokol[23], who persuaded him to study law. It should be noted that Resler commenced his studies on 1 December 1917, a date that did not coincide with the start of a standard semester. This was because special shortened courses had been brought in for soldiers, which enabled them to quickly gain an overview of the subject sufficient to pass examinations. Hence early in 1918 Resler attended courses in a number of topics, while the Royal Imperial Ministry of Cultus and Education's ordinance no. 5161 of 18th February 1916 excused him from a further two semesters of attendance and the requirement to attend lectures in a number of other topics. This meant that Resler could already proceed to the final examination in history of law, which he took on 17 April 1918 (after only five months of study) and passed successfully. He then also passed the examination in Church law, this time with distinction.

Resler continued with his studies straight away, and on the basis of a further ordinance no. 9252 of 12 April 1918 he was granted a further semester of exemption on 22 June 1918. After the Czechoslovak Republic gained its independence, it is possible that Resler would have been granted exemption from a further semester of study. Kamill Resler graduated as a Doctor of Law on 9 December 1920, after a shorter period of study than one could ever expect a legal degree to require.[24]

23   The Sokol (or Czech Sokol Community, as it was officially called) was a Czech gymnastics organ-isation whose aim was to boost Czech national self-realization, and which was founded in 1862. One of its mottos was "Healthy body, healthy soul." For more on the Sokol, see Mark Dimond. *The Sokol and Czech Nationalism, 1918–48* in Mark Cornwall and R. J. W. Evans (eds.) *Czechoslovakia in a Nationalist and Fascist Europe, 1918–1948*. Oxford: Oxford University Press and British Academy, 2007.

24   AHMP 16; Index, NM; AUK, Kamill Resler: Běh života [Life story].

AS A SOLDIER

Although Resler knew enough of suffering and never wanted to become a soldier, he always considered it his duty to take up arms, especially when his fatherland called on him to do so.

He joined the First World War from its outbreak – in August 1914 he was called up to the Austrian military as a "Bosnian hunter." He served on all fronts, from Russian Poland to the Volyn province[25] and Albania, with two regiments; this included three years serving in the Bosnia-Hercegovina First hunters' battalion. Resler remembered that they had been distinct from other soldiers by the accessories on their uniforms: "Instead of brick-red epaulettes, theirs were hunter green, and officers had a pin on their cap in the shape of a hunting horn and eagle."[26] After completing training as a reserve officer early in the war, he spent most of the war serving as platoon commander and was gradually promoted from aspiring cadet to lieutenant and later first lieutenant. He also received training in machine-guns and in 1918 became commander of a machine-gun company.

In 1917 he was taken ill with malaria and spent several months in hospital. Considering what activities he could take up to pass the time, he decided to start studying at the Law Faculty.[27] After 17 months in hospital he was named commander of the firing range and weapons and ammunitions store, and did not return to the Austrian Front.

He brought back several songs from Albania, which were later sung at the Reslers' home, and kept in contact with a number of acquaintances from his time there. In 1960 he was still exchanging letters in Croatian with Džambo Tadija, a wartime friend.[28] In addition to Croatian, he also learned German very well during the war, in particular while he was in the Austrian hospital.

On 31 October 1918, three days after the independent Republic was declared,[29] Resler informed the commander of his battalion that as a result of the constitutional change he would be leaving the battalion, and Austrian military service. As the commander did not object, he left on 1 November and returned to Prague, where he immediately reported for duty to Josef Scheiner, who was the chief governor of the Czechoslovak armed forces. And so on 6 November he became dispatcher to General Diviš.

---

25 The Volyn province is a region on the Ukraine – Poland – Belorussia borders, which had several tens of thousands of Czech inhabitants.

26 PNP 111, Letter to Jaroslav Křižan on 16 June 1951.

27 VHA, Osobní výkaz nadporučíka v zál. JUDr. Kamilla Reslera [Resler's military reserves record].

28 NM 214/154. For more on their relationship see Jozo Džambo. *Advokat koji je volio knjige. Život češkoga pravnika i bibliofila Kamila Reslera (1893-1961). Přednáška v České Besedě v Sarajevu, 28. dubna 2016* [a lecture for the "Česká Beseda" in Sarajevo, 28 April 2016].

29 For more on the establishment of Czechoslovakia see Hugh Agnew. *The Czechs and the Lands of the Bohemian Crown*, Stanford: Hoover Press, 2004, chapter 11.

Military identification papers. (NM)

Resler during the First World War. (heirs)

In his "Bosnian hunter" uniform
during the First World War. (heirs)

He was to meet the 88th infantry regiment in Pardubice as they returned to Beroun, a town close to Prague, and accompany them to Moravská Ostrava, so that they were ready for duty in the Těšín area.[30] And above all, he was to inform the regiment's (Austrian) commander that he must hand over command to the highest Czechoslovak officer. The train was to wait for Resler in Pardubice, but in Pečky he found out that the men had disobeyed their orders and were continuing to Prague. The railway crews held up the train so

30 Nowadays, the north-eastern city of Ostrava is the third largest city in the Czech Republic. Těšín is a region of Silesia, to which both Czechoslovakia and Poland laid claim at the end of the First World War. An armed conflict over control of the region took place in 1919.

that Resler arrived in Přelouč well before the soldiers from Pardubice, even though it was much further for Resler from Pečky.[31]

As their train approached, the bright red on the sides of the carriages was visible from far away; this was the colour of the revolution. Resler "was not deterred by the red colour, although it belonged to a political party and not to the government who had sent him." Once the train had stopped, Resler attempted to talk to the colonel, but the soldiers' accusatory shouts and lack of discipline made this difficult. Eventually, after he had explained the order, the colonel informed him that he would be unable to carry it out on account of his men's injuries, lack of discipline, insufficient weapons, and this was confirmed by the Czech lieutenant colonel, whose name happened to be Rössler.

Despite this, Resler insisted that the order must be followed and command handed over – which was extremely painful for the Austrian officer. Despite the personal risks involved, he decided that as a foreign national and the long-term commander of the regiment, he would personally hand over the regiment to the new government, and wanted to do so in person to General Diviš. Upon being told this could not be, he was most disappointed. Although Resler fully understood him, he had to insist on the orders being carried out.

The colonel did then eventually hand over command to lieutenant colonel Rössler, but he in turn repeated that the regiment could not carry out the order- the soldiers wanted to go home to Beroun, and nothing would stop them. Moreover, once the ill, injured and unfit soldiers had been discounted, apparently nearly no-one would be left. Hearing that, Resler gave up trying to persuade the regiment as a whole, and instead decided to form a voluntary unit, later known as the voluntary platoon of Brickmakers, who would report for duty in the Těšín area. He gave Lieutenant Colonel Rössler the task of taking care of the rest of the regiment and reporting their failure to follow orders.

Resler stood on the flat freight wagon and addressed the gathered soldiers (around a third of the regiment) with the words "on behalf of the National Committee [the temporary government] I greet you as free men of the free Czechoslovak nation," which was met with a burst of cheering. After pointing out that the new government included workers' representatives, he called on the soldiers to report themselves for service as volunteers. 59 soldiers signed up, to whom he expressed his recognition that "they had found in themselves the strength to resist, after so much hardship, the opportunity of returning home and seeing their loved ones, and to take upon them new – and likely

---

31   For an idea of the distance between the stations mentioned: Prague (0 km) – Pečky (48 km) – Přelouč (91 km) – Pardubice (106 km).

tough- duties." Resler established that the voluntary platoon would be on first-name terms with one another, and would address one another as "brother." Other commands typical of the Sokol were also taken on, as were Czech military commands necessary for their immediate work.

For the remainder of the journey to Pardubice, Resler spent his time getting to know each soldier's story. Once they had arrived in Pardubice, they gathered the equipment they needed in the Pardubice armoury, ate in the school canteen, quickly practiced the most crucial drills with their weapons, and set off for Ostrava. On the way, they passed by stations that had been decorated in German colours and symbols, and also encountered Czech soldiers who had been tasked with occupying the regions they travelled through. In Moravská Ostrava Resler handed over the troops, signalling that the authorities in Prague knew how hard the situation there was, and on 8 November 1918 he hurried back to Prague. These events were significant for Resler, since small acts at that revolutionary time were capable of bringing about great changes. As he later wrote, "That is why the next generation will not even be able to imagine the troubles we had to go through, even to set the smallest cogs of the new national constitution in motion."[32]

On 15 November 1918, a week after his return from Ostrava, Resler joined the I[st] regiment of the Freedom Guards (*Stráž Svobody*),[33] where he served as First Lieutenant until 1920, as commander of the 2nd company, commander of the 6th company 2nd battalion, and later commander of the 3rd field company 1st field battalion.[34] While in Bratislava, when they were not in the field, Resler became involved in setting up the Sokol there, where he trained young boys.

In 1919 (probably on 7th June) he was severely injured in a clash with a division of the German army under Mackensen[35], which was returning to Germany from Romania via Hungary and tried to cross the Czechoslovak border at Komárno and Hetíno in Slovakia. He suffered a serious break to his left thigh bone, which left his leg shortened by 3–5 cm. Amputation was considered. Eighteen years later, Resler described his feelings about the operation in a letter to a friend who was to undergo serious surgery: "as a former soldier I see these things impassively. I myself have been under the scalpel several times, and once they threatened to amputate my leg at the thigh, but I always

32   *Rakovnické listy*, vol. II, nos. 43, 44, 45.
33   For more on the Freedom Guards see Pavel Jaroslav Kuthan. *V těžkých dobách (2/20): První dobrovolníci*. [In hard times (2/20): The first volunteers]. [online]. [accessed 2017-11-28]. Available at: http://www.valka.cz/clanek_11043.html.
34   VHA, Hauptgrundbuchblatt, Záznamní list 1 [military record].
35   Part of the German army, returning to Germany, which was commanded by August von Mackensen. In the end the troops returned via Vienna. The exact date is not known, but Resler is recorded as having been company commander until 7 June 1919, and from 8 June 1919 until 25 May 1920 his records show that he was undergoing treatment in hospital. VHA, Osobní výkaz nadporučíka v zál. JUDr. Kamilla Reslera [Resler's military reserves record].

Military identification papers. (NM)

In the uniform of a member of
the Freedom Guards after the
First World War. (heirs)

The Commander with his men (Resler in the centre) in the Freedom Guards. (heirs)

approached these matters calmly, simply asking the surgeon whether he understands his craft, and then thinking no more of it and leaving the responsibility to the doctor. I only thought about how to put the whole problem most swiftly behind me."[36]

Resler spent a month in the garrison hospital in Prague, for which he paid 232 Kč, and from that time onwards he wore raised heels on his left shoes. While Kamill was in hospital in Prague recovering from his broken leg in 1920, his mother came to see him. She was accompanied by her niece, Resler's cousin, a pretty girl nine years younger than him called Libuše Donátová. Resler fell in love with her on the spot and she felt the same.[37] This did not much impress their parents, on account of their close blood relationship, but Kamill and Libuše did not allow this to come between them.

Wedding photo. (heirs)

Resler's wife Libuše. (NM)

Resler married Libuše in Chrudim on 28 June 1924. One of their witnesses was his old friend Jiří Scheiner. None of their parents were present at the wedding; we do not know whether they were invited, but both sets of parents did send warm congratulations to the newlyweds.

Kamill Resler was very much the head of his family, and his wife and children would never have dared oppose him, as concerned taking on certain defence cases or in any other matter, unlike the impression given in the film *Ex offo*. The depiction given in the film was the result of the filmmaker's

36   PNP 75, Letter to Karel Štika on 13 July 1937.
37   Pavel Muchka: *Kamill Resler, právník a bibliofil* [Kamill Resler, lawyer and bibliophile]. Bachelor's dissertation (hereafter "Muchka") 17, Hradec Králové: Univerzita Hradec Králové, Filozofická fakulta, 2009.

artistic licence, at a time when he did not know the reality of Resler's family relationships.[38] He had two children with Libuše: Blanka Kamilla Reslerová was born on 18th March 1925 and Kamill Jiří Resler (who sometimes wrote his first name with just one 'l' and left out 'Jiří') on 10 June 1927.[39] Both children attended the French primary school and French gymnasium (secondary school) in Prague, so as to receive a broader education, until the Germans closed these schools in 1940.[40]

While serving in the Czechoslovak armed forces, Resler was twice verbally appraised. Major Heller judged him to be an energetic and enterprising officer, well educated and knowledgeable in general as well as specialised matters. He was confident in leading a division, and had the most desirable influence on those in his command. He was found to be competent at leading a company of officers. His supervising officer noted in his file that he was: "An officer serviceable in any situation, intelligent and keen. Recommendable." Similarly, at the end of his active service, his notes read: "First Lieutenant of the reserves Resler is a good officer. Suitable for promotion."[41] In 1924 Resler was promoted to Captain, and in 1934 to Staff Captain of the off-duty infantry.[42]

When he joined the reserves he received an allowance for injury, of some 400 crowns per year,[43] which was raised slightly after a few years. In 1940 he put in a claim for 2 200 crowns compensation for having had, in 1939, to surrender the weapons he had at home – two military pistols, one automatic, and three military rifles.[44]

Despite this, Resler never gave up being a soldier, as can be seen from his post-war attitude. On 22 May 1945 he wrote to his peer Václav Adamec: "There is no command yet for us older ones to sign up anywhere, and at the moment there is no need. There are plenty of keen, young men who should be given priority. Even so, the Sudetenland will need serious attention and may need many men; if they call us up, we should go."[45]

---

38 *Ex offo*, [film]. Directed by Jaromír Polišanský. Czech Republic, Česká televize, 1998. Screenwriter Jan Drbohlav had the idea of making a film after seeing an exhibition about Kamill Resler, organized by the National Museum. This became a top priority for the creative team at Czech Television in 1998. Letter from Blanka Brunnerová to Jan Drbohlav, NM.

39 KNM 1, Protektorátní doklady [identity papers].

40 AHMP 16, Přihláška pro důstojníky, rotmisty a poddůstojníky aspiranty v záloze [application to serve in the reserves].

41 VHA, Záznamní list 1, Osobní výkaz nadporučíka v zál. JUDra Kamilla Reslera [Resler's military reserves record].

42 AHMP 16, 17, Promotion decrees.

43 VHA, Výkaz 5303 [military statement].

44 AHMP 17, Compensation claim.

45 PNP 103, The Sudetenland comprised regions primarily inhabited by the German-speaking population, whose cession was the main topic at the Münich conference in 1938. Letter to Václav Adamec on 22 May 1945.

In 1947 Resler specifically applied to remain in the reserves. As he explained in a letter in September 1948, he only asked to retain his officer status because he considered it his duty to the nation.[46]

While serving in the army, Resler earned the following awards: large and small medals for bravery, the Karl Troop Cross, a victory medal and a badge for 1918–1919 volunteers.[47]

JUDR. KAMILL RESLER'S LEGAL PRACTICE

As previously mentioned, in late 1920 Kamill Resler graduated as a doctor of Law and on 17 November 1920 he entered legal practice at the office run by JUDr. Josef Scheiner the elder and JUDr. Maximilian Leiser, as the latter's trainee. He had already worked for the firm as a clerk, after receiving an invitation from Scheiner while he was in hospital in Prague with a war wound to his leg, in Autumn 1919. At that time, Scheiner was Supreme Commander in the armed forces and Resler, with whom he was already well acquainted, was among his troops. Upon discovering that Kamill was wounded and in hospital, he visited him and offered him a position at his legal practice.[48] Resler's military service with the Czechoslovak forces contributed one year, one month and one week towards the minimum training time for his legal qualification.[49] Hence Resler completed his 5-year legal training on 10 October 1924, and as he had already taken his bar exam on 6 July 1923 and passed with merit, he was then admitted to the bar.

Once his name had been inscribed on the register of lawyers, Resler set up his own legal practice. This was in part thanks to an interest-free loan worth 60,000 Kčs which he received from the Ministry of National Defence. His father and father-in-law acted as guarantors for this loan.

Resler's office was first located in Prague's Vinohrady quarter, at Fochova 39, but after two years, Resler relocated it to Na Zderaze 11, between Karlovo náměstí and the river Vltava.[50] Resler tended to go to the office after the end of his meetings and court sessions, rather than in the morning. He worked late into the evening, and often also on Sunday.[51]

The most important figure in his office, after Resler himself, was his secretary Erna Jánská (who was also an editor for Hyperion publications), whom

---

46   AHMP 17, Statement by JUDr. Kamill Resler.
47   The Karl Troop Cross was awarded to soldiers who had spent 12 weeks serving on the front, and participated in at least one battle. It was named after the Austro-Hungarian Emperor Karl I.
48   Jiří Kotyk: *JUDr. Kamill Resler.* [online]. [accessed 2017-11-28]. Available at: http://archive.is/2013.01.05-210038/http://www.kpp.iipardubice.cz/1123596021-judr-kamil-resler.php.
49   ČAK, Application to be registered as a barrister.
50   NM, Envelope marked KR: office at Zderaz.
51   Blanka Brunnerová's personal recollections, Muchka, p. 19.

he employed as soon as she finished at business college and until his office closed. He had a very close relationship with Erna, and repeatedly pleaded with her not to divorce her husband Karel Jánský, of whom she was extremely jealous. When she died, he gave the eulogy at her funeral.

For most of his legal career, Resler employed several trainees at his office, including in particular JUDr. Jiří Mašek and writer and trade union worker Jaroslav Čecháček, who worked for Resler primarily to ensure he had cover during the Second World War. In the '30s Resler also trained JUDr. Miroslav Houska, who was later to become Consul in the USA.[52]

He was kind to his employees and took on trainees even though they caused him certain difficulties. For example, he employed JUDr. Čestmír Müller in mid-December 1946, even though this meant that he had to pay a whole year's extra fees to the bar. If he had waited until the new year before taking him on he would have saved this money, but Müller needed to complete his training, and so Resler offered him the place. Only later, in 1948, did Resler request that the training fee for Müller be waived on account of his short period of employment, and the executive board of the Czech Bar Association granted his request.[53]

Resler's practice was an open place, where many people met. While Resler worked and wrote in his own study, the practice had three further rooms. In the late afternoons, people would come in, to ask Resler's advice or simply "meet and converse with people of sound mind."[54] Occasional guests of this kind included, for example, the writers František Halas, Konstantin Biebl, Karel Konrád and Jindřich Hořejší, and from time to time Josef Hora and Jaroslav Seifert. Visiting artists included Karel Holan, Jindřich Štyrský, Toyen and others.

The light atmosphere in the office is also evident from a warmly critical letter that Resler received from his employee G. S.: "Having nothing useful to do in the office, I got bored. I came home, sat down to lunch, and three times in a row was dragged away from my plate by the collar and taken to the telephone, although I did my best to resist. While my food was getting cold, I learnt the joyful news that you had managed to trip on the stairs, but forgot to slide down. And lo, my heart rejoiced that I have some fun again and will have some errands to run. I strictly forbid you to return to these uninhabitable rooms at Na Zderaze, until you obtain a special ticket, i.e. a properly signed certificate from the doctor stating that you may once again move freely in the world, extort money from clients and have inappropriate fun with courts and other authorities. Until such time, I intend to make myself

---

52   PNP 111, Complete list of employees, NM; Personal note from Blanka Brunnerová.
53   ČAK, Request for training fee to be waived.
54   NM, Bidlo's Zderaz sketches and files, p. 5.

comfortable here as is proper of a G. S. and do not require your presence. Rest well for as long as you need, put on some weight and get your face back into shape. For the nation!"[55]

THE SOKOL'S REACTION TO RESLER'S DEFENCE OF KIESEWETTER

When Resler took on the defence of Kiesewetter, part of the population had a spiteful reaction, much as they did later when he defended Frank. In one telegram, Resler mentions that he had to "fight against many of my friends in order to be able to carry out my work according to my own honest convictions."[56] These friends included members of the Sokol organization. What reaction did they have to his defence of Kiesewetter?

Resler was never excluded from the organization, although many journalists believed he was. He was, however, demoted from the committee of the Prague Sokol and banned from being elected to any other role within the organization for one year, because they maintained he had not behaved sufficiently patriotically. A motion to exclude him entirely was defeated in the committee by 17 votes to 14. In response to this vote, the 14 members of the committee who had voted to exclude Resler, led by one of the first presidents of the Sokol Dr. Jaroslav Urban, resigned. The committee's decision was not taken amicably by all, as can be seen from the headlines of an article published in the *Haló* newspaper on 16 April 1936: *Advocates of the Third Reich in Prague's Sokol,* and one in the *Express* on 15 April: *Defender of "loyal" Germans not expelled from Sokol.*[57] Resler appealed against the committee's decision at the General Meeting of the Prague Sokol, but his appeal was rejected.[58] Nevertheless, the Prague Sokol later cancelled his punishment, after the public prosecutor had withdrawn his charge against Kiesewetter and it was thus clear that Resler had acted honourably.[59]

The biggest conflict, however, took place quite apart from the debates over Resler's possible exclusion. It began on 25 January 1936, two months before the charges against Kiesewetter were dropped, at a meeting of the committee of the Prague Sokol concerning Resler's defence of Kiesewetter. Resler expressed his willingness to forfeit his legal fees from the case, as a gesture to show that he was not profit-seeking. He wasn't sparing with his words, and went so far as to describe his feelings for his country by saying that he was prepared even to die in its defence. Former town councillor Václav Štěpánek then let rip at Resler and aired several examples of other barristers who had

---

55   NM, Letter to Resler on 26 March 1941.
56   PNP 33, Telegram. 16 March 1936.
57   *Expres.* 15 April 1936, vol. IX., no. 88, p. 1.
58   NM, Letter to Erna Jánská on 11th March 1936.
59   České slovo, 25 March 1936, p. 5.

turned down the chance to defend in cases concerning crimes against the Republic. He called Resler a defeatist, which Resler was not willing to accept; Resler therefore requested the committee to judge whether this had been a libellous statement on Štěpánek's part. Yet at an extraordinary meeting the committee decided that Štěpánek's comments had been "fair, brotherly, and in line with the organization's values."

One of the Sokol members congratulated Resler on his success in the Kiesewetter trial and advised him to have sympathy for with those who couldn't understand that everyone has the right to a defence lawyer; even so, he also advised him not to remain engaged in the matter until its final settlement. Not for the sake of his own satisfaction, but for the sake of justice.[60] He believed that Resler was trying to secure justice.

The committee's decision about Štěpánek's comments angered Resler so much that he decided to file a legal complaint against Štěpánek for slander. He believed that it was "a question of whether public matters in Czechoslovakia should be decided with understanding and calm deliberation, or whether it is in the national interest for big, empty words to be used at such moments." Resler was of the opinion that defeatism was "an insubstantiated or exaggerated fear of the dangers of war – accompanied by an attempt to avoid them, even dishonestly. Ours would be a case of defeatism if someone, considering the relative military strength of Czechoslovakia and Germany – and aware only of Germany's advantage – expressed weakness, fear and misgivings, and advised not to fight, to avoid a war, and to negotiate with Germany even if that involved undignified compromises." Yet Resler could not find signs of this in his speech, indeed on the contrary, he had declared that he and the Czechoslovak nation would fight to the last for their honour. Hence he considered that "the use of the word 'defeatism' in this situation must be regarded as an offence."

The District and Regional Criminal Courts in Prague both found the complaint to be unjustified. Although the courts did not find any evidence of despondence or defeatism in Resler's speech, they considered that his words had included "early signs of a certain skepticism and weakness." Resler used these excerpts as part of his new year greetings in 1939, which he entitled *Hlas v hluku zalehlý* (A Voice Resounding in the Noise). He also added part of the text of a letter he had received: "That which in 1936 was defeatism or the early expression of skepticism and weakness became the nation's ultimate aspiration in September 1938, and what is far worse and was at that time so unimaginable a notion we could not have entertained it even fleetingly, this became – a thousand times alas – the fate of a nation betrayed and abandoned

---

60   PNP 33, The word "justice" was written with a capital letter. Letter to Resler on 13 March 1936.

by all, and her last resort." He concluded the short booklet with these words: "Faith, strength, determination and luck in the year 1939."[61]

In the wake of these cases, Resler gave up his activities in the Sokol and on 14 December 1936 officially left the organization. His affairs with the Sokol nevertheless continued to affect him in other areas. He came to generally dislike club life, and this led him among other things to refuse to walk in pride of place at the head of the 3rd Company of the Ist Freedom Guard regiment in 1937.[62]

Even twenty years later, he still had certain reservations about the Sokol. In 1957 he declined an invitation to the birthday party of one of his fellow soldiers of the Ist Freedom Guard regiment, both because he was not in Prague at the time, and because he anticipated that many Sokol members would be present. He supposed that his presence would not be well viewed, and so simply sent a card instead – which was very warmly received. The friend who had invited him responded to his comment, and indicated that based on the mood in the group, "you should not remotely suspect even one of the excellent Sokol members of your home regiment in this sense."[63] As proof, about 30 of the members present at the party signed a friendly letter to Resler.

Years later, Resler recalled this case in an article about František Bidlo: "At one point I had a bitter relationship with a large organisation of which I had been a member, as a result of my defence in a political criminal case – they reproached me not for the way that I defended, but simply *because* I had defended, and successfully. There was much that was awkward in our bitter clash, but much more that was laughable, even pitiful."[64]

In connection with the Kiesewetter case and its repercussions in the Sokol, Resler requested print corrections from numerous newspapers. In one case he even requested a correction of a correction, when the České slovo paper printed one correction alongside another objectionable article. In the column *Zábavy pražského advokáta* (Pleasures of a Prague Barrister) they remarked that "Of course, the evening České slovo is not intimidated. We would like to tell you openly, sir, that you have made yourself a reputation that is unfortunate not only from the Sokol's perspective, but also from a higher perspective."[65] Resler received similar comments from the daily *Telegraf*, which printed a correction and added to it this editorial comment: "Lawyers sometimes like to dance between words. It is true that he did not take on the defence of a traitor, only of a person accused of a crime against the Republic.

---

61   PNP 113, The quotations are taken from Resler's text *Hlas v hluku zalehlý* [A Voice Resounding in the Noise].

62   PNP 103, Letter to the 3rd company on 19 November 1937.

63   PNP 103, Letter to Resler on 20 October 1957.

64   NM, Bidlo's Zderaz sketches and files, p. 21.

65   *Večerní České slovo*, 24 June 1936.

(...) Dear sir, do you regard such gimmickry to be respectable?"[66] Ironically, his friend responded with the following:

Jiný v lebku by si vpálil
chladného kus olova
Resler opravami pálil
Českého zvlášť do Slova.

Pláče Šalda, pláče Borin[67]
na redakčním dvorku.
Odvážejí redaktory
na magorku."

Another might have reckoned
suicide the best way out
but Resler used corrections
to shoot Czech in its Word.

Salda's sulking, Borin's sorry,
team morale is low.
The men in white coats
have come for the editors.

By requesting these corrections, he fulfilled the Sokol's requirements, which were, as mentioned, to defend justice and the truth, and to speak out.[68]

IN THE SOKOL

Although relations between Resler and the Sokol turned somewhat sour following the Kiesewetter trial, the preceding decades had seen Resler take a very active part in the organization, which he loved dearly. He had first become involved in the Sokol during his teenage years, at the same time as he began associateing with anarchist-socialist groups. He officially joined the Czech Sokol community at the age of sixteen, "a little early, which was only possible by slightly cheating," as he wrote in a letter to Kristian Franta. In his own notes he describes it thus: "My two younger brothers[69] trained with the Sokol juniors from 1903 to 1907, when we lived in Nusle, whereas I started

---

66   *Telegraf*, 26 June 1936, no. 145.
67   Czech journalists and critics.
68   AHMP 14, Request for corrections in the Prague edition of *Národ Karlu Čajčíkovi* on 30 March 1936.
69   Resler had, however, only one younger brother Antonín. See below.

to train at the Sokol in Královské Vinohrady in 1907, when I was thirteen.[70] In the autumn of 1908 a schoolmate of mine, Jiří Scheiner, asked me to join the Tyrš institute [the Sokol]. (...) They didn't address us as children, but rather as younger friends. My first instructor was Vilda Vajner, a mechanic from Nusle whom I knew, and who took to me. The warm and friendly behaviour of the instructors fast built up our self-confidence; these were members of a club where the motto 'liberty, equality, fraternity' was lived out for real. (...) Soon enough we – I was the youngest – aspired to be full members. We felt this need particularly strongly once our older friends had already become members, and so a few of us decided to try applying for membership as early as 1909. We added a year to our age; at first I wrote that I was born on 23 December 1892, but that wasn't enough. (...) The member who saw me at the headquarters, sympathised with my desire to feel like a man, and wanted to help, and so he came up with the idea of adding a year to my age. (...) He did so, but it still wasn't good enough! Even then it looked like I was only 17. So I stuck with the 23 December 1892. In the end, when they saw how eager we were, they allowed us to join anyway and gave us membership cards on which they had added the word 'pupil'. We breezed into the gym in autumn 1909 with lively determination; I was really only 15 ¾ at the time. We extended our circle of acquaintance in particular with a group of slightly older technicians. (...) One evening (in 1910) Jiří Scheiner invited me to join his group, which was known as *Parta Noha* ["Foot Band"]. I asked whose idea it was, and why the group had such a stupid and inelegant name. He told me that Pepík Rosa was the mind and soul of the venture and benevolently refuted my aesthetic objection to its name, saying: "well, it's all just for fun anyway." I didn't ask about the purpose; that was clear: to train with the group for an additional hour in addition to the obligatory hour with the association, and to organise friendly meetings, discussions and excursions."[71] Young Kamill regularly went to the countryside with *Parta Noha*, most often to the village of Svatá, near Beroun[72], where the Scheiners had their summer residence. It was there, in the former hunting lodge, that Jindřich Fügner had first met Miroslav Tyrš in 1860, and where they had later made plans to found the Sokol. Resler enjoyed playing the guitar there, and his Sokol friends gave him several nicknames, such as 'Camillo furioso'.

In 1912 Resler took part in the All-Sokol *Slet* (a mass gymnastics festival organised by the Sokol) on Letná[73], where among other things he performed

70   Nusle and Vinohrady were independent towns at the time, but are now areas of Prague.
71   Family archives, typed copy of Kamill Resler's notes made by his daugher Blanka Brunnerová. Cited in Muchka, pp. 11 and 12.
72   A town 25 km south west of Prague.
73   An area of Prague and the place where the Sokol's competitions and many other demonstrations were held.

as a militant in a re-enactment of an ancient battle between the Greeks and the Persians.[74] He would attend his second (and last) slet twenty years later.

Within the Sokol circles, he befriended the Scheiner family; he also worked for Josef Scheiner after the war, and after completing his studies trained as a barrister under him. Their relationship was close and brotherly, despite an age difference of 32 years. Josef Scheiner was a long-standing associate of the Sokol's founder, Tyrš, and had been president of the Czech Sokol Association since 1906. During the war he was arrested together with Dr. Kramář, a politician and the first Czechoslovak Prime Minister, and after the war he became the Chief Commander of the Czechoslovak Armed Forces.[75] Resler had great respect for Josef Scheiner, whom he saw as a strong, manly, courageous, cultured, proud and yet unpretentious man. After Scheiner's funeral in early 1932, Resler expressed his deep thanks to fellow Sokol member Albert Pražák for his eulogy, which had rightly touched upon Scheiner's greatness, and likened him to Tyrš: "Your speech was capable of kindling a spark in the hearts of men, and it must be kept, so that it will still be here when people ask for it. That may not be straight away, but one day they will, for sure." Resler asked Pražák for permission to publish the speech – but this was too great a task for Pražák, who preferred to leave the speech as something for those present to remember, with its imperfections and improvisations.[76] Resler was also a close friend of Scheiner's son Jiří, and indeed Jiří was Kamill's best man at his wedding. After they had both died, their descendants became closer still – a few decades later their grandchildren married one another.

Resler as a member of the Sokol. (NM)

With members of the Sokol, 1931. (AHMP)

---

74   NM, An article entitled "Všesokolské slety" [All-Sokol Slets] with his daughter's notes.
75   *Národní listy, Večerník,* 11 January 1932, p. 1, available online at kramerius.nkp.cz.
76   PNP 72, Letter from Resler to Pražák on 5 March 1932.

Resler wrote and published his first book for the Scheiners; this was *Codex mejdanensis*, written in 1919 during his long and uneventful stay in hospital. A second edition was published in 1921, and the book later came out in a special print run of 35 copies in 1931, with 17 illustrations by František Bidlo on handmade Dutch paper.[77]

CODEX MEJDANENSIS[78]

The book sets out the rules for a gathering (or party – *mejdán*), at which the main activity involves card games. First of all, it focuses on defining the *mejdán*. What is it? "A gathering of people in honour of the owner of the club, for the purpose of entertainment at others' expense, and in particular the cultivation of fine national games." (§1) "The day for the *mejdán* is set by the club owner. The event begins at eight o'clock in the evening. Arrivals later than nine without due apology are to be punished as the club owner deems appropriate, by a fine to be donated to a charitable cause. Amorous goings-on are exacerbating factors." (§2) "If rations are raised, the *mejdán* is known as a feast." (§3) The following are notable among the basic provisions: "Strange habits shall not be tolerated, but otherwise each may amuse himself as he wishes; with consideration for the wear and tear caused to the ladies present." (§4) "Do not go to the *mejdán* penniless!" (§23) "Shut up, windbag!" (§24) "Cheating is not punishable, as a rule, if it goes unnoticed. However, if it is discovered, the cheat is to be penalized with penalty kicks as the club owner judges appropriate, with consideration for the offender's build and physical condition. Penitent confessions have no effect on the extent of the punishment." (§26) Furthermore it is established in §39 that "no one may request, that [kicks] be changed into another punishment, such as a fine." §36 sets out a rule known as "Yum" or "He who gives late gives double." "Anyone who, without due advance justification, does not put down the required bet before the cards are dealt, or before they are passed, and is then reminded with the word "Yum!," must put down twice the amount. Diverting players' attention away from the bet by appropriate means (in particular by recounting indecent anecdotes) is to be encouraged. Anyone wrongly saying *Yum!* shall be required to pay a fine equal to the amount that the person he wrongly *Yummed* would have put down. Mistaken *Yums* are considered wrongful *Yums*." Resler also covers the interpretation of a number of terms, so as to avoid their (mis)guided abuse: "Moral support is to be given to punished players, but the command 'Grease your wheels, squeaky!' must under no circumstances lead to the improper use of dog fat." (§83) Certain expressions, on the other hand, are explicitly permitted: "Encouragement with phrases like 'And we're off! The puppy's in the pond', as a gesture of joyful participation in the game is permit-

---

77   VCM, List of books published.
78   PNP 111, *Codex mejdanensis* and *Kdo je kdo* [Who's who].

ted." (§86) Players were not left in any doubt as to essential principles of health and safety (§92): "Getting the other players wet is to be encouraged for the sake of their hygiene. A player who is undressed must be left at the least with clothing sufficient that he does not cause a public scandal. In any case, he must be allowed to keep his eyes, so that he can have a good cry." According to §99, however, "Shrieking, howling, purring, moaning, groaning, whining, hissing and despairing, rolling one's eyeballs, having lank beards or bristly stubble, sighing, grimacing or making sour faces will be tolerated only within the limits of decent manners." And the end of the party doesn't go forgotten: "The *mejdán* ends when the guests leave; the departure of family members is of no importance." (§108) "Upon leaving all should undergo a thorough bodily check, unless they are in a revolting state." (§102).

For the second edition of the Codex,[79] published on St. Joseph's Day in 1921, Resler further specified and extended some of the regulations. For example he extended §99 to include weeping, wailing, squealing and lamenting and to §101 he added an explanatory note: "Players are reminded of the traditional saying, 'poverty does not bring honour' and should reject the saying spread with Bolshevik enthusiasm, 'Poverty does not lose honour, kiss our pockets, rich ones!'." Similarly, four union representatives were chosen. Among them, JUDr. Vojta Fifka was elected representative for grease and dirt (added to §39 a)). Barrister Fifka died (imprisoned by the Gestapo) in Prague's famous Pankrác prison on 22 December 1941.

All the players had several nicknames. Resler's were: "Camillo Furio, Orlando furioso, Bothersome, Stinging hornet, Rolandus impertinensis, Hoppocamelos nassabercensis, Camillus lascivus, Ruffian, riding page, Chief Partner at Potasch & Perlmutter Ltd., Camil.

CLUBS AND ASSOCIATIONS

Although Resler´s departure from the Sokol three years before the start of the Second World War marked the end of his participation in non-literary groups, he made up for this by redoubling his activities in literary associations – as an active member, organiser, and strong supporter.

The most important association among them was the *Spolek českých bibliofilů* (Society of Czech Bibliophiles), established in 1908, in whose organisation and leadership Resler was long involved. This group was so important to Resler that he did not mind gently laying into his friends when its interests were concerned. In the late '50s he wrote to Karel Čechák: "I hope I have persuaded you (...) that I separate my personal relationship with you, which is very good, from my attitude to your activity in the SCB, which you have

---

effectively helped to bring into decline and for which I judge you harshly. I hope that this letter will not damage our good mutual personal relations."[80]

In 1950, the Ministry of Information and Public Culture appointed the Society of Czech Bibliophiles as official publisher of bibliophilic books in close collaboration with the publishing house Československý spisovatel.[81] Hence, the society succeeded all other publishers of bibliophilic books.[82]

The Society of Czech Bibliophiles still exists today, and describes this period in its history as follows: "It must be appreciated that the Society of Czech Bibliophiles managed to survive at all between 1948 and 1989, and that it did not perish like numerous other societies, but made the most of all available loopholes in the restrictions so as to publish a series of fine books, together with the Československý spisovatel publishing house (1950–1958) and the Museum of Czech Literature (1960–1992), several dozen of which were of a comparable standard to those produced before the war, and that in choosing works to publish the Society never compromised the humanistic and democratic traditions for which it had stood from its outset. The Society even managed to publish a number of works by silenced authors."[83] Resler had a part in that, too.

During the '50s, Resler published three works with the Society, all of which narrated someone's life story – *Sborník na památku Karla Dyrynka, knihtiskaře, tvůrce písem, knihomila a člověka* (Anthology in Memory of Karel Dyrynk the Man, Writer, Publisher and Bibliophile), *Buřiči a stříbrný vítr* (Rebels and the Silver Wind) and, together with J. Picek, *Spolek českých bibliofilů Methodu Kalábovi k 70. narozeninám* (The Society of Czech Bibliophiles on the Occasion of Method Kaláb's 70th Birthday).

Resler was also one of the founders of the Scholarly Literature Society at the Czechoslovak Academy of Sciences. He took on the role of treasurer for the Society, and was later chairman of its review board. He did his best to support young scholars, always allowing them to access his resources and campaigning for them to be fairly paid for their work.[84]

At times he considered his membership in these groups to be a way of promoting his political views. After Minister Moravec's hateful speech against Czech writers under the Nazi occupation, he signed up out of solidarity as a member of the *Syndikát českých spisovatelů* (Czech Writers' Syndicate),

---

80 PNP 69, Letter to Karel Čechák on 29 April 1960.
81 Decision on 26 January 1950 no. 46.580/48/III.
82 PNP 73, file no. 463/52, Letter to the residential officer of the Distric National Committee in Prague, .
83 On the history and activities of the Society of Czech Bibliophiles see their official web pages. Available at: http://scb.wdr.cz/scb_historie.html [accessed 2017-11-28].
84 PNP 91; Resler's literary worksAHMP 16, Letter from the Scholarly Literature Society to Resler's widow on 14 July 1961.

which he remained until 1949. The Syndicate was replaced after February 1948 by the *Svaz československých spisovatelů* (Czechoslovak Writers' Union).

LEGAL PRACTICE DURING THE FIRST REPUBLIC (1918–1938)

The Kiesewetter trial was the most important of Resler's cases during the First Republic, but many others also came to his desk. A number of these, in particular those that reveal Resler's character and opinions, are described below. Resler did not specialise in any particular legal field, but he did work on a large volume of criminal cases and represented many of his acquaintances in matters related to their inheritance.

He enjoyed his work, although it certainly was not easy. After more than thirty years of legal study and practice, he described his work as a barrister in one letter thus: "Helping those around you to achieve justice when unjustly prosecuted by flawed human society is beautiful and rewarding work, but fighting for justice with common sense and skill against cold hard power is sometimes extremely tough and gruelling."[85]

One of his first private cases involved negotiations with the creditors of Josef Florian's publishing house *Dobré dílo* in Stará Říše in the Jihlava area. Despite his own rather reserved approach to religion, Resler much admired Florian for his determined approach to publishing religious literature. When Resler went to Stará Říše to meet Florian, he had to walk the best part of eighteen kilometres on foot, as the railway line only went as far as Okříšek. The negotiations with the creditors turned out well in the end, not least thanks to Resler's approach, and this paved the way for a long friendship with Florian. Their friendship remained strong despite the fact that, according to Resler, their opinions on various social questions were not always the same, and when it came to religion there was an unbridgeable gulf between them. Nevertheless, Resler appreciated the importance of religion in the grounding of the Czech nation.

Although Resler frequently reflected on metaphysical questions, he never settled within a church. He came from a catholic family, as did his wife, who later joined the Czechoslovak Church (nowadays the Czechoslovak Hussite Church),[86] but his own attitude to life rather distanced him from religion. He officially left the Roman Catholic church when he was eighteen, and remained

---

85   NM, Letter to Norbert Felach of Brno.
86   The Czechoslovak Church was established in 1920 by a group of priests and lay people who split from the Roman Catholic church. It is committed to professing the legacy of Jan Hus and the Hussite movement, and is a specific Czechoslovak church.

a non-believer from that time onwards.[87] As he himself said, religion was something that almost no-one understood, and which his generation saw as something akin to "abandoned children's toys. For us, religion was something for grannies with candles, beggars at church doors, sacristans and priests. We let them cheat at cards, with some reservations, and without much understanding we observed their easy sexual affairs, which they often carried on publicly and without evident embarrassment, and we then observed their piety during services and 'prattling from the prayerbook' with unconcealed hatred. In the end we looked on all of this with a sympathetic haughtiness."[88] This opinion of course stemmed in part from his anarchist views. Even so, it was to be somewhat changed by one of his first clients.

The client in question was the catholic thinker and publisher Josef Florian, a long-time friend of Resler's. "If we ever discovered what religion really was, then it was all thanks to you [Josef Florian] and your colleagues, who built up that which all Czechs, and indeed some Slovaks, nowadays refer to lovingly and respectfully as the 'Stará Říše.'[89] (...) This does not apply only to me, but to many others here, who are as aware of it as I am, and who appreciate your work even in those parts where they remain your irreconcilable opponents. (...) For others you have renewed something that had been buried or lost behind the magicianry of mindless ministers."[90]

After Florian's death, Resler emphasised this even further: "Anyone who is familiar with J. Florian's work must concede that it presented him with, and in the literal sense uncovered, a different catholicism, one that was fresh, living, decisive and uncompromising, yet at the same time immensely deep and broad, capable of inspiring him to the highest of goals, of reshaping individuals' lives and the lives of whole communities in the spirit's image, and must admit, that Josef Florian's work wiped away from his not unjustified ideas all the mould, rust and leprosy that had been left by all those petty and troublesome devotees of the great and powerful faith on which human learning has been built for two thousand years."[91]

Resler never considered himself a Christian and later wrote that he remained uncompromisingly opposed to religion. Nevertheless, he understood and respected Christianity when it was truly lived and applied, rather than automated and vacant.

---

87   NM, Notice of leaving the church, letter to the chairman of the district council in Královské Vinohrady on 5 November 1912.
88   PNP 113, Letter to Josef Florian on 5 October 1940.
89   Florian lived in the village called "Stará Říše" and there published a series of books entitled "Good work".
90   PNP 113, Letter to Josef Florian on 5 October 1940.
91   Kamill Resler: "Josef Florian zemřel před rokem (29. 12. 1941): Jan Konůpek pro Starou Říši a o Staré Říši," in Marginálie 16 (1943), p. 55, cited in Muchka, p. 19.

During his visits to Stará Říše, Resler gradually got to know a number of thinkers of the time, whom he had not had the chance to meet within the anarchist circles. One of these was the catholic writer, artist and thinker Bohuslav Reynek, with whom Resler formed a life-long friendship, and who also became one of his clients.[92] When Reynek was making preparations for his wedding in the French town of Grenoble, he consulted Resler as to the documents he would need in order to be able to marry in France. Resler also represented Reynek in a few cases related to non-payment; one of these was against Reynek's debtor František Hezina, a factory owner from Humpolec, and one against bookseller J. Milešek from Bratislava, who had owed Reynek the sum of 88 crowns for over a year, according to surviving records. Resler's legal intervention had the desired effect, and all the money owed was eventually paid. As an expression of his gratitude, Reynek later gave Resler one of his artworks.

When, in 1960, Resler asked him for a depiction of certain past events, Reynek's response was: "My dear Doctor, upon your request I began to look into the past, but found that dead dogs were baring their teeth at me from the verges down memory lane, and there were so many of them that I had to stop straight away for fear of becoming ill (even physically so). The illness is no metaphor, but reality, and I am sharing it with you for information. My wife says that she will write something about her work; when that will be, though, I do not know. I greet you warmly and thank you for remembering me, B. Reynek."[93]

As a result of his regular contact with artists, and thanks to the fact that Resler himself was also an artist at heart, he often represented artists in his legal work. Among them were the fine artists František Bidlo, Karel Holan, František Tittelbach, Karel Kotrba, Toyen, and writers St. K. Neumann, F. X. Šalda, Josef Hora, Jindřich Hořejší, Petr Bezruč, as well as several architects, actors and politicians. In many cases, Resler represented these artists as an act of friendship and free of charge.

It was thus that during the 30s and 40s he handled communications with the revenue authorities over matters concerning pension taxes for František Halas, whom Resler also counted among his personal friends. When Halas married in 1936 Resler wrote to him that "it comes round to everyone in the end, and so, as this white card tells me, you will no longer walk the path of life alone, as you have done so far; that is as it should be, and I wish you all happiness on your new journey together." After Halas' death in 1949, of which Resler learned while reading the newspaper *Rudé právo*, he wrote to his widow: "The

---

92   NM, Transcript of the programme *Advokát, který měl rád knížky* [A barrister who liked books], produced by Pavel Kosatík, Český rozhlas Vltava, broadcast on 18 June 1995 at 8.00 pm., p. 8.
93   PNP 52, Letters between Reynek and Resler.

necessities of life required of him that he become that which he least knew how to be – an official. And yet he led his office with a broad outlook, in the interests of his sector, which upheld and gained the esteem of all who had reason to contact the office. / In him I have lost a sincere friend, a man whom I deeply respected both for his poetry, and for his character; a man of whom I was genuinely very fond."[94]

In 1929 following a recommendation from Karel Novák, an operations controller at the state printers in Prague, Resler took on the defence of Novák's deputy, Vilém Kohout, who was accused of stealing passport blanks. Kohout passed these passports on to a secret communist group, which printed leaflets and pamphlets. One of the passports was also used by Czech communist journalist Julius Fučík for his secret journeys from Russia to Czechoslovakia. Fučík showed it to Resler when they were travelling to Prague together by train on one of those journeys. Although Kohout admitted his guilt in the preliminary proceedings, Resler succeeded in obtaining his acquittal.[95]

This case is particularly interesting in that Resler only wrote openly about it at the end of the 40s, when it began to be fashionable to mention cases relating to the defence of communists or work with communists. No other documents related to it survive in his archive.

Another of those whom Resler met at Florian's in Stará Říše, and who later became his client, was František Mastík of České Budějovice,[96] the owner of Izmael publishing house and editor of *Gedeon* magazine, whom Resler also often met in Prague. In 1934, he was accused of homosexuality, or rather of the crime of unnatural fornication with a person of the same sex according to § 129 point b) of criminal act no. 117/1852 ř. z. (imperial code)[97] The entirety of the prosecution's argument fit on one side of paper.[98] Resler's defence argumentation largely relied on experts. In his observations on their reports he wrote: "The question of sexual abnormality is not generally a question of everyday medicine, but rather a question for a specialist and complex field of medical science: sexual pathology." This was his way of pointing out the insufficient expertise of the experts appointed, who were experts neither in this field nor in psychiatry.

The experts in question were police doctors who had been nominated against Resler's will, while he had proposed true experts. He considered their judgements to have been drawn up in a "very rustic manner." According to Mastík's previous military records, he had suffered from severe psychopathy

---

94   PNP 69, Letters between Resler and the Halas family.
95   NM Appeal against being excluded from the bar.
96   The largest town in South Bohemia, known as Budweis in German.
97   PNP 109, Case filed at the Regional Criminal Court in Prague.
98   PNP 109, Obžaloba sp. zn. Krajského soudu trestního v Praze Tk X 3589/34 [court document – accusation].

from birth – although the new experts did not make reference to this. Resler's defence emphasised the difference between "a congenital disease or the result of criminal perversions,"[99] making a clear distinction between innate homosexuality, which in Resler's opinion was not punishable, and criminal perversion. On Resler's instigation a new expert was also called, whose report was in Mastík's favour.

During the trial, Mastík was concerned that the case would be discussed in public, but Resler reassured him that this would not happen: "doctors, judges and my colleagues are all legally bound to strict confidentiality and will be careful not to disclose anything." Even after the Mastík's partner was sentenced to three months in prison, the case did not arouse any outside interest, and no one attended the hearing. Mastík complained in one letter to Resler: "I still cannot rid myself of the impression that society is cruel to people like me."

František (who took the name Chrysostom) Mastík was ordained in 1943 and celebrated his first Mass in the most famous of Czech Catholic churches, St. Vítus Cathedral at Prague Castle. On that occasion, Resler wrote to him: "I have come to realise that you have chosen the right harbour in which to anchor the barge that is your life, so often tossed about by storms and inclement weather. I sincerely pray that it will find there quiet and peace of heart, with all my best wishes."[100]

Resler was in general very lenient with his artistic clients. For example, he had an agreement with the writer S. K. Neumann that Neumann would pay him when he was able to – and that time eventually came only after Neumann's death. Similarly, when he represented the publisher *Družstevní práce* against B. M. Klika's company in 1928, he only asked the publishing house for a tenth the amount they were expecting. To thank him for the favour, they offered him a work from their fine art collection.[101]

RESLER'S OTHER CLIENTS

A number of cases – both well known and less well known – about which records were retained in Resler's estate are outlined below. In some of these cases it has not been possible to identify the individuals involved fully, and we only have basic information about them. This is true of the state of Resler's records more generally, and thus holds throughout the following chapters as well.

---

99 PNP 109, Final three points of case filed at the Regional Criminal Court in Prague.
100 Letters between Mastík and Resler, PNP 109. For further information about František Mastík see Ivan Slavík. *Kdo byl Chrysostom Mastík?* [Who was Chrysostom Mastík?], *Box* 3/1993, p. 130–131.
101 PNP 111, Letter to Resler on 4 April 1928.

DEFENCE OF DOCTOR ARNOŠT DVOŘÁK[102]

Six years after establishing his own practice, Resler began work on one of his most publically renowned cases, and one that tested his knowledge of military law: the defence of Lieutenant Colonel MUDr. Arnošt Dvořák, the recruiting doctor for the Supplementary District Command of Greater Prague, who had treated Resler in Vienna in 1917, and whom he also knew from the Union café. Dvořák was on trial for abuse of professional power, for having deemed recruits unsuitable for service and sent them to hospital for further examinations.

The Divisional Court in Prague nevertheless found that from a medical perspective Dvořák's decisions had been sound, that is, that at the time the recruits in question were not in a position to carry out military service. Although Dvořák had personal relationships with a number of the excused individuals' families, and had borrowed small amounts of money from them, the court considered that this had not influenced his decisions, and so he had not committed the crime of abuse of professional power. The only fault they could find with him was occasional carelessness in describing his medical findings in the individuals' files. From a legal perspective, then, Resler was fully successful, which must certainly have pleased the Minister of National Defence, who enquired as to the state of the case every day.

Dvořák further considered suing the journalists who had written about him. However, articles on his case had appeared in nearly every magazine in Prague and beyond, and so he would have had to bring about a hundred lawsuits. This would have been a long and costly procedure, and would have brought his case to light once more, so he was not keen to go down that route. Especially since many of the magazines had corrected their reporting mistakes, either during or after his trial. The provincial military command also recommended that he refrain from suing, and the commander refused to agree to his doing so, as he did not consider it to be in the interest of the armed forces.

That was the end of Dr. Dvořák's case. However, the case did further result in some information that led Resler to ask the disciplinary committee of the Bar Association in Prague to look into his friend JUDr. Mellan's affairs. According to Resler's information, one of Mellan's employees had found out from the Divisional Court, where he had previously worked, that Dr. Dvořák had been

---

102 PNP Arnošt Dvořák, inv. no. 432–510. The case is also described in Jan Hrubý. *Aféry první republiky* [Affairs of the first Republic]. Prague: Práce, 1984, although in a somewhat sensationalist manner. The author attempts to persuade the reader that the case was consistently manipulated, and that only the communists stood against such corruption. Without much analysis of the legal arguments he draws the conclusion that Arnošt Dvořák was guilty. Although the book is ideologically biased, it nevertheless provides some further detail on the case.

arrested, and had repeatedly attempted to force him to accept representation by Dr. Mellan. Kamill Resler had no qualms about making a complaint against his friend – since he believed he was not playing fairly.

When he had to attend a meeting linked to the Dvořák case and could not join the family in the countryside for his daughter's 6th birthday, he wrote Blanka a lovely letter in which he recalled another of her birthdays and the fun they had had. He wished her as much fun every birthday as then.[103] Together with that letter, he also wrote to his wife to tell her that the case with Dr. Dvořák had ended well, and that he would come to join the family soon.

Resler was often busy with his work, but did his best to spend his free time with the children and to show them that he cared about them. The extent to which he cherished even the smallest things is shown by the fact that he kept a note from his daughter Blanka in his archive; it was written on his name day in 1934, and read: "Dear Daddy, we are glad you came to see us so that we could tell you on your name day how much we love you and how happy you make us when you're with us."

DEFENCE OF BEDŘICH KALDA VS. THE CZECHOSLOVAK STATE[104]

Dr. Kalda, consul of the state of Cleveland, was accused in 1935 of embezzlement, which he had allegedly committed by pocketing money that had been intended for Czechoslovak citizens. Resler represented him, and consulted on the case with Opava-based senator and barrister JUDr. Josef Lukeš, who had been a member of the National Assembly's foreign affairs committee for 10 years, and knew the whole Kalda family well. Lukeš believed that Kalda had most likely spent more money on the promotion of Czechoslovakia, then known as propaganda, than he had been authorized to. However, this would have been consistent with the wishes of the parliamentary foreign affairs committee, which had criticized the Ministry of Foreign Affairs several times for allocating too small a budget for propaganda. Kalda was highly regarded by Czechoslovaks living in Cleveland, who wrote numerous letters in his support. His young son also died during the trial, a further reason why Resler had to try hard to keep Kalda "in such a state of mind as to be able to summon enough moral strength to defend himself firmly and confidently in court." Hence why in a letter to Kalda's brother, an architect working in Zagreb, Croatia who covered part of his brother's legal costs, Resler asked him to write to Kalda to encourage him.

Resler praised the judges who presided over this case: they were "two of the best judges of the time, noble and righteous people." The case was also

---

103   NM, Letter to daughter Blanka on 17 March 1931.
104   PNP, Kalda Bedřich, inv. no. 2278–2538.

a matter of interest for the politicians of the day, and indeed president Beneš himself, the first Czechoslovak minister of foreign affairs, reported that he would be happy to see the matter resolved *ad exemplum*.

At the main hearing the public was excluded, probably because the case touched upon matters of foreign policy. The prosecutor therefore had to make extra efforts to enable representatives of the Finance Prosecutor's Office and Ministry of Foreign Affairs to be present, which he did by including them in the case as civil claimants. The court rejected their original claims for 300,000 Czechoslovak Crowns (Kčs), but accepted a revised claim for 150 Kčs. Resler described the hearing as "a rough beating." He was so sure of the outcome that he stated: "unless justice is a wholly relative term, the matter is ripe for all evidence to be rejected and an acquittal issued."

When Dr. Lukeš praised Resler's legal prowess, he responded thus: "I am however afraid that you are overestimating the significance of my part in the matter. I am doing what a simple citizen would; I have no other option than to appeal on the law against the powerful central authorities, who, as can be seen from the progress of this case, have willingly resorted to means that are undignified for such a high office. The power of this authority does not dazzle me personally, and I am not used to backing off in the face of such things. And according to the law, the court should not and must not allow that power to dazzle it."

The Regional Criminal Court in Prague judged, on 7th April 1937, that Kalda had used all the money in question for state matters, but for matters other than those for which they were intended (as Dr. Lukeš had supposed), and therefore found him guilty of embezzlement and sentenced him to a suspended sentence of one year in prison. The court also stated that the crime could not be considered dishonourable and therefore Kalda's right to vote could not be taken away. However, he was required to pay damages amounting to more than 300,000 Kčs. Resler submitted an appeal against the court's decision, as did the state prosecutor. The Supreme Court however, as that of last instance, rejected both the appeals. Resler demanded public corrections from all newspapers that had written dishonourably of Kalda. He sought approval for this from the ministry; this was granted, but only after a week, which Kalda considered to be too late for the corrections to be issued. As a result of his assertion that the ministry had made the claim of embezzlement for 150 Kčs purely as a distraction, and had thus falsely accused Kalda, Resler was charged by the District Criminal Court in the tenth district of Prague; the ministry believed this to constitute defamation. Yet Resler's reason for claiming this was simple: a representative of the ministry had once stated that the 150 Kčs were embezzled, but while under oath as a witness had declared that he was unable to prove this, and that he simply believed it to be the case. Resler was represented by his friend JUDr. Antonín Švehla in this dispute.

Resler was acquitted, not on the basis of the matter itself, but on the basis of a formality regarding who should represent the ministry in such cases. The state prosecutor appealed, but the Regional Court returned the case to the District Criminal Court for a second time. This did not change the outcome; Resler was once again acquitted, and although the state prosecutor appealed once again, the Regional Criminal Court in Prague confirmed this judgement. Resler thus emerged in spring 1940 from a legal process that had lasted three and a half years and resulted in an important verdict despite the rather unimportant case. This was the Ministry of Foreign Affairs' way of expressing the extent of its sincerity and dignity.

The President of the Republic announced an Amnesty on 7th October 1938, which pardoned Bedřich Kalda – he was cleared of his criminal sentence, but this did not extend to the payment of damages. He continued to pay these as his means allowed, and in 1942 Resler represented him in an executory dispute. He even sent a request for clemency to the President of the Protectorate, Hácha, but whether this was granted remains unclear.

THE CASE OF THE MÁNES ARTISTIC ASSOCIATION[105]

One of the longest cases Resler was involved in concerned the exclusion of painter Karl Holan the younger and a group of other artists from the Mánes Association of Fine Artists in 1930. Disputes had arisen around the construction of the new Mánes building in Prague. Karel Holan and others had pointed out inconsistencies in the accounting of building work costs, and this was not well received, in particular by the Association's chairman, architect Otakar Novotný,who was the new building's designer. However, it turned out that excluding certain members in order to silence opposition within the group was not valid. According to the group's statutes, members of the Association could only be excluded if they had been artistically inactive, which was not the case here. The dispute continued, with a number of judicial instances, until 1st December 1939, when the court finally ruled in Resler's favour.

---

105   PNP, Karel Holan; Muchka, p. 21–22.

2. AFTER MUNICH

SALUTE THE FLAG! AND OTHER WARTIME BOOKS

The Kiesewetter trial was the prelude to the end of the First Republic and an independent Czechoslovakia. After Austria's annexation to Germany in March 1938, it was Czechoslovakia's turn. Fearing for his family's safety and because of the danger of air raids in Prague, Resler moved his wife and children to their cottage in Zadní Třebáň on 2 September 1938.[106] Six days later he laconically noted "München" on a scrap of paper, followed on 30 September by "fall" and on 1 October "the Germans occupy Šumava."[107] He recorded his personal views on the political events taking place in a short verse, written in his diary on 13 October:

Dopředu nelze a nelze zpět,
přede mnou, za mnou podlý svět
vpravo i vlevo zrada i klam –
ještě své tvrdé pěstě mám.

No way forward and no way back,
Ahead and behind the world is black.
Betrayed and deceived on every side –
At least my fists are not yet tied.

During the pre-war period, Resler was particularly active as a writer. In 1938 he published the previously mentioned booklet *Hlas v hluku zalehlý* (A Voice Resounding in the Noise), a discussion of defeatism. In mid-1938 Resler had the idea of putting together a collection of poems as a reaction to Germany's threats in the days surrounding the Munich agreement. This idea occurred to him after reading Karl Rohan's poem *21.V.1938* and Hora's *Noc*

---

106 NM, Life story 1934–1942.

107 München here is a reference to the München Agreement, by which France, Great Britain, Italy and Germany obliged Czechoslovakia to annex the Sudetenland to Germany. For more on the München Agreement, see Hugh Agnew. *The Czechs and the Lands of the Bohemian Crown*, Stanford: Hoover Press, 2004, chapter 12. Šumava is a forested area in south Bohemia, which was part of the Sudetenland, and is also known as the Bohemian Forest.

z 20. května (The Night of 20 May).[108] These poems were the first in a "continuous poetic diary, which is still being written. This diary boldly reflects the whole nation's attitude to the historic moment, their love for their homeland, and for diligent creative work, their awareness of fatal danger, their faith and firmness – their men's true determination to fight, if necessary, their women's bravery and submissiveness; then the harshest disenchantment and utter bitterness in the moments when they saw that they had been betrayed and abandoned. (...) Once more – after Godesberg[109] – that nation plucked up its courage, with new-found faith and the greatest of effort, as it assembled young and old under its banner, in the night of 23 September 1938 in a unique display of discipline and unity. All the nation's ammunition, and all her hearts, were then at the frontier, among the boundary stones. Only within a week came Münich. After that, the nation saw that the big states' betrayal had become reality, that they had lied about their care and allegiance to her, and that twenty years of her hard work was in ruins, its effects for the most part lost, her dreams for the future dashed."

Why did Resler choose poets and poetry for this reaction? "Even during this period, when politicians and representatives of the people were crippled by the pressure of events and kept quiet out of dread for the future and their responsibilities, poets continued to accompany the people and were the spokespeople for their feelings, their confidence, their hope, their disillusionment, their pain and their firm, unshakeable faith in their own strength and future."[110]

He wanted to publish this collection of poems in 1939. It took him a great deal of work to obtain permission for publication from each of the poets involved. He included stamps for the reply with some of his requests, as he knew that many writers would not be able to afford them. He could only hope that this would not offend them.[111] He tried to include poems from regions other than Bohemia; he had a handful of Moravian poems in the selection, and just a few Slovak verses, which he cherished all the more for their small number.[112] Censorship under the Second Republic slightly interfered with his work, but the greater blow came after 15th March 1939 when the work, which was already typeset and partially printed, could not be completed. The typeset form remained at the print works and was destroyed after the attempted assassination of deputy Reichsprotektor Reinhard Heydrich on 27 May 1942. Resler later defended the censorship under the Second Republic as civically

---

108 PNP 71, Letter to Karek Rohan on 7 September 1945.
109 This was the location of Hitler's meeting with Chamberlain on 22 September 1938, which sparked the second mobilization in 1938.
110 1938. PNP 74, Kamill Resler (ed.). *K poctě zbraň.* [Salute the Flag!] Prague: Václav Petr, 1939.
111 PNP 64, Letter to Bohuš Beneš on 23 March 1939.
112 PNP 64, Letter to Andrej Kostolný.

courageous, as the censors had only forbidden a small number of poems or parts thereof from being printed. Resler had nevertheless tried his best in various ways to get around this, and when a poem that he had chosen for his collection had been banned, he had replaced it with a different poem by the same author.[113] In a few cases, whole verses of poems were removed by the censors, as in the case of Jiří Mašek's poem *Jiný přítel není* (There's No Other Friend) where the following was removed:

Na účet náš přátelé mír psí
ukramařili v zmatku bědném.
Byli jsme národem. Jsme knirpsy?
Tu urážku jak Guezi zvednem.[114]

In woeful chaos our friends
Have made us a doggy peace.
We were a nation. Are we dogs?
We'll rise to the insult like Guezen.

Elsewhere, it was sometimes just one line that bothered them, as in the case of the poem *Milostná písnička* (A Love Song), where for the sake of decency the censors removed the words "and a bosom like a bayonet."[115]

Dr. Plechatý of the press office of the Presidium of the Ministers' Council read Resler's book and did not find in it anything objectionable, as he wrote in his letter to the Ministry of the Interior's Central Censorship Committee. He only confiscated S. K. Neumann's poem for its communist-campaigning tendencies, and suggested that it might be a good idea to exclude one further poem for the same reason.[116]

Although the book was never published, Resler claimed 3000 crowns in expenses from publisher Václav Petr in October 1940, based on their contract. At the same time, he offered that this sum could be paid to him in books, "so that the matter could be resolved from your side without great sacrifice, and I would also receive indirect compensation for the costs that I incurred for this, which in reality came to at least twice the present amount."[117]

---

113   PNP 57, Letter to Josef Knap on 7 February 1939.
114   PNP 63, Právo lidu, 10 October 1938.
115   PNP 63, *Pondělní ranní noviny*, 24 October 1938.
116   Presidium ministerské rady, tiskový odbor, č.j. 45/60-39 [Documents from the Presidium of the Ministers' Council], PNP 68. For more on censorship during the Second Republic, see Jan Gebhart, and Jan Kuklík. *Velké dějiny zemí Koruny české: Svazek XV.a 1938–1945* [The Great History of the Lands of the Czech Crown: volume XV.a 1938–1945]. Prague: Paseka, 2007, pp. 144–146.
117   PNP 73, Letter to Václav Petr on 14 October 1940.

When the War was coming to an end, Resler contacted Václav Petr and asked him whether the book might be finally published. He agreed, and together with Cyril Bouda, who took care of the book's graphical and decorative layout, had the book prepared for publication before the liberation.[118]

As a result of this preparation, *K poctě zbraň praporu!* (Salute the Flag!) was the first book released after the liberation, and came out in a print run of 7 700 copies.[119] Resler hoped that the book would fulfil its original ambition, even then, and help the nation to return to its roots. In it he therefore called for Czech bravery, nobility, iron discipline, honour and dignity. He thought that there was not, and never would be any nation that would honour its flag like the Czechoslovak soldiers did. The book was designed to strengthen the nation during the tragic year 1939, but could achieve its goal even after freedom had been restored, by instilling new hope in the nation. It is symbolic that Resler concluded his foreword to the publication with praise for the USSR, thanks to whose protection the Czech people had been able to return to their daily work and to building their nation.

Resler sent his book to a number of key figures of the post-May 1945 events. He included a personal letter with copies sent to the American ambassador Stenhartt and the British ambassador Nichols, whom he asked to pass three further copies on to Prime Minister Attlee, wartime Prime Minister Churchill and former Foreign Secretary Anthony Eden, and to the French ambassador Keller, whom he asked to graciously accept the book despite it containing some bitter words against France, which "were the result of the painful disappointment of Autumn 1938 in a nation that had always esteemed and loved France and the French above all others."[120]

IN POLITICS

This book was by no means Resler's first political act; he had been involved in political life from a young age. He became a fan of social democracy at the age of thirteen after coming across a red poster while out on errands around town, which advertised a meeting of the Social Democrats and laid out in black print a brief summary of the party's aims. He found himself agreeing with what he was reading, but as he felt he was too young to become a member of a political party, he decided instead to throw his youthful energies into promoting these ideas. This decision came after a debate with his older cousin, Bohumil Neumann, who was working as a bookbinding apprentice

---

118 Muchka, p. 58.
119 PNP 91, List of publishing activities.
120 NM 214/129–132.

in Chrudim and whom Resler later described as a proletarian. Bohumil explained to him that the issue was more complex than it might at first seem, in particular because political parties were largely divided along ethnic lines. This made Resler rethink, and he decided (partly on account of his young age) to hold back for a while. A year later, however, he attended a meeting of the *Dělnická Mládež* (Workers' Youth) and joined their association *Zemská všeodborová jednota dělnické mládeže národně-sociální* (the Provincial All-Union Unit of the National-Socialist Workers' Youth) using a pseudonym. As that association's activities were gradually closed down by the police, Resler then joined another group, *Klubu mladých* (Youth Club), led by Vlastimil Borek, which brought together anarchist-communist, anarchist-socialist and liberalist youth. That club was also dissolved after a short time.

As an anarchist, before the First World War. (AHMP)

Before the First World War. (heirs)

As a member of the *Dělnická Mládež*, Kamill used the pseudonym Karel V. Branald, inspired by a sign he had once seen for a certain Mr Branald's employment agency. Although he kept quiet about his membership, his parents soon found out and Kamill was in serious trouble with his father, who was a national democrat. What was more, membership in this kind of group was forbidden in the disciplinary code for secondary school students. After the club disbanded, Resler attended meetings of Vilém Körber's *Politického dělnického klubu* (Workers' Political Club) in Prague between 1910 and 1914.[121]

During this period, Resler's attitude to life was largely formed by political literature. One of the first political textbooks he read, at the age of fourteen, was entitled *Omladina a pokrokové hnutí: trochu historie a trochu*

---

vzpomínek (The Youth and Progressive Movements: a little history and a few memories). He gave this same book to his son in 1950, so that he could learn from it too.[122]

Resler was an active supporter of anarchism. At the age of sixteen, he began to write articles for the anarchist-communist magazine *Mladý průkopník [The Young Pioneer]*.[123] One of his articles from 1910 was for example entitled *Národnost, mezinárodnost, beznárodnost* (Nationality, Internationality, No-nationality).[124] As a result of his activities in the anarchist movement, he once met Franz Kafka.[125] Thirty years later Resler recalled how honest the people were whom he had met in this context: "Michael Kácha (...) was a shoemaker, to whom I came full of my sixteen-year-old's worries and desires, to warm myself at the 'poor workers' fireplace,' and in whom I found a man for whom I felt a deep, heartfelt fondness, and whom I deeply respected. In recognition of our mutual brotherly-fatherly bond, I – when there was no one more appropriate – gave the eulogy at his funeral after the war, and published an article in his memory."[126]

RESLER'S FAMILY

Resler was born on 23 December 1893 in an area of the eastern Bohemian town Pardubice known as the *Zelené předměstí* (Green Suburb), house number 110.[127] Imperial Royal Professor Jaroslav Antoš from Chrudim was witness at his baptism into the Roman Catholic Church. The fact that his first name Kamill was written with two "l"s was unintentional – it was a mistake local chaplain Alois Ulbrich made while writing the birth certificate. All Resler's ancestors were from eastern Bohemia: both his parents came from near Nasavrky, a small town near Chrudim to the South of Pardubice; his father's family was from Nasavrky itself, and his mother came from the neighbouring village of Ochoz (now part of Nasavrky). Resler himself wrote of his family's origins: "Our oldest ancestor was a metalworker, his descendents labourers

---

122   KNM 1, P. A. Veselý. *Omladina a pokrokové hnutí: trochu historie a trochu vzpomínek* [The Youth and Progressive Movements: a little history and a few memories], Prague 1902, with an inscription by Resler.

123   AHMP 14, Rozklad a odvolání adresovaný Akčnímu výboru Advokátní komory pro Čechy, II. [Appeal documents].

124   VCM , Articles by Kamill Resler.

125   O. Kosta. "Hledání a bloudění Franze Kafky [Franz Kafka's Searching and Wandering]," *Nový život, měsíčník pro literaturu a umění*, no. 10 (1958), p. 784.

126   VCM, "Michael Kácha, průkopník krásné české knihy" ["Michael Kácha, Pioneer of a Beautiful Czech Book", in XXIV. ročenka českých knihtiskařů [XXIVth Czech Bookprinters' Annual], 1941.

127   NM, Baptism Certificate.

and cottagers in the Chrudim area, near Nasavrky, the second most heavily Czech-speaking area of Bohemia after Čáslav."[128]

Resler took great interest in the origin of his surname. His grandfather on his father's side had still used the Germanic spelling Rössler, although his father wrote his name Ressler, and Kamill rather hoped that the name might be linked to well-known figures Ressel and Roezl.[129] When, during the Second World War, he attempted to draw up his family tree in order to apply for recognition of Aryan origin, he discovered that he had no blood relationship to these individuals.[130] There were thus two possibilities left for where his name had come from: *Rössler* in German means "poor tawer," or leatherworker, while the German word *Ross* means "steed".

Kamill Resler was his parents' fifth child of six. The first three children died in childhood: the eldest Zdenička of diphtheria at the age of four, the second Bedřich at six months, and the third Marie two days before her first birthday and just half a year before Zdenička. Kamill's elder brother Josef, a lieutenant in the 11th infantry regiment and commander of the 4th company, was killed on the front line in 1915 in Halič, nowadays on the Poland/Ukraine borders. Only Kamill's younger brother Antonín lived as long as he. Antonín became a composer, and his compositions were played in Bohemia's most renowned concert hall, the Rudolfinum. Kamill became a relative of František Palacký[131] when Antonín married Palacký's granddaughter.[132]

While Kamill was stubborn and untamable from a young age, and outspoken and uncompromising as an adult, Antonín was more concerned with creature comforts and simple pleasures than intellectual satisfaction. Kamill remembered one occasion when young Antonín had preferred to stand behind his father rather than his brother, to be on the safe side. That didn't mean, though, that he didn't go in for daredevil adventures – at the age of just five, he killed a large adder with a stick, for which his brother rather envied him.[133]

---

128 AHMP 16, Kamill Resler: Běh života [Life story]. The areas around Chrudim and Čáslav were heavily Czech areas; in 1910, more than 99.5% of their populations spoke everyday Czech. There were numerous areas like these, with the most heavily Czech-speaking being the area of Sedlec near Sedlčany. *Statistická příručka království Českého* [A Statistical handbook to the Bohemian kingdom], ed. 2nd, prepared by Zemská statistická kancelář království Českého, issued in Czech, Prague: knihkupectví Františka Řivnáče, 1913, pp. 2–15.

129 Both were famous Czechs. Josef Ressel was the inventor of the screw propeller. Benedikt Roezl was a Czech explorer and plant collector – one of the most famous collectors of exotic plants, in particular orchids. See e.g. M. C. Kline. *Benedict Roezl – Famous orchid collectors.* Amer. Orch. Soc. Bull. 32, no. 8 (1963).

130 AHMP 14, Místopřísežné prohlášení, 17. VII. 1939, Rodokmen a Místopřísežné prohlášení k provedení vládního nařízení ze 4. července 1939 č. 236/1940 Sb. z. a n. [official family origin declarations]; NM 216/257, Report by Resler's daughter Blanka Brunnerová.

131 František Palacký was a Czech historian and politician, known as "the Father of the Nation."

132 NM 214/103, Rozpracovaný rodokmen [family tree].

133 NM, Kamill Resler: Antonín Resler.

Shortly before the Second World War, Kamill and Antonín lost their parents. Resler's mother Antonie died on 8 August 1938 and was cremated. Her sons asked those who wanted to contribute to funeral flowers to make a donation to the national defence effort instead.[134] Her husband, Kamill's father Josef, died exactly a year and a day after her, on 9 August 1939. He suffered a heart attack during a dispute with the priest in Nasavrky, where both he and his wife had wanted to be buried. The parish priest was refusing to have anything to do with Antonie's remains, because she had been cremated. At Josef Resler's funeral Kamill's old friend and renowned Czech poet Petr Bezruč gave a eulogy.[135] Antonie's urn was eventually committed to her husband's grave in 1941 after an agreement was reached with the parish priest; it is not clear if this was the same priest, or another. Her two sons did the deed in total secrecy at a time when no one was at the cemetery. Both Resler's parents' remains are to this day in grave no. 407 in Nasavrky, near the grave where his grandparents are buried.[136]

In addition to some old family properties in Nasavrky, Kamill and Libuše also owned and took care of a small house in Zadní Třebáň[137] (Hlásná Třebáň – Roviny, no. 77), and spent more of their time there. Resler spoke of the work he did there as "slave labour." In 1951 they were ordered to partially demolish the house, whose roof had partially fallen in, but the family instead re-built the damaged part and renovated the house. In Zadní Třebáň, Resler tried not to do anything related to law. In a letter he sent in 1940 to J. L. Krejčí in Brno, he wrote: "So far I have not written to anyone from here, and I am not going to either; I am going to chop wood and work with a hoe and spade, so that I need not think about many other pressing matters."[138]

By comparison, the Reslers took little care of a plot of land that they also owned in Radotín, now a district of Prague. As the plot was as yet unused, Kamill offered it to writer Karel Dvořáček in 1944 for development. He offered to pay for the plot to be fenced in, and for a cottage to be built on it for the Dvořáčeks' use – on only one condition, that Resler approve in advance the plans for the landscaping and placement of the cottage. Resler did not want any money in return for their use of the land; it was good enough for him if they cultivated the land and took care of a garden there. However, in summer 1944 Karel Dvořáček was arrested for a second time for failing to report a crime; or, more specifically, for having known about an organization and not reported it (a crime according to section 139 of the Imperial Code),

---

134 NM, Funeral announcement.
135 PNP 109, Eulogy; NM, Handwritten note on folder "Reslerovi Donátovi".
136 NM, Letter to the local priest on 27 May 1941; handrwritten undated letter from the priest to Kamill.
137 Zadní Třebáň is a village located 20 km south-west of Prague.
138 PNP 109, Letter to J. L. Krejčí on 16 July 1940.

and was sent to prison, first in Wrocław and later in Zwickau. While there he suffered starvation and was forced to carry out hard labour, and, since he had severe lung disease, died before an appeal Resler wrote or the intervention of Resler's barrister colleague in Berlin were able to save him.[139]

ROLE IN THE BAR ASSOCIATION

After practising as a barrister for over 10 years, Resler began to feel he was ready to take up a role in his profession's Association, and so from 1932 until 1935 he was a deputy member of the disciplinary board of the Bar Association for Bohemia and Prague, and from 1935 until 1946 deputy prosecutor for the Association. It certainly helped that in 1931 he was elected to the examiners' panel for judicial entrance examinations for one year. Furthermore, on 14 January 1939 he was elected as a substitute to the Permanent delegation of Bar Associations in the Czechoslovak Republic in Prague, which was a sort of joint representation of the Bar Associations (at that time only Czech and Moravian Associations), but with no legal basis. As prosecutor for the disciplinary board, Resler attended 212 hearings.[140] In particular, he dealt with disciplinary appeals that were brought to the Supreme Court, which served as the disciplinary court of appeal in matters related to barristers and aspiring barristers.[141] From Resler's surviving records we aren't able to report the entirety of his results in appeals for this period, however his notes on cases from some of the pre-war and wartime years have been preserved. In the period 1936–1940, Resler took 39 appeal procedures to the Supreme Court and achieved complete success in 19, and partial success in 10. 5 were rejected and 5 ended for other reasons (e.g. the charges were dropped, the case was discontinued, or the case was transferred to a German court). Most of Resler's appeal cases on which records survive concerned the disciplinary offence of discredit and disrespect of status.[142]

On 18 March 1946, Resler resigned from his position within the Association in response to his unlawful appointment as an *ex officio* defence counsel. That did not mean, though, that he neglected his duties. At the following

---

139 PNP 69, Letter to Karel Dvořáček on 9 May 1944; letter from his wife Ž. Dvořáčková on 18 March 1945.

140 AHMP 12, Dozorčí stížnost na rozhodnutí výboru Advokátní komory [complaint] on 16 March 1946.

141 These procedures were two-instance. For more information see e.g. Lenka Řehulová. *Profesionální etika advokáta a kárné řízení jako důsledek porušení povinností advokáta v podmínkách právní úpravy České republiky.* [Barristers' Professional Ethics and Disciplinary Proceedings as the Result of Breaching One's Duties as a Barrister in the Law of the Czech Republic]. Dissertation. Brno: Právnická fakulta Masarykovy Univerzity, 2012/2013.

142 PNP 78, List entitled "Odvolání, Množství podání".

meeting, he sent in a response to a case that had been on his desk. It wasn't in his nature to walk away from work in progress.[143]

Several times, Reslcr also experienced disciplinary proceedings from the other side – that is, as the accused. Since he held an official role within the Czech Bar Association, his cases were heard before the Moravian Bar Association to ensure fairness. In one case, in 1947, he was found guilty of discredit and disrespect of status, after he had launched legal action on behalf of his client against the opposing counsel, for the lawyer in question to surrender some letters, even though Resler knew that the lawyer had only had the letters entrusted to him. Resler was required to pay a fine of 1 000 Kčs.[144] He appealed against this decision[145] and the Supreme Court acquitted him, noting that he had had a duty to "defend his client's rights against any individual zealously, faithfully and conscientiously." This decision was supported by the fact that the letters in question had been stolen from Resler's client. The Supreme Court made its decision on 29 December 1948 – two days before a key date in his legal career.[146] Resler was also acquitted in all of the other relatively unremarkable disciplinary cases concerning him.

PROTECTION OF JEWS DURING THE WAR

In the period just before the war, Resler was not particularly active on the political scene, other than as a writer. As deputy prosecutor for the Bohemian Bar Association in Prague, however, he was fearlessly active. In particular, he brought charges against antisemitic excesses by the group of so-called Aryan barristers, and continued in this even during the German occupation. Resler's estate included records of two proceedings.

Conditions were never easy for lawyers of Jewish origin in Czechoslovakia. Some felt that they were primarily Czechs or Germans, others primarily Jews. There was a general dislike for them in the Czech society, which became evident in the Hilsner affair (similar to the Dreyfus affair in France). During the Second Republic Jews were gradually forced out of various professions, including the Bar, largely for economic reasons;this came to an end with the German army invasion on 15 March 1939.[147]

---

143 PNP 78, Letter to the Bar Association delivered 26 March 1946.
144 PNP 78, Nález Moravské advokátní komory, sp. zn. DR 24/44 [court document].
145 ČAK, Letter dated 4 June 1947. In one letter, the president of the disciplinary board of the Moravian Bar Association also considered it evident that Resler would appeal.
146 PNP 78, Rozsudek Nejvyššího soudu, sp. zn. DS II 18/47 [court document].
147 Jakub Drápal. "Postup advokacie proti židovským advokátům [The Bar's Move Against Jewish Barristers]," in Marcela Zoufalá, Jiří Holý, and Pavel Sládek (eds.). *Rozpad židovského života: 167 dní druhé republiky.* [The Disintegration of Jewish Life: 167 Days of the Second Republic]. Prague: Academia, 2016.

In one case, Resler launched disciplinary proceedings against Aryan barrister JUDr. Čeňek Bruno, who had distributed whistles to obstruct Jews from speaking during an extraordinary General Meeting of the Bar Association Prague on 5 February 1939. When the Bar Association's disciplinary committee discontinued the proceedings on 18 March 1940 – in Resler's view wrongfully, since it had already decided on 1 June 1939 that there were grounds for disciplinary proceedings – he made a complaint to the Supreme Court.

Similarly, on 17 February 1939 he proposed charges against JUDr. Antonín Hübschmann, who had driven some Jews out of a café in October of the previous year. However, the disciplinary committee called off the proceedings given the difficult circumstances, and so Resler made a complaint to the Supreme Court on 15 March 1939, when the Germans were already in Prague. After a few months, the court asked him whether he wished to persist with the case, to which Resler replied on 25 September 1939 that he did.[148] The Supreme Court then rejected his complaint.[149]

JUDr. Hübschmann's fate after that was peculiar. After his antisemitic statements and acts, he eventually found himself in a concentration camp, where he apparently turned himself around, expressed regret for what he had done, and started to help the Jews. After his release he continued with these efforts to help the needy, sometimes providing them his services *pro bono*. Despite this, he was detained for a few months after the war, and while waiting for his trial before the Extraordinary People's Court to begin he worked in the coal mines, where he was praised by his workmates. The court found that he showed remorse for his actions and that he was a changed man, and so although it found him guilty according to the Retributive Decree, it did not sentence him to any punishment.[150]

Resler was also active beyond the duties of his professional roles. At a time when the media were attacking Jews, Resler spoke on behalf of the Bar Association in Prague at the funeral of the Association's prosecutor JUDr. Oskar Taussig, who was of Jewish origin, because no one else was willing to do so.

He also did his best to intervene in the fight over Jewish barristers. The Bohemian Bar Association, based in Prague was one of the bodies (together

---

Helena Petrův. *Zákonné bezpráví.* [Legal Injustice]. Prague: Auditorium, 2011, chapter II.5. For more on Jews in Czechoslovakia, see J. Láníček: *Czech, Slovaks and the Jews 1938–48: Beyond Idealisation and Condemnation.* BasingstokeL: Palgrave Macmillan, 2013, and L. Rothkirchen. *The Jews of Bohemia and Moravia: Facing the Holocaust.* University of Nebraska Press, 2006.

148 NM; AHMP 14, Rozklad proti rozhodnutí Akčního výboru Advokátní komory pro Čechy [appeal].

149 PNP 78, Seznam odvolání, stížností a obnov [list of appeals and complaints].

150 PNP 78, undated newspaper article entitled "Uniknou fašisující advokáti potrestání" ["Barristers with fascist tendencies escape disciplinary proceedings "] by Dr. Paleček, which probably appeared in Rudé Právo. The article is against JUDr. Hübschmann and so it does not seem that its author would sided with him, for example concerning helping Jews in the concentraton camp.

with the Medical Chamber) that began to restrict Jews from practising their profession of its own initiative.[151] Already on 14 October 1938, the committee of the Union of Czechoslovak Barristers, a key association of barristers in Czechoslovakia, decided that the number of Jews at the Bar should be proportional to the number of Jews in the population. Resler attempted to prevent this from being implemented. At a meeting of a key group of barristers, he pressed for a unanimous resolution "that representatives of this group who are on the committee of the Union of Czech Barristers will vote against the mass exclusion of Jews and will do their best to look closely into each case in which a Jewish member of the Union is considered for exclusion, to prevent Nazi views from affecting the Union".[152] As he wrote after the war, he succeeded in maintaining this position for a few months. How successful they were in preventing the mass exclusion of Jews from the profession we may only speculate; nevertheless it is true that during the Second Republic no mass exclusion took place. That came only on 11th January 1939, when the Union's committee decided to exclude a number of Jewish barristers, and approved a report on Jewish-Czech barristers' ethnical difference, although this decision was taken amid numerous procedural errors and mix-ups, which should have made it invalid.[153] Even so, a ban from practising as a barrister could only be handed out by the Bohemian Bar Association itself, in Prague. There, the Jewish question was addressed at an extraordinary general meeting on 5 February 1939, but it was not until 15 March 1939 that the Bar Association's board decided to pass a resolution banning all non-Aryan barristers from practice.

Along with all other barristers, Resler too had to prove that he was not a Jew, and so in July 1939 he submitted a solemn declaration as to the origins both of his own ancestors and his wife's.[154] One of his wife's ancestors had been born a Jew and later baptised, but luckily for him, the parish records showing this had been burnt and so he was not persecuted.

During this period he often wrote to his Jewish friend, the dentist and bibliophile MUDr. Otto Stern, who lived in the South Bohemian town of Tábor. He was expecting a similar fate for doctors as for barristers, although he considered it reasonable that Jewish doctors should be allowed to continue to treat patients as long as the patients were also Jews. Nevertheless, if that were the case he would not have had enough patients to keep his clinic in Tábor open.[155] Dr. Stern died on 6 June 1942 in Oranienburg. After the war Resler placed a column in the Tábor region social democratic weekly paper "Jiskra,"

---

151   Both associations apologised for this more than seventy years later. For more on this topic see Helena Petrův. *Zákonné bezpráví* [Legal Injustice]. Auditorium. Prague, 2011, chapter II.5.
152   NM, Rozklad proti rozhodnutí Akčního výboru Advokátní komory pro Čechy [appeal], point 4.
153   Helena Petrův. *Zákonné bezpráví* [Legal Injustice]. Auditorium. Prague, 2011, p. 80.
154   ČAK, Místopřísežné prohlášení [solemn declaration].
155   PNP 54, Letter from Otto Stern on 19 March 1939.

in which he described the late Dr. Stern as follows: "When we realise that he was a practising Jew, belonged to the intelligentsia that that Nazis hated, and was a Social Democrat, there is no need for further comment. He had to lose – Doctor Stern's tragic fate was sealed on the day he was arrested. It was difficult to hope that he would return. That conscious hopelessness was the saddest part."[156]

Of about 640 Jewish barristers practising under the Bohemian Bar Association before the war, only 21 returned for the Association's first post-war general meeting on 17 June 1945. Others did return later, but Resler notes that the number was negligible. He names eight of them, as friends of his and of Paul J. Edwards, who had emigrated to the USA before the war.[157]

---

156 "Nezapomenutelný ironik [An unforgettably ironic man]," *Jiskra* XVI, no. 8 (22 February 1946), p. 1.
157 PNP 91, Letters to Paul J. Edwards.

3. DURING THE WAR: 1939–1945

RESLER'S "PROTECTORATE FUN"

In March 1939, Czechoslovakia was occupied by the German army, and the Czech lands became the Protectorate of Bohemia and Moravia, while the Slovaks formed their own independent state.[158] Resler attempted to take life in the Protectorate somewhat dispassionately, and work in his own way towards undermining the protectorate's systems. Well aware of the risks this entailed, he committed a number of minor and less minor violations of regulations, which he himself termed his "protectorate fun" and in later memoirs he added that he "certainly did not attach any importance to them, even though in certain situations they could have had unpleasant consequences".[159]

He started with his own office. As Resler himself writes, he was unsuccessful in an attempt to persuade the Bar Association's Protectoral Board of the usefulness and sense of having a bilingual sign for his office, and so the sign outside his office was only in Czech.

Then, in 1940, just like old times, he sent a request on behalf of a client for print corrections, this time to the resistance magazine *V boj*, simply in order for it to be printed, and therefore prove that even a resistance magazine issued secretly and at in danger of death would still comply with the Czechoslovak law.

Another of Resler's favourite misdemeanours against the protectoral system was that during the occupation he refused to pay taxes, and encouraged others to do the same, so that the Germans could not use the money. After the liberation, however, he immediately paid 70 000 crowns to the new Czechoslovak Republic, in an effort to support the new state.[160]

After the attack on deputy Reichsprotektor Reinhard Heydrich the atmosphere was very tense. Resler's office was located just a hundred metres from

---

158 For an analysis of the occupation and the situation in Slovakia see Hugh Agnew. *The Czechs and the Lands of the Bohemian Crown*, Stanford: Hoover Press, 2004, chapter 12 or Peter Demetz. *Prague in Danger*, New York: Farrar, Straus and Giroux, 2008, chapter I.

159 NM, Rozklad proti rozhodnutí Akčního výboru Advokátní komory pro Čechy [appeal]. Unless stated otherwise, this section and sections "Wartime conditions and the resistance" and "Court cases and disputes during the war" are based on this source.

160 PNP 91, Letter to Paul J. Edwards on 24 June 1946.

the attackers' final hiding place, and he described the situation in one of his letters as follows: "My head is still on my shoulders and I sincerely hope I will keep it there. I am an insignificant person and have never been concerned with so-called 'public affairs'. On 18 June 1942 I wasn't able to get to my office until 14.30, as the streets around it were occupied and attention focused on the Dientzenhofer church of St Charles Borromeo in my street.[161] The beautiful building is in a lamentable state. All the glass has been smashed out of its five slender, pretty windows, it looks like a burned-out factory, but it isn't scorched."[162]

At the obligatory gathering of lawyers to express feigned grief over the death of Reinhard Heydrich, Resler did hand in his numbered summons at the Smetana Hall, but afterwards slipped out through the staff entrance to a café on the other side of town, where he composed a poem for his friend František Bidlo.[163]

When it came to military matters, Resler was brave, but scorned medals, which he referred to as metal trinkets. In 1939 and 1940, however, he obtained forbidden Czechoslovak military badges for ten friends and ex-soldiers, which it was by then illegal to wear, including the particularly strictly prohibited so-called entente medal For Civilisation 1914–1918. He gave these to some of his friends ceremonially, in his office, to encourage them in their fight against German oppression.

During the occupation Resler collected protectoral and German posters, most of which he probably obtained by taking them off public walls. These included[164] a poster about the closure of universities on 17 November 1939, and a decree dated 15 March 1939, according to which Konrad Henlein became the "chief of civil administration." In the same way, he procured a declaration by Richard Bienert from 27 November 1939 on respecting symbols of the Reich[165] – the right-armed salute was left to individual discretion – and a warning from von Neurath against acts of sabotage, which stated at the end that "responsibility for all acts of sabotage rests not only with their perpetrator but with the entire population." Further acquisitions included orders on keeping weapons and on not wearing badges with Czechoslovak themes, and posters with the slogans "Singing strictly forbidden! *Gesang behördlich verbo-*

---

161 This church was the hiding place chosen by the Czech parachutists who carried out an assassination attempt on Reinhard Heydrich, a key representative of Nazi Germany who was serving as deputy Reichsprotektor in Prague at the time. The parachutists were found, and having no way to escape, they all either shot themselves or were shot by the Gestapo. In 1935 the church was reconsecrated to Ss. Cyril and Methodius, and since then it has been used by the Orthodox Church.

162 PNP 69, Letter to Zdeněk Řezníček on 22 June 1942.

163 NM, Bidlo's Zderaz sketches and files, p. 37.

164 PNP 52 and 53.

165 Resler himself deliberately wrote the word "reich" with a lowercase "r".

ten!" and "The Reich will win for Europe on all fronts against Jews, plutocracy and Bolshevism."

WARTIME CONDITIONS AND THE RESISTANCE

Besides his "fun" Resler was also active in the resistance movement. This began not long after the country was occupied, when he helped a group of ten men from one division of Lieutenant Josef Balabán's regiment. Balabán was a resistance fighter and one of the so-called "Three kings." Resler arranged for someone to defend their friend, who had been arrested by the Germans. After they had been found out, and were fleeing for the border, he provided them with half the funds they needed, while JUDr. Antonín Švehla provided the other half, in total more than 15,000 crowns. In the evening, however, when they were supposed to collect the money, only their sergeant Hynek Pletánek came, to inform Resler that the others had had to leave Prague. He took just 1,500 crowns for his own needs. In the end, all ten men were caught by the Gestapo and the People's Court had them (according to one account, all ten, according to another, six of them) executed.[166]

Kamill Resler was active from the start of the war in the resistance group ÚVOD (Ústřední vedení odboje domácího, the Central Leadership of Home Resistance). He most likely became involved with the group through his former fellow student Jiří Sedmík, who was Beneš's secretary and diplomatic advisor to the Ministry of Foreign Affairs for a time.[167] Sedmík had founded the resistance group *Politické ústředí* (Political Centre), together with ex-chancellor Přemysl Šámal, and was also a member of the resistance group led by the police advisor Karel Jaroš, through which he became involved with the resistance group *Obrana národa* (Nation's Defence). These two groups *Politické ústředí* and *Obrana národa* later joined together with the *Petiční výbor Věrni zůstaneme* (Petition Committee We Remain Faithful), to form ÚVOD. Sedmík's

---

166 VHA, Vyjádření j. č. 110.903/P.K. 1948 [military report], point 51. Resler describes this differently in another document, where he states that the ten men were from Balabán's regiment under lieutenant colonel Josef Mašín and that six of them died. No studies of the resistance movement refer to this group in detail. Similarly, Resler's involvement in the resistance movement, including holding meetings at his offices, is not mentioned even in Jan Gebhart, and Jan Kuklík. *Velké dějiny zemí Koruny české: Svazek XV.a a XV.b 1938–1945*. [The great history of the lands of the Czech crown: vol. XV.a and XV.b 1938–1945]. Prague: Paseka, 2007; Karel Pacner. *Československo ve zvláštních službách: Pohledy do historie československých výzvědných služeb 1914–1989, díl II 1939–1945*. [Czechoslovakia in the special services: Perspectives on the history of Czechoslovak intelligence services 1914–1989, part II 1939–1945]. Prague: Themis, 2002. Nevertheless it is evident from Resler's documents that these events did take place and that there were other witnesses to them. For more on the resistance movement see V. Mastný. *The Czech Under Nazi Rule: The Failure of National Resistance 1939–1942*. New York, NY: Columbia University Press, 1971.

167 Eduard Beneš was Minister of Foreign Affairs and later President.

wife wrote that Resler "was one of my husband Jiří Sedmík's longest-standing and most dependable friends; my husband was arrested by the Gestapo in 1940 for his part in the Czech resistance movement, and executed in 1942. (...) After my husband was arrested, Dr. Resler was in close contact with those of my husband's colleagues who had remained free, and became involved in the Preparatory Revolutionary National Committee. On its behalf he visited my husband in prison in Berlin, and arranged for financial support for persecuted members of the resistance and their families. His office was used as a meeting place for members of the resistance."[168]

Resler's role in ÚVOD was to oversee the provision of facilities for other members, and to take care of their and their families' legal affairs if they were persecuted. Members' wives were also informed that he held this role. This legal aid was, though, more often simply a pretext for the chance to support surviving family members financially and remain in contact with them.

Resler used his excellent German skills to gain the trust of the Germans, who were less suspicious of people who spoke fluent German.[169] His daughter, Blanka Brunnerová, believed that it was thanks to her father's defence of banker Kiesewetter and the Sokol's subsequent accusations that he stayed clear of the German authorities' radar.[170]

Resler did not only help members of ÚVOD, but also people from other resistance groups. In particular, he assisted the Jermak partisan fighters, illegal KSČ (Communist Party) organisations (e.g. *Včela*), and several relatives of arrested, imprisoned or executed Czechs who were not part of any organisation. He provided all this legal support entirely for free. Resler believed that the mere presence of a defence lawyer was crucial, since they were at least familiar with the system and could, within reason, prevent certain excesses. This was also behind his negotiations in 1940 with ministerial counsellor Červinka of the Presidium of the Ministers' Council and JUDr. Appel from Brno about whether the Council might secretly arrange to defend Czechs within the Reich and cover the costs of their defence.

Towards the end of the war, Resler was considered one of the key informers of the illegal Czech National Committee, the main resistance force at the end of the war. At the end of April 1945 renowned Czech architect Ladislav Machoň asked him on behalf of the Košice government to obtain some details about Prime Minister Richard Bienert's journey with other representatives of the Protectorate to make peace with the Allies. They had never arrived

---

168 Ladislav Tunys: *Noc před popravou. K. H. Frank a jeho obhájce* [The night before the execution. K. H. Frank and his defence counsel], Prague 1995, pp. 54–55. *Biografický medailon – Jiří Sedmík (1893–1942)* [Biographical Profile – Jiří Sedmík (1893–1942)]. [online] [cit 2014-02-21] Available at: http://www.ustrcr.cz/cs/jiri-sedmik.

169 AHMP 14, Testimony by Ivan Petr.

170 VCM, Resler's biography, as written by his daughter.

at their destination as they were detained at Kesserling's headquarters in Aichach.[171] Resler also arranged for representatives of the People's Party to be included in the Czech National Council.[172]

As well as participating in the resistance and helping in a legal capacity, Resler also helped others on a personal level. In Spring 1940, when no-one else was willing to do so, he spoke at the funeral for proletarian editor Michael Kácha, and published a booklet in his memory on the anniversary of his death. He became legal guardian to Alena Sedmíková, the daughter of his friend Jiří Sedmík, who was executed on 18 December 1942, and to Marie Beranová, daughter of warehouse worker Včela, who was executed for communist acts on 25 October 1944.[173] Furthermore, he provided legal support to a number of people who were in hiding from the Germans for years. During the war he also stored and concealed property belonging to *Rudé Právo* editor Vlastimil Borek[174], who had shaped him politically in his youth.

Despite his substantial financial outlays during the war, Resler's estate increased in value by 162,846 crowns, in major part thanks to inheritance of 93,300 crowns.[175]

In a letter to his former colleague JUDr. Ewald Stein, who had emigrated to the USA, he described the situation during and after the war. Many of their colleagues had not survived – they had been executed, beaten to death or gassed in the concentration camps. Resler himself had not got into any particular personal difficulty, although he was interrogated a few times by the Gestapo. Half of those interrogations were on account of him defending Jews, which was seen as a smirch on his clean slate as a barrister. In particular, the Gestapo questioned him about his defence of MUDr. Bohuslav Vrbenský, Ing. Vlastimil Borek and several other Jews under the Protectorate. His other Gestapo interrogations were on the orders of Gestapo officer Dr. Brandová, who suspected Resler of abusing his authority by using blackmail.

From a material perspective, Resler's life during the war was neither easy nor particularly difficult. While his family was taken care of, he suffered from

171   For more on this mission see Jan Gebhart, and Jan Kuklík. *Velké dějiny zemí Koruny české: Svazek XV.b 1938–1945.* [The great history of the lands of the Czech crown: vol. XV. b 1938–1945]. Prague: Paseka, 2007, pp. 534–535.

172   Historical studies do not even refer to Resler's involvement in this manner, although they do address the participation of members of the People's Party in the Czech National Council, see Jan Gebhart, and Jan Kuklík. *Velké dějiny zemí Koruny české: Svazek XV.b 1938–1945.* [The great history of the lands of the Czech crown: vol. XV. b 1938–1945]. Prague: Paseka, 2007, p. 435.

173   ČAK, Žádost o vydání potvrzení spolehlivosti pro poručenské soudy [guardianship application].

174   Jiří Kotyk. *JUDr. Kamill Resler (1893–1961), oběť šikany komunistického režimu.* [JUDr. Kamill Resler (1893–1961), bullied by the communist regime]. [online]. 10 August 2011 [accessed 2017-11-28]. Available from: http://www.kraj.kppardubicka.cz/stranky/cti-prispevky.php?id=JUDr._Kamill _Resler_(1893%961961),_obet_sikany_komunistickeho_rezimu.

175   AHMP 16; VHA, Přihláška pro důstojníky, rotmistry a poddůstojníky aspiranty v záloze [application to serve in the reserves], point 54.

hunger at times. He recalled that during the war he could only get potatoes and disgusting food that was neither nourishing nor satisfying. Even after the war, in March 1946, Resler wrote that there was only very occasionally any nourishing food on offer in the pubs.[176]

FRANTIŠEK BIDLO AND HIS ZDERAZ SKETCHES[177]

Resler met illustrator and caricaturist František Bidlo during French classes at the secondary school in Vinohrady, which they both attended. During the '30s their paths crossed several times, and they gradually grew to be close friends and began to comment on each other's lives in a harsh but well-meaning manner. In Bidlo's case, these comments usually took the form of sketches with captions, depicting key events in Resler's life or making fun of him.

He was assisted in this by a number of others, notably Resler's trainee JUDr. Jiří Mašek. Together, they made a satirical booklet for Resler in 1937 called *Ballada o duši Kamilla Reslera, doktora práv a advokáta* (A Ballad about the Spirit of Kamill Resler, Legal Doctor and Barrister), in which his character and habits were mockingly presented.

Of course, the Kiesewetter trial and Resler's departure from the Sokol didn't pass Bidlo and Mašek by. On that occasion they wrote the brochure *Letopis o junáckém zápolení ... Léta Páně 1936* (Chronicles of a Scout Fight ... AD 1936). Resler wrote of their work: "They were not kind to me, and gave me a ruthless thrashing in their creations, but they were even more merciless to the smalltown setting from which the whole thing had emerged."

In late 1938 Bidlo gave Resler a Nazi book that he had mischievously decorated with pictures and captions, including Resler's name. Resler could not afford for the book to end up in a second hand bookshop, and so had to accept this Trojan horse of a gift. Keeping hold of it was a risk to his life, but at least tasted a little of rebellion.

When Resler and Bidlo felt the need to clear their heads of the dismal atmosphere of the inter-war period, Resler had Bidlo illustrate a 1934 booklet of erotic poems. Bidlo illustrated the romantically indistinct deeds in the poems in the most unrefined manner. While Resler criticized him for being overly crude in his depictions, Bidlo was superbly pleased with his perfect execution of the task he had been set.

At the end of 1938 or in early 1939, Bidlo was to publish a book entitled *Diktátoři* (Dictators), which would have mocked Adolf Hitler, among others. However, the publishers decided not to release the book, given the international situation, and on 17 March 1939 returned the proofs to Bidlo's legal representative. That representative was in fact just a dummy figure, as it was Resler who took care of all his legal work; the

---

176   NM, Letter to Ewald Stein on 29 March 1946.
177   NM, unless otherwise stated, the information in this section is taken from Bidlo's Zderaz sketches and files.

reason for this arrangement was that the owner of the publishing house disliked Resler and refused to have anything to do with him.

Less than an hour after the "legal representative" saw the drawings (on 17 March 1939), he brought them to Resler, saying that he did not want to have them in his house because simply possessing them could lead to severe punishment. Bidlo began to destroy them in Resler's office, but Resler prevented him from destroying all of them. Naturally, the publisher did not ask for the deposit to be returned, as drawing attention to the work and its planned publication could have been detrimental.

A further series of sketches that Bidlo produced for Resler, this time together with JUDr. Antonín Švehla and with text by Jiří Mašek, was "The song of the raven's father." In this song Resler was depicted as a forgetful barrister who leaves his daughter among his files and goes to buy naughty images of women while cavorting with witches. The daughter grows up and has to beg for her living, when a gentleman takes her in, clothes her and makes her into a beautiful young woman. After they meet again, the father is suddenly filled with pride for his daughter and she banishes him. "The moral of the story is: Don't meddle in the world of law, if you conceived it near Beroun, then make it look presentable."[178] Resler considered the subject matter "inappropriate and the graphical represenation not fitting," even though Mašek's voice succeeded in turning it into a kind of fairground song. The two authors' skills hadn't managed to edify the low subject matter, and so Resler gave his judgement on the work's quality after fruitlessly attempting to explain it "in a few words, which did not please them (...). The thing was, that on top of everything it emerged that there was no alternative but that I should pay for the drawings myself. In the end, they didn't care about that too much, but it was a waste of Mašek and Bidlo's effort to produce such inane nonsense. (...) At the same time, Bidlo would never have put up with anyone else taking such liberties with me, and would have crushed anyone who dared to do so, as he reserved the right to taunt me exclusively for himself and Jiří Mašek."

For Christmas in 1941, Bidlo gave Resler a sketch depicting "four pale faces with their ears to the radio, wide open eyes and closed lips, with a clock on the wall, the short hand pointing to seven, the big hand to six, and a golden five-point star in the sky outside the window. 'I bring you News, listen carefully!'"[179] To understand the joke, one needs to know that from half past six until seven o'clock each evening there was a broadcast from Moscow, and that the Nazis would punish anyone found listening to it with death. In Resler's view, "to produce such a sketch, daring even to include the Soviet star, required admirable insolence, scorn for danger and even the willingness to trifle with one's life at a time when the Nazis were brutally enforcing their power and red and black placards announced new executions almost every day." Of course, by simply keeping these drawings, Resler was taking similar risks.

---

178   NM 217/369.
179   This mimics the opening line of a traditional Czech Christmas carol.

Bidlo asked Resler on several occasions to compose poems to go with his drawings, after his previously stalwart co-author Mašek had gone AWOL. After one of those occasions, when Resler had hurriedly put together a lousy quatrain for Mrs Buňka Halasová, the writer and later Nobel Prize winner Jaroslav Seifert happened to come to Resler's office. Resler and Bidlo sat him down in a small room, gave him a pen and paper, and briefly explained the problem, adding that they would not let him out of the room on any account until he had written a festive poem for Mrs Halasová. "The poet had such a delicate constitution that he was unable to put up a fight, did not manage to protest at all, and so submissively sat down at the table and pondered for a while, how to begin. (...) I watched Seifert for a while, and saw how he concentrated on his work; from the few movements and gestures he made, I could feel his intense irritation, which surprised me for such a light and quick-witted poet." After reading Seifert's poem, Resler asked Bidlo to give him back his lousy quatrain. When Bidlo refused, saying that he would use it anyway, Resler proposed that he should call the sketch "Don't go to the blacksmith's apprentice, if you can go to the blacksmith." Bidlo's likeness of the stout and muscular Seifert was dignified and without caricature, but the "blacksmith's apprentice" came off notably worse.

During the decade that led up to the war, Bidlo ruthlessly attacked the Nazi regime's leaders, orientation and acts. Still, the Nazis left him alone for five years of the war, on condition that he kept quiet in public. As he explained himself: "these regimes consider artists to be some sort of nutters, so they leave them in peace." Even so, on 15 January 1945 he was arrested by the Gestapo for a trivial matter that was long past: in January 1944

František Bidlo's illustration of Resler. (NM)

A caricature of Resler. (NM)

POZDĚJŠÍHO MUŽE. SOKOL UKOVAL JEHO NERVY V OCELOVÉ PRUŽINY SCHOPNÉ SNÁŠET I KONCI: PIENTY A ZASTUPOVAT KARIKATURISTY, ANAR: CHISTÉ NAUČILI HO VÁŽITI SI ZÁSAD. VOJNA DALA MU TO NEJVYŠŠÍ : BLESKOVÝ ÚDER A HNED PODAT STÍŽNOST !

František Bidlo's illustration of Resler. The text goes: "The Sokol forged the nerves of steel that he needed to cope with his trainees and represent caricaturists. The Anarchists taught him to stick to his principles. Military service trained his highest skills: strike quickly and put in a complaint straight away!" (NM)

he had said something against the Nazi leaders, in the Procházkova pub in Prague XII. Bidlo died in Terezín.[180] That, though, is another immensely sad tale, as Resler put it.

COURT CASES AND DISPUTES DURING THE WAR

In one of his manuscripts for *Radio Prag*, Resler described conditions for barristers under the Protectorate.[181] Who could defend at which courts? There were great differences between Czech and German barristers in particular, in that ordinarily Czech barristers could not defend at German courts, while German barristers could defend at all courts; this privilege was extended to just a couple of dozen Czech barristers. In Spring 1939 the German Bar Association in Prague recommended 30 barristers who would be able to defend at the *Landgericht*, the German provincial court, in Prague. Resler was the only one of these who was not approved by the Reich ministers. Why this was, we do not know. Resler was therefore among the third class barristers,

---

180 NM, point 36, Also known as Theresienstadt, this is a town in northern Bohemia, where there was a concentration camp. Rozklad proti rozhodnutí Akčního výboru Advokátní komory pro Čechy [appeal].

181 AHMP 15, Article for Radio Prag, German original and Czech translation.

although as he snidely commented, many Czech barristers in this category became visibly more self-assured once a fourth class was formed – of four Jewish defence laywers at the Provincial court. Since Resler was not allowed to defend before German courts, he had to hand certain cases over to his colleagues, among them his former trainee JUDr. Antonín Jelínek.[182]

In order to be able to practise as a barrister during the war he, along with all other barristers, had to sign an oath worded as follows: "I declare that I will obey the Führer of the German Reich Adolf Hitler as protector of the Protectorate of Bohemia and Moravia, that I will support the German Reich's interests to the benefit of the Protectorate of Bohemia and Moravia, abide by the orders of the head of the Protectorate of Bohemia and Moravia and his government, comply with the law and carry out my official duties diligently." Resler signed this on 24 May 1940. He was aware that he could do far more as a barrister than as a civil citizen, and so signed this oath despite the fact that it went against everything he believed in.

Although Resler did not speak out on the position barristers found themselves in under the Protectorate, he took a clear attitude to judges. If a judge were to find himself judging according to a criminal code which contravened human rights, he should resist it and refuse to judge. Such a judge would surely object that it was not easy to refuse and that such refusal would have bad consequences, but Resler argued that "no-one has the right to buy his own success through criminal acts. If any activity goes against one's conscience, one must not take it on, even if that could have serious consequences. The Third Reich would surely not have the judge in such a case executed, and a man of noble mind and a sense of what is right must in such cases risk the consequences, even if those include a concentration camp. If anyone judges wrongly, they must also bear the consequences."[183] Resler probably took a similar attitude to other legal professions. It is worth noting that Resler himself followed these principles in his practice. If he had been taken by the Gestapo, he would likely have been executed rather than sent to a concentration camp.

Resler judged other barristers against a benchmark appropriate to the times and the regime, too. Some of his criteria were, of course, common and necessary in the profession not only under the Protectorate but also at other times. A barrister needed to have good knowledge of political life and foreign affairs, to have life experience and legal erudition, skill as an orator, and be exceptionally quick and astute with a high level of tact, so as not to arouse public opinion against himself and his status. These characteristics, which

---

182   PNP 103, Letter to Jaroslav Hrkal on 19 October 1944.
183   AHMP 15, Article for Radio Prag, German original and Czech translation.

were required of those defending Nazi officials after the war, were what Resler considered should be required of any ordinary barrister.[184]

In his piece for *Radio Prag*, Resler also addressed the classification of two branches of the German court system – the civil judiciary, which from his own experience, in particular based on his case against members of the NSDAP, was very properly run, and the criminal judiciary. Administrative enforcement of sanctions without a trial before a judge and with inhumane consequences, such as he considered the case in the eradication of the villages of Lidice, Ležáky and Zubří, could not even be considered criminal justice.

Resler found it difficult to make generalisations about criminal procedures. On one occasion he wrote that the German occupying powers were so "thorough" (he later crossed out this word and replaced it with "open"), that they forced all newspapers to print a warning that those committing crimes against the Reich would be ruthlessly prosecuted. Yet he claimed that the Czechs did not believe that it would be "that bad."[185]

He found out just how bad it would be when he represented his cousin's husband (who was also a good friend of his) at the Extraordinary Court in Prague, which was located at the *Strakova Akademie*, nowadays the headquarters of the Czech government. The previous hearing was delayed, and so Resler witnessed a case in which the State Prosecutor proposed the death penalty for four young lads who had self-harmed in order to get out of a few weeks of work at a Prague factory. He could not comprehend why the death penalty should be handed down for this type of offence – but it was. Since Resler couldn't believe this, he noted the workers' names and those of the German lawyers. After the war, Resler brought these names to the authorities' attention via his contact officer Bohuslav Šedivý.[186]

Following that shocking verdict, it was his cousin's husband's turn – Ferdinand Routner. He had let an officer of the Czechoslovak intelligence service sleep at his house several times, and this officer had been condemned to death and had then gained survival by informing on others. Ferdinand Routner was his seventeenth and final victim. The presiding judge took Routner's statement as an admission of guilt, although it was nothing of the sort – in the end the State Prosecutor had to help Routner by persuading the presiding judge that the accused had not admitted anything. Even so, an indirect and contradictory statement by the Gestapo commissioner was sufficient for him to be sentenced to death. Resler recalled the case thus: "I was present for many death sentences, but none that were given so carelessly as this. It was a murder I observed that day." Presiding judge Dr. Bellman was condemned after

184 AHMP 16, Complaint delivered to the Disciplinary Board on 25 October 1946.
185 AHMP 15, Article for Radio Prag, German original and Czech translation.
186 PNP 91, Letter to Bohuslav Šedivý on 8 October 1945.

the war to 25 years' imprisonment for three well-known death sentences, and in 1955 prematurely handed over to the government of the Federal Republic of Germany. It emerged that he had handed out 110 death sentences in total.

Because he defended Jews, Resler was interrogated a number of times by the Gestapo, and the Nazi weekly tabloid *Stürmer* prepared an article at one point in which they intended to brand him a Jew-supporter. Resler had, for example, agreed to defend the late JUDr. Otto Taussig's daughters in their dispute with renegade Češka Matkovská, who had worked for the German secret service since 1938 and put pressure on Resler not to defend the daughters. The Gestapo summoned Resler three times, and in the end commissioner Schreiber made it clear to him that this was a matter of interest to the Reich, and that the Gestapo would step in if he didn't give up the defence. Resler did back out of the case, but made arrangements with the Bar Association to provide the daughters with a duty lawyer, JUDr. Lomberský, for whom Resler prepared the appeal, as he would not otherwise have managed it in time.

While practising under the Protectorate, Resler also came into contact a number of times with the collaborationist organisation *Vlajka* (The Flag), which was the Czech Nazi movement.[187] He argued a case against a key member of the *Vlajka* association, Jan Rozsévač-Rys in order, in his words, to distract him for a few months and prevent him from persecuting Jews. He managed to make an out of court settlement, but Rys later rescinded that agreement, giving rise to a court hearing. During the hearing the accused once again agreed to a settlement – he sent an apology to all those to whom the original accusatory letter had been sent, and paid legal costs amounting to 2,500 crowns. The dispute concerned the expulsion of a group of former *Vlajka* members.[188] Resler was not the only one trying to keep Rozsévač-Rys busy; for example, the central police bothered him in various ways on Prime Minister General Eliáš's orders.

When he had the opportunity to bring legal action against *Vlajka* again in further cases, Resler was undecided. Resler's employee JUDr. Jiří Mašek advised writer Václav Černý to sue the organisation, which had offensively branded him a Marxist and Masaryk sympathiser in reaction to his essay *Rasismus, jeho základ a vývoj* (The Roots and Development of Racism). However, Černý did not want to get into a legal dispute, and preferred to let them "go to hell." Resler also disadvised him from entering into legal proceedings – the article's author had deliberately set out to attack Černý, irrespective of his work's critical reviews. Resler warned him, though, not to respond to the article anywhere other than in *Vlajka* itself, if he were to respond at all. From Resler's knowledge of the *Vlajka* movement and those involved in it,

---

187 For more on *Vlajka* see Milan Nakonečný. *Vlajka*. Prague: Chvojkovo nakladatelství, 2001.
188 PNP, Kretší Jindřich, inv. no. 6917–6941.

it was clear to him that the article had been written primarily as a provocation. Despite that, he did not recommend suing for defamation – it was, after all, a matter of opinion, and Resler pointed out that "legal proceedings and in particular trials are a cumbersome machine and these days very slow-moving." Although he had prepared a request for print corrections, in the end given the situation he advised Černý that it would be best to let the matter go unnoticed: "silence is also a response, and in certain situations it can be the most appropriate one. In similar situations many who have found themselves the object of insulting articles have simply not responded, and as a result, *Vlajka* has been rather reluctant to touch on them again."

DEFENCE OF THOSE ON DEATH ROW[189]

During the war, Resler defended at least 63 people who were later executed by the Germans. These included his friends and relations, as well as people he had not previously known. He worked on their defence together with German barristers, a number of whom were good friends of his, as he wrote to his friend and client Jiří Scheiner in Buchenwald.[190] He already had experience of working with foreign barristers from before the war, when he had worked on a tough financial case with a barrister from Milan.[191] During the war he also worked with Dresden-based lawyer Gerhard Poege and barristers Dientz, Haller and Stein; naturally, they did not work for free. Resler wrote expert reports for a number of these colleagues after the war, defending their merit, in particular in relation to cases like that of Resler's close friend Ferdinand Routner. Barrister JUDr. Magerstein "demonstrated great conscientiousness, extraordinary concern and personal courage, while from other German barristers I saw only superficiality, carelessness and fear,"[192] wrote Resler.

For those who were executed, Resler handled and forwarded their final letters and last wishes to their relatives. Hence dozens of letters survive in Resler's archives from those on their way to execution, from which it is easy to recognise their situation and mood. In preparation for their death they were often permitted to attend a church service and speak to a priest, to write to their family (sometimes only one letter every six weeks) and to receive parcels of clothes and food. Their remains, though, were not repatriated. If

---

189 Unless otherwise stated, the materials in this section, in particular family letters, are located in PNP 35.
190 AHMP 14, Letter to Jiří Scheiner on 12 October 1939.
191 PNP 69, Letter to the General Consulate of the Czech Republic in Milan.
192 AHMP 14, Document dated 14 October 1946.

friends and family wanted information about the body, they had to turn to the relevant People's Court.

Even before the war was over, Resler received numerous letters of thanks from those he looked after. Although all these letters were important to him, those he received during his own low patches – during his defence of K. H. Frank, the German minister of state for Bohemia and Moravia, and after 1948 – touched him the most. He never asked those whom he had helped to write him references, even though this could at times have helped him. In his application to retain his military position in 1948, he wrote that he would consider it undignified for a Czechoslovak officer to ask for statements three years after the war from those he had helped, or from their surviving relatives. Similarly, it was unthinkable for him to ask them to confirm that he had worked for them free of charge, or that he had assisted some of them financially.[193]

Below, I describe a number of Resler's cases to which some reference is made in his archives, in alphabetical order. I do not provide accounts of these cases in their entirety, but give an indication at least of the fragments of information about them that Resler had chosen to preserve.

FRANTIŠEK BERAN

In some of his cases, Resler advised the accused's family about how they could visit their relative after his death sentence. In general, this was possible in two situations – either during court hearings or in private, which could sometimes be arranged for spouses. In Beran's case, Resler tried to negotiate this with the help of German barrister JUDr. Poeg. Once Beran had been sentenced to death, Resler wrote a request for mercy on his behalf, which he sent to the German barrister. His request was not met, however; Beran was executed and Resler had nothing to present to his client's wife except his death certificate and a translation of his final letter. After the war, Resler arranged for František Beran to be awarded the 1939 Czechoslovak Military Cross for his activities in the communist resistance movement.

IRENA BERNÁŠKOVÁ

Some German nationals, in particular lawyers and clergymen, behaved extremely sensitively even towards Czechs. One of these was Lohoff, the senior pastor at the Berlín-Plötzensee prison, who when informing executed Irena Bernášková's family of her last hours concluded with the words: "I send you my heartfelt wishes that God might grant the deceased eternal rest, and

---

193   VHA, Vyjádření k j. č. 110.903/ P.K. 1948 [military report].

give you comfort and strength in your grief." Almost all those who were condemned to death spoke of their family. They worried about their future well-being, and about detailed arrangements for them, which provided a welcome distraction from the thought of their impending death. It was always very difficult for them if they did not have news of their families. Irena Bernášková put it in these words: "I am suffocating under a growing mountain of terrifying thoughts! But my rebellious spirit is gathering the vital strength to flee." Some of those sentenced did not want their families to know the truth of their situation, and Irena Bernášková was one of them: five days after she was sentenced to death, she wrote that she had "only" been sentenced to life imprisonment.

ANNA DOUŠOVÁ

Resler's client Anna Doušová was sentenced in August 1940 to one year in prison for assisting in an act of treason, but since she had already spent three quarters of the year in prison, she was released shortly afterwards. Her husband was not so lucky. He was tried only later, in Dresden, and JUDr. Dietz, the barrister there, attempted to arrange for his wife to visit him. For that to be allowed, though, he needed to cite an important family or proprietary reason why such a visit was necessary. Resler offered Anna a consultation, so that they could come up with a reason that would be genuinely convincing. In his letter to Anna, he observed that "purchasing a house" might be a possible reason, or "to see his son." The visit was eventually permitted. She received a pass to enter the Reich, and travelled with her eight-year-old son to see her husband in August 1941. In April 1942 she visited him once more, although for that she had to think of new reasons, both for the visit itself and in order to obtain an entry pass – the two permits were unconnected.

On 28 December 1944 Resler informed Anna Doušová of her husband's death: "These were tough years, but through them the hope remained that he would return home. Now that is over, and you will bring up the children alone. That is a substantial task in itself and I wish you the strength to accomplish it honourably. Both I and my family send you our sincere condolences."

GISELA GOLDSCHRAISÁTOVÁ

Resler was involved in a lawsuit concerning the Jewish origin of his client Gisela Goldschraisátová's child, in which he attempted to prove that the child's true father was a different man than that written in the Jewish birth register. Judge JUDr. Miloš Wirth deliberately delayed the hearing, altered the outcomes of the questioning, and eventually found that the child did not have a Jewish father. The Reichsprotektor, however, quickly nullified the verdict and ordered the case be heard at a German court. Even so, thanks to the delay of several months, Resler's clients were not deported; this may have saved their lives.[194] Unlike the others in this list, both Goldschraisátová and her child survived the war.

JOSEF HOJNÝ

It was difficult for Resler to make contact with Josef Hojný to begin with, since it was not clear where he was. Resler negotiated for him to sign a power of attorney so that barrister Dr. Rolf Haller from Prague could represent him at the People's Court. After that, Dr. Haller could not obtain the necessary details and so instead recommended Berlin-based defence lawyer Rudolf Schmidt. Although his relatives received a message saying that he was in Münich, Resler was informed by the Berlin lawyer that he was in the Plötzensee prison near Berlin, and that his sentence would most likely not be enforced. In the end it turned out that he really was in Münich, and Resler made contact with his lawyer JUDr. Dominik Micceli, to whom he sent a power of attorney for the relatives, so that he could file a plea for mercy on their behalf. In a letter to the relatives explaining the case's progress, he included this surprising postscript: "I know that the Reich barristers carry out their duties extremely properly and conscientiously, and that you can trust Mr JUDr. Micceli to do everything that is within his power."

Resler usually asked his condemned clients' relatives to send him a description of their life, which he needed in order to compose a plea for mercy. He was particularly keen to know whether the person in question had ever expressed friendliness towards German nationals, and whether they had had help in personal matters. While during the war everyone attempted to mention times when they had behaved in a friendly manner towards Germans, even in trivial matters, this trend entirely reversed after the war, when it was much more beneficial to show that you had been friendly towards the Republic and unfriendly to the Germans.

Josef Hojný's mother was allowed to visit her son in Münich, although only for twenty minutes, during which time they had to speak German to one another without an interpreter.

Resler wrote, after completing the plea for mercy, that: "Everything that could have happened has happened, and there is nothing left but to wait and trust that the sentence will not be enforced." He wrote this in response to an impassioned plea from Hojný's mother: "Honourable Doctor/ I entreat you, save my only son / with deep respect / Aloisie Krupce."

---

194   AHMP 14, Lawsuit concerning ancestral origin.

Like Irena Bernášková, Josef Hojný hadn't felt able to tell his mother during her visit to him in Münich that he had been sentenced to death. Resler only found out about his execution from the newspapers. He then attempted to learn from Dr. Micceli what his last moments were like and where he had been buried, for the family's sake.

FRANTIŠEK KORDA

In this case, too, Resler did his best to think up various reasons why Korda in particular should be granted mercy, and so asked the family to provide him with detailed information. He cited the fact that Korda had been a soldier during the war and had been awarded a badge of honour. Even so, he was executed. In a letter to his mother after his death, Resler wrote: "It would be pointless to try to console a mother and child who have lost their closest relative." He enclosed Korda's final letter and a translation of it. At the same time, he wrote to the Münich prosecutor to request the details of the execution. He also assisted Korda's widow, Marie Kordová, with her application for a widow's pension.

ADOLF PLACHÝ

Dr. Plachý was arrested because a document that the Germans found in Paris stated that he had been part of the foreign resistance since 1938. According to barrister Hugon Jaria this was a serious crime and the death penalty was to be expected. He was charged, but the People's Court's documents were damaged in an air raid on Berlin on 3 February 1945. The trial was therefore postponed, and the hearing never took place, thanks to which Adolf Plachý survived the war. After the war he served in a key role at the Ministry of Foreign Affairs, and in 1949 he went into exile.

LADISLAV RAŠÍN

JUDr. Ladislav Rašín, son of the first Czechoslovak Minister of Finance Alois Rašín, was arrested by the Gestapo in 1939. Resler was in contact with his wife and with one German Freemason, who Rašín knew and who was able to visit him in prison. From him, Resler learned that Ladislav Rašín had been sentenced to execution and that this should take place after the standard preparatory period – twelve days. During that time, though, an order was issued to postpone the execution – most likely thanks to his wife's intervention – and a few weeks later he was granted mercy. His death sentence was changed to fifteen years hard labour in prison. In the end, though, even this amended punishment was simply a postponed execution; the words "Return undesirable" were written on his file, indicating that the punishment was to have the same outcome, if by a different method. Ladislav Rašín died in hospital in Frankfurt am Main on 20 March 1945, just days before the allies liberated the city; he had spent three years in a German prison and, as Resler wrote in one letter to his wife Karla Rašínová, had himself never found out that he had been sentenced to death.[195]

JANA TUHÁ

Dr. Poeg in Dresden took over Jana Tuhá's defence from Resler. He requested a fee of 5,000 crowns, but was willing to accept a lower figure. He also asked Resler to send an invoice for his services, but both during and after the war Resler replied stating that his services were provided free of charge. Families sometimes asked how much they should pay the German lawyers, and according to Resler's records, they always paid up.

RESLER'S STORIES OF A COLLEAGUE IN BERLIN[196]

In one account of wartime events, Resler described his experience of a professional visit to the Plötzensee prison in Berlin. The brief account, written in the form of a dialogue between the Czech barrister and his Berlin colleague, clearly depicts Resler's memories of the barrister with whom he worked on cases involving the death penalty. It portrays the Berlin prison and their treatment of those preparing for execution.

After the sentence was issued, it was usual to petition for mercy, which usually took three months, sometimes less. After a plea for mercy had been turned down, the convicted individual would have about twelve days to live. The evening before the execution all the documents were examined once again, after which the death sentence was read out to the convicted prisoner, informing him that mercy had not been granted and that early the following morning he would be executed. The prisoner was allowed to spend limited time with a priest and to write a final letter. Resler then describes the execution procedure itself in detail, stating that from the moment the individual stepped over the threshold of the execution chamber there were just fifteen seconds before they were beheaded by the guillotine. Blood then gushed, regardless of which there would be less than three minutes before the next prisoner was executed.

---

195   PNP 91, Letter to Karla Rašínová on 23 August 1945.
196   AHMP 5, Tales of a Berlin defence counsel.

The Berlin barrister in the account, who was most likely one of the German lawyers Resler collaborated with, attended his clients' executions; these were nine Czechoslovak officers. He describes their behaviour as heroic, stating that they walked straight up to the guillotine without the slightest signs of discomposure. Only two allowed their despair at the sentence to show on their faces, but even these kept themselves together and went calmly to their death with dignity.

We can compare this account with Resler's impression when he visited the Plötzensee prison once more, again for a client who had been condemned to death, on 11 (elsewhere noted as 10) November 1942. The client in this case was Jiří Sedmík; he had expressed a wish for Resler to visit him, which was conveyed to Resler by his friend Ivan Petr, who thought that Sedmík had contacted other agents of the secret Czechoslovak Communist Party (KSČ) through JUDr. Sekanina, without telling his colleagues. Sedmík's German barrister succeeded in negotiating an hour-long visit for Resler thanks to a kind recommendation from the prison administrators, who were significantly influenced by the chief teacher at the prison and Nazi dissident Christian Nissen. Sedmík explained to Resler in their coded conversation that everyone he knew was either dead, in prison, or had fled abroad. Five weeks later Sedmík was executed.[197] Resler described the small building in the prison courtyard, where the execution chamber was, as "an ordinary, uninteresting building, which gave nothing away of the frightful rituals to which it witnessed, the thought of which accompanied me late into the night on the long train journey from Anhalt station through a neverending land ruled by a government of lies, violence and darkness."

ORDINARY DISPUTES

Of course, Resler continued to take on ordinary cases during the war, and when he charged a fee for them it was these that made most of his living. These included numerous inheritance proceedings. A typical example, although one for which he did not charge a fee in the end, were the inheritance proceedings following the death of Czech painter Jindřich Štyrský, which Resler handled between 1942 and 1945, both as executor of Štyrský's will and as legal representative to his only inheritor, the painter Toyen (Marie Černínová). Kamill Resler retained Jindřich Štyrský's residence papers in his archive. Štyrský died on 21 March 1942, and the value of his net inheritance was just 92.20 crowns. Although Resler suggested Toyen should apply for an

---

197   NM, point 32, Rozklad proti rozhodnutí Akčního výboru Advokátní komory pro Čechy [appeal].

extra public funeral allowance for him, she declined this option saying she would be ashamed to ask for money.[198]

Another client, also of the creative professions, was the writer Jakub Deml. He turned to Resler for help when he was required to pay pension tax on his earnings for 1940, which amounted to 46,000 crowns. For a piece of work that he had worked on for four years he had to pay tax of 8,486 crowns, which he said he could not afford; he believed that the fee should have been divided over four years and the tax charged accordingly.[199]

A further category of cases for which Resler never charged a fee were those in which he helped his colleagues' families. In 1943 he assisted Opočno barrister Karel Dražďák's 73-year-old widow to obtain an extraordinary allowance. Mrs Josefina Dražďáková had been widowed already twenty years, and lived in extremely destitute conditions. She turned to the Bar Association with a request for financial support, since her husband had been a key figure in the life of the Bar in his time. Thanks to Resler's interest and action, she was successful in obtaining higher allowances.[200]

In disciplinary proceedings, Resler represented a consultant in the surgical department of the Čáslav hospital, MUDr. Jan Kafuněk. [201] The accusation against him concerned unprofessional and negligent treatment in surgical and gynaecological cases; Kafuněk was dismissed by the Provincial Authorities in Prague for extremely poor and unprofessional treatment of fractures and other medical operations. Resler appealed against that decision to the Supreme Administrative Court. Meanwhile, however, Jan Kafuněk was arrested by the Gestapo on 16 January 1943, and accused of involvement in the resistance movement and membership in the Rotary Club; he was subsequently imprisoned in Kolín, Terezín, Birkenau and Auschwitz, where he died on 4 May 1943, either of typhus fever or of a lethal injection, according to his fellow prisoners. Resler nevertheless continued to manage his affairs. The result was that in 1946 Kafuněk's widowed wife and son received his consultant's salary, on account of his unfair dismissal, and further contributions. The Provincial National Committee in Prague eventually officially overturned the dismissal on 23 February 1948, at which point Resler's complaint to the Supreme Administrative Court (which he had submitted in case the Provincial National Committee decided otherwise) became void. Resler continued to advise Kafuněk's widow even after 1948, albeit for free and, in his words, "only out of kindness." He did, though, ask her to pay his legal fees from the post-war period during which he had provided full legal services, given that

---

198 PNP, inv. no. 5706–5752.
199 PNP 48, Letter from Jakub Deml on 11 August 1941.
200 PNP 111, Letter to Josefína Dražďáková on 15 July 1943.
201 PNP, Kafuněk Jan, inv. no. 2198–2277.

thanks to him arranging her compensation, she had the means to pay them. He modestly added that he would be content with very low monthly instalments.

Alongside many painters and writers, several actors also made use of Resler's services. In 1941 Resler took on the defence of actor Stanislav Neumann, son of writer Stanislav Kostka Neumann.[202] He had been offered the title role of Sharpsight in the film *Long, Broad and Sharpsight*, and had accepted, but in the end the Nationalfilm company instead decided to give him a minor role as Second Doctor. This would have meant that he lost out on a considerable portion of his fee, and so when communication with Nationalfilm broke down, he turned to the Českomoravské filmové ústředí (Bohemian and Moravian Film Union) with a request for conciliation proceedings. Eventually the film company gave in, and agreed to pay Neumann 10,000 crowns for giving up his rights and 400 crowns for his legal costs. Resler continued to manage S. Neumann the younger's affairs until his death, as we will see in the final chapter of this book.

In 1942 (AHMP)   During the second world
                                 war. (NM)

AFTER THE WAR

When the war ended, Resler's active involvement in the resistance movement continued. He did not, however, take part in the Prague Uprising against the German powers, which lasted from 5 to 9 May 1945. Although it may sound strange, he continued to go to work in his office near *Karlovo náměstí* every day during the uprising, since he lived in a quiet part of Prague where there

202 PNP, Neumann Stanislav – actor, inv. no. 3959–3999.

was no fighting. His son, on the other hand, was held by the Wehrmacht in the *Dejvice* district for about five hours on 7 May 1945.[203]

The end of the war was an interesting time for Resler for several reasons – first of all, because it brought an influx of new work. As early as 12 May he began to represent the first of his clients who was accused of collaborating with the Germans. This was the deputy director of the National Gallery and chief commissioner of the State Printing Works, Karel Novák, who had been dismissed by the company's board. The Ministry of Information confirmed Novák's dismissal and the employment tribunal called off his case at the end of 1946 based on section 22 of act no. 143/1946 Coll. on employment relationships affected by the national revolution, according to which all court proceedings concerning the termination of employment due to suspicion of unpatriotic practices were to be closed. Resler did not manage to avoid a hearing before the Regional Civil Court for Prague city by citing Presidential Decree no. 105/1945 Coll. on cleansing commissions for the re-evaluation public employees' actions. Resler believed that his client fell within the scope of this decree as an employee of a state-owned company, and therefore could not fall within the scope of act no. 143/1946 Sb., since the act stated this explicitly. The court nevertheless decided that according to section 17 of Decree no. 105/1945 Coll. this argument was not valid, and declared the case closed. Section 17 related to disciplinary matters and was just a few paragraphs long. The court did not further specify its reasoning, and left those concerned to choose an appropriate interpretation, even though no such interpretation could be made from that section. Post-war justice could sometimes be this unjust and dismissive. Not only was it impossible to achieve a proper judicial review of post-war redundancies, but some courts would not even provide sufficiently comprehensible reasoning for their decisions.[204]

After the war, Resler continued to represent many of his pre-war clients. These included Czech Germans who had maintained their allegiance to the Republic and wanted to remain its citizens. One of these was factory owner Josef Etrich, from the East Bohemian town of Jaroměř, whom Resler had represented before the war in cases relating to promissory notes. Although he was a member of the Sokol, since 1939 Josef Etrich had officially been a German and a member of the NSDAP. He claimed that he had not protested when assigned German citizenship, because his friends had asked him to remain in charge of the factory and help the Czechs. He was signed up to the NSDAP by gardener Marx, who he claimed had terrorized the whole of Jaroměř. He

---

203 AHMP 16, Přihláška pro důstojníky, rotmistry a poddůstojníky aspiranty v záloze [application to serve in the reserves], point 54.

204 PNP, inv. no. 4968–4999. For more on the post-war decrees, see Jan Kuklík. *Czech law in historical contexts*. Karolinum: 2015, chapter 17.

was, however, an inactive member, and said that he had never attended the party's meetings or worn its badge. He lived with a Czech woman, whom he wanted to marry, but he would only have got permission to do so if she had accepted German citizenship, and therefore they had decided to postpone the wedding.[205]

At the end of 1946, the District National Committee in Jaroměř rejected Etrich's application for confirmation of his loyalty to the state because the Provincial National Committee had recommended that such confirmation should not be granted. Resler appealed against this decision on Etrich's behalf. However, in the meantime the Local National Committee in Jaroměř commanded, in a notice printed in the paper *Rudé právo* on 16 March 1947,[206] that Josef Etrich be treated in the same way as other Germans. They claimed that he had long behaved like a German and supported the German cause. His only reason for wanting Czechoslovak citizenship was "evidently" in the Local National Committee's eyes for property restitution, specifically the restitution of the Jaroměř factory.

The Ministry of the Interior rejected Resler's appeal and so Resler turned to the Supreme Administrative Court, which overturned the Ministry's decision on 19 February 1948, stating that the decision had been taken without due scrutiny. This was because the Ministry had not inquired into whether supporting underground military groups in one's business, putting up with Russian prisoners of war and partisans in one's district and hiding weapons – all of which Etrich had done – could be considered active participation in the fight for Czechoslovak liberation. If so, that would have given him Czechoslovak citizenship.[207] Sadly, Etrich did not live to see another decision made – he died in hospital in Caracas, Venezuela, at the end of 1949, having left for America in October 1948 trusting people he should not have trusted. He lost 35 kg in six months due to problems with his prostate and lungs, which eventually led to his death. And that was the end of a Czech about whom Resler wrote in 1949 that "even within the new conditions in the Czechoslovak Republic (...) no-one could say that his business activities went against his employees interests."[208] The fact that someone who had supported Czech employees during the war and was himself a Czech at heart was hounded out

---

205 PNP 69, Josef Etrich, "On my Loyalty to the State," May 1945. This condition isn't reported in relevant studies, so it is unclear whether he invented it or whether it may have been imposed by local officials. See e.g. Renata Veselá. *Rodinné právo v době protektorátu.* [Family law in the protectorate]. [online]. 2010 [accessed 2017-11-28]. Available at: http://www.law.muni.cz/sborniky/dny_prava_2010/files/prispevky/08_promeny/Vesela_Renata_(4462).pdf.

206 Rubrika Zasláno, *Rudé právo*, 16 March 1947, p. 5.

207 PNP 69, Rozsudek Nejvyššího správního soudu č. j. 903/47-2 [court decision].

208 PNP 69, Letters between Resler and Salma Etrichová.

was most likely the result of jealousy over his Jaroměř factory and a general hatred against anyone who was formally a German.

After the war, Resler also once again resumed his work for translator Pavel Eisner, who was of Jewish origin. He rejected a payment of 2,000 crowns from Eisner in June 1945, on the grounds that Eisner had previously given him many books, which were worth more than the legal services Resler had provided. The two were soon close friends, and Eisner even dedicated one chapter of his book *Na skále* (On the Rock) to Resler. Eventually, he asked Resler to help Miss Krticzková, who had looked after the Eisner family's property during the war, supported them and sent them parcels in Terezín. Miss Krticzková had been informed on by the concierge and a servant at the property, who had also stolen from her, and as a result she received a summons to the detention camp from which deportations were organised. Eisner believed that this was out of jealousy, because Miss Krticzková was a co-owner of the house in Prague 3.[209]

THE ATTEMPT TO CONVICT TRAITORS

Together with the rest of the nation, Resler shared the feeling that those who had done wrong for several years without punishment should not escape justice. He himself pushed for investigations into cases when he was convinced that the individuals in question had acted malevolently during the war, and similarly willingly represented those who wanted to trace unknown perpetrators of wartime crimes like denunciation, and have them tried. Thus, for example, he had Josef Rozsévač (alias Jan Rys, as previously mentioned) questioned before the Extraordinary People's Court in Prague just a day before he was sentenced to death. The proceedings, which Resler had initiated, were however called off by the court, because it had failed to establish who had informed Resler's client – the head of the National Museum, PhDr. Miloslav Novotný.[210] Resler had previously represented Novotný before the war.

Resler also petitioned himself for a number of trials to be held. One of these was against the manager of the company Pev, for which Resler had served as legal representative and board member since 1926. Resler claimed that manager Martin Theileis had bankrupted the firm for his own profit during the occupation and had threatened the other employees with imprisonment if they got in his way. He had done this in cooperation with JUDr. Jan Procházka, with whom he had signed a very unfavourable contract for legal representation. However, the Gestapo had arrested Theileis on suspicion of

209 PNP 69, Letter from Pavel Eisner on 9 October 1946.
210 PNP, inv. no. 5064–5070.

other crimes before he was able to withdraw the money. He was not put on trial, but sent to a detention camp and after the war he claimed he had been mistreated by the Gestapo.[211]

After the war, Resler proposed to the Bar Association's disciplinary committee that they should punish JUDr. Procházka, who Resler believed had behaved perfidiously during the war, even though he had then publicly participated in the general post-war effort to "cleanse public and professional life." Resler proposed that the case be taken to the public prosecutor at the Extraordinary People's Court.[212]

He also asked the authorities whether they knew of Major Jaroslav Novák, who had published a book during the war in which he enthusiastically endorsed German rule over the Czechs.[213] Similarly, he also drew their attention to Müller, an inspector of the civil guard whose trickery had contributed to the execution of Resler's friend, resistance fighter Jan Smudek.[214] During Müller's trial, however, Resler reported that the chief witness had not been questioned at all, and the public prosecutor therefore closed the proceedings.[215]

Not all of Resler's efforts were intended to punish; often he also made an effort to point out and uphold the status of those who had served the Republic throughout the war. Hence as early as 11 May 1945 he pleaded with Augusta Müllerová, who had become a member of the Czech National Council, on behalf of the Secretary of the Central Union of Pharmacists, who, based on Resler's information, had only been in contact with a few Germans as a means of cover and to enable him to fight for the Republic.[216] While defending several other individuals who had been publicly active under the Protectorate, Resler soon learnt just how difficult it was to explain this line of argument.

---

211   PNP, inv. no. 5294–5302.
212   PNP, inv. no. 5294–5302.
213   PNP 91, Letter to Bohuslav Šedivý on 8 October 1945.
214   PNP 78, Submission to the Committee for Internal National Security on 17 September 1945.
215   PNP 78, Letter to Karel Vojtěch on 20 August 1947.
216   PNP 75, Letter to Augusta Müllerová on 11 May 1945.

4. THE KARL HERMANN FRANK CASE

Karl Hermann Frank was a clerk and bookseller, who had a glass eye and was therefore not accepted for the front line during the First World War, despite twice signing up for service voluntarily. During the war he also attempted (unsuccessfully) to study Law for a year at the German University in Prague.

From 1919 onwards he was a member of the German National-Socialist Workers Party, which supported the cession of the Sudetenland to Germany. After the party was banned in 1933, Frank transferred to the Sudeten German Party, together with other party members. Thanks to a timely affiliation with his peer Konrad Henlein, Frank succeeded in being elected to the Czechoslovak parliament in 1935 for the Sudeten German Party (SdP), and also became chairman of the SdP parliamentary club. With Henlein, he urged for the Sudetenland to be joined to Germany, as a result of which an arrest warrant was issued for both of them, on the very same day that the Sudeten German Party was dissolved, 16 September 1938. His approach, however, impressed Heinrich Himmler, who promoted him in Autumn 1938 to SS-Brigadeführer.[217]

In 1939, Frank was appointed Police Leader and Secretary of State for the Reichsprotektor's office, which gave him significant influence in devising and shaping German occupational policy under the Protectorate. His ambition was to command the Protectorate of Bohemia and Moravia, but he was repeatedly unsuccessful at achieving this. After Reichsprotektor Konstantin von Neurath was dismissed he expected to be named Reichsprotektor, but instead Reinhard Heydrich was given the role. Then, when Heydrich was assassinated in May 1942, Kurt Daluege was appointed Protektor, and although he was dismissed in 1943 due to illness, the position was then taken up by Wilhelm Frick.

In 1943 Frank did at least become the Reichsminister for Bohemia and Moravia, which gave him greater authority and effectively made him the highest-ranking German official in the Protectorate. At the same time, he was appointed SS-Obergruppenführer, the General of Police in the Protectorate

---

217   For more on the Henlein movement see Mark Cornwall. "'A Leap into Ice-Cold Water': The Manoeuvres of the Henlein Movement in Czechoslovakia, 1933–8," in Mark Cornwall,and R. J. W. Evans (eds.) *Czechoslovakia in a Nationalist and Fascist Europe, 1918–1948.* Oxford: Oxford University Press and British Academy 2007.

and head of the higher SS in Bohemia and Moravia. Frank "was responsible or co-responsible for almost all the German occupational government's victims. (...) It would be wrong to reduce Frank simply to a state criminal and mass murderer working from a desk (though he was that too), given that he did his best, both for ideological and opportunistic reasons, to develop Protectorate policies wherever possible along moderate lines. The policies were undoubtedly murderous and their final aim just as contemptible as those in the rest of occupied Europe, but under different leadership they might well have turned out far more brutally"[218].

Frank was one of the most important Nazi figures both before and during the war, and always stood firmly on the side of his superiors. Before the war he was Konrad Henlein's closest colleague, and during the war he was especially loyal to Hitler and Himmler. Even so, that did not mean that he carried out all of their orders without any objection; on the contrary, in several cases he softened what he saw to be too severe a decision. Although he himself saw Czechs, Jews, Sudeten German democrats and communists as enemies and was not afraid to take a brutal stand against them, he attempted to run the country rationally, and this guided his actions. Primarily, he would disregard morality in favour of rationality when that meant achieving one of the German Reich's two key aims in Bohemia and Moravia: peace and orderly production. Frank took a milder approach towards the Czechs than the Nazi governors in the other occupied territories precisely because he wished to successfully achieve these two key goals. It helped that he did not see the Czechs as inferior, but as a valuable people. Much though the Czech nation was to be eradicated in the long run, this was to be for the most part as a result of Germanization and not through extermination or forced expulsion. Thus, although Frank was a criminal and a mass murderer, he implemented the Nazi policies – for which he was also judged – more mildly than he was instructed to, and in comparison to other Nazis.[219]

When the end of the war came on 9 May 1945, the police and American soldiers arrested Frank in Rokycany at about 11 o'clock. After a number of months in American prison and interrogations in Wiesbaden, the Czechoslovak government requested that he be tried in their courts, and following lengthy negotiations between General Ečer and the Americans this was per-

218 René Küpper. *Karl Hermann Frank (1898–1946): Politická biografie sudetoněmeckého nacionálního socialisty*. [A political biography of the Sudeten German National Socialists]. Prague: Argo, 2012, pp. 243, 247.

219 René Küpper. *Karl Hermann Frank (1898–1946): Politická biografie sudetoněmeckého nacionálního socialisty*. [A political biography of the Sudeten German National Socialists]. Prague: Argo, 2012, pp. 243–247. For a more detailed presentation of K. H. Frank I recommend this work, which was originally published in German: René Küpper. *Karl Hermann Frank (1898–1946): Politische Biographie eines sudetendeutschen Nationalsozialisten.* Munich: Oldenbourg Wissensch, 2010.

mitted. He was handed over at Prague's Ruzyně airport on 7 August 1945 and taken straight to the Regional Criminal Court's prison at Pankrác, where he was taken into pre-trial custody as standard for crimes within the remit of the Great Retribution Decree.[220]

While in prison, Frank was not allowed to have contact with the other prisoners, and for his "daily walks he was assigned a courtyard to which no other prisoners had access; hence this courtyard became known as Frank Square".[221] Frank was interrogated from September 1945 until 15 February 1946. The full transcript of his interrogation was published as early as March 1946, as *K. H. Frank's Confession*.[222] Frank had responded to the questioning extremely openly, after some initial wariness, and attempted to shed light on many events. The book therefore came to be extremely useful during the trial, when both parties carried it with them and referred to it regularly.

On 4 March 1946 public prosecutor JUDr. Jaroslav Drábek and his deputy JUDr. Jan Gemrich charged Frank before the Extraordinary People's Court in Prague. The charges were on ten counts and were accompanied by an extensive fifty-five page interpretation. On 15 March 1946, seven years after the occupation of the Second Czechoslovak Republic, K. H. Frank appeared before the Extraordinary People's Court in Prague; the charges were read out to him, and the presiding judge JUDr. Vladimír Kozák asked Frank whether he wished to appoint his own defence lawyer, or whether one should be appointed by the court – *ex officio*. Since Frank responded that he did not know how these matters were usually handled in the court, the judge informed him that he would be allocated a defence lawyer by the court, with whom he would be able to consult before the planned start of his trial on 22 March 1946.

JUDr. Vladimír Kozák, the presiding judge at the Extraordinary People's Court in Prague, chaired the trial. His substitute was the court chairman, JUDr. Jaroslav Novák. The lay judges were Václav Koubek, František Klika, who was taken ill on 3rd April and replaced, Alois Fiřt and JUDr. Vladislav Sutnar. Their substitutes were Antonín Blažek, Růžena Rollová and František Červinka. The Court Clerk was Dr Hugo Zeman. Various interpreters were involved, including Dr Felix Gráb for a significant portion of the trial.[223]

---

220 Presidential Decree no. 16, 19 June 1945, hereafter simply "Retribution Decree" or "Great Retribution Decree".

221 Karel Zajíček. *Český národ soudí K. H. Franka*. [The Czech nation tries K. H. Frank]. Prague: Ministerstvo informací, 1947, p. 17 (hereafter "Český národ soudí").

222 Karel Výkusa. *Zpověď K. H. Franka*. [K. H. Frank's confession]. Prague: Cíl, March 1946.

223 Český národ soudí p. 80.

THE *EX OFFICIO* APPOINTMENT

Early 1946 was not, for obvious reasons, a favourable time to take on the defence of Nazi criminals, and certainly not voluntarily. After the war a number of newspapers, leaders of political parties and even some barristers on the Bar Association's board had attempted to establish a policy by which Czech barristers could not voluntarily defend traitors, but could do so only if the court ordered them to. In some cities (such as Pardubice), this policy was indeed adopted.[224]

A difficult task therefore emerged at the Bohemian Bar Association in Prague when, on 15 March 1946, Frank was told that a defence lawyer would be appointed for him within six days. Several barristers refused to take on the case voluntarily, including JUDr. Antonín Švehla, who stated that he was unwell. JUDr. Jaroslav Mellan claimed that if the Bar Association appointed him he would strip naked, throw a sheet over his shoulders, walk out onto the riverside and shout: "I am Jesus Christ!"[225] If he had really done so, this would have been a sign of insanity, and would have disgraced the Association. The President of the Bar Association, JUDr. Antonín Klouda, who had been imprisoned at the Büchenwald concentration camp during the war, was aware of the significance of the case and the need for Frank to be properly defended, not just for show. The long process eventually resulted in Kamill Resler, who was five years older than Frank, being appointed for the defence. Why did they choose Resler? It was partly down to luck.

On Friday *15 March 1946* the presiding judge at the Extraordinary People's Court, JUDr. Kozák, asked the Bar Association not to delay in appointing a defence lawyer for K. H. Frank. That afternoon, Resler happened to come into the Association's offices, in order to hand in some disciplinary reports. He got talking with the gentlemen of the board about the difficulty of appointing someone to defend Frank. He told them that it was pointless to ask someone to take the case on voluntarily, because "no Czech could willingly do that and if someone did, he would risk justified disapproval from the public and especially the media, and would bring utter discredit upon himself." President Klouda then arrived, and also discussed with Resler whom he should appoint to the defence. Resler insisted that choosing the next barrister on the register, in alphabetical order, was the fairest (and standard) approach, to which Klouda countered that the chosen barrister must not be just an ordinary barrister, someone who would sit and observe the trial and might end up agreeing with the prosecution. The other lawyers who were present at the time (Tarabrin and Konečný) advised the President of the Association to ask the Ministry of

224 AHMP 12, Podání s č. j. A 8926/46 Advokátní komora [official document].
225 AHMP 12, Lecture *On the Demise of K. H. Frank*, (hereafter "Demise") p. 17.

Justice to appoint their salaried barrister.[226] Resler was then asked whether he would be willing to take on the case, to which he responded absolutely not, since as the Bar Association's deputy prosecutor he was exempt from court defence duty, and the Association would seriously breach its code if it appointed him despite this. Klouda then asked him how he would respond if the Association were to impose the case on him, disregarding its own rules. He was referring to the possibility that he could appoint Resler as Frank's defence lawyer regardless of the Association's code, and that if Resler refused to carry out the duty then he could disqualify him from practice as a barrister. Resler responded that this would constitute "a deliberate contravention of a valid code, that he would consider it wrong and would resist it by all legal means available to him, and that he would cope with the consequences of doing so." To the direct question whether he would defend Frank, if his means of resistance did not work out and he ended up having to take on the case, he stated that "every defence lawyer is bound by professional duties and must carry out every defence properly and conscientiously; that applies to me too." With that, he considered the matter closed, and left.

President Klouda, on the other hand, immediately left for the Ministry of Justice, where the Minister of Justice Prokop Drtina requested that a barrister be appointed to the case without reference to the usual order of priority.[227] The same day, the Ministry of Justice instructed the Bar Association (as its supervising body) to appoint an exceptionally competent barrister to the case, and quickly.[228] By coincidence on the same day, 15 March, Ivan Suk gave Resler a copy of his book *Reportáž o Norimberku* (A Report on Nuremberg), little knowing what an omen it was of what awaited him.[229]

On *16 March* Kamill Resler received an order, with a letter from the Ministry of Justice attached, appointing him to defend K. H. Frank. Although it should have been the court itself that appointed the defence counsel, he was in fact appointed by the Bar Association using a form pre-prepared by the Extraordinary People's Court.

The same day, Resler submitted a complaint to the Ministry of Justice about the Bar Association board's decision. Beneath his copy of this complaint he noted in pencil: "Submit first thing in the morning to Prague II, Vyšehradská street, no. 16 (beneath Emausy) 16. 3. 1946."[230]

226 Jiří Kotyk. *JUDr. Kamill Resler (1893–1961), oběť šikany komunistického režimu.* [Kamill Resler (1893–1961), Bullied by the Communist Regime]. [online]. 2011 [accessed 2017-11-28]. Available at: http://www.kraj.kppardubicka.cz/stranky/cti-prispevky.php?id=JUDr._Kamill_Resler_(1893 %961961),_obet_sikany_komunistickeho_rezimu.

227 AHMP 12, Podání Reslera doručené AK 23. 8. 1946.

228 Rozhodnutí NS se sp. zn. Ds I 16/46 [court document] p. 3.

229 KNM 1, Ivan Suk. *Reportáž o Norimberku: 1945–1946.* [A report about Nuremberg: 1945–1946]. Prague: Nová osvěta, 1946, Book with personal inscription.

230 AHMP 12, Complaint on 16 March 1946.

Čis. jedn. Ls IX 1527/46

Ustanovení zástupce chudých.

Hlavní líčení o — veřejné — obžalobě

veřejného žalobce

proti K.H.Frankovi

pro zločiny proti státu dle §u 1,2,3/1,5/2,5/1 lit.a/,5/2 lit.a/
6,7/1, 7/2, 7/3, 8/1,a , 9, 10, 11,z.ze dne 24.I.46 ve znění vyhlášky
ministr. vnitra, ze 18.II.1946 č.23 Sb.zák a nař.
konati se bude dne 22.března 1946   do pol. o 10   hod. u tohoto

soudu v jednací síni čis. porotní, čís. dveří přízemí   posch.

Ve shodě s výborem advokátní komory zřizujete se zástupcem

chudých a obhájcem výše jmenovaného .

Obžalovaný jest   ve vazbě   na svobodě a bydlí

vzdejšího soudu .

Mimořádný lidový soud v Praze XIV.
odd. IX. dne 18.března 1946.
Krajský soud trestní v Praze XIV.,

oddel   dne

Trest. řád č. 95 č. — Praha-kr. — (Ustanovení zástupce chudých a vyrozumění jeho o hlav. přelíčení.)

Tiskárna Protektorátu Čechy a Morava v Praze. — 5278-39.

Resler is named defence counsel to K. H. Frank. (AHMP)

On *17 March* Resler complained to the Extraordinary People's Court that they had not kept to the formalities of appointment, and attempted to obtain a declaration from the court that the appointment had been unlawful and invalid.[231] The court responded to this by sending Resler a second order of appointment, which it issued itself and not through the Bar Association.

On *18 March* the Bar Association received Resler's official appeal against its previous decision, which its board then rejected on 21 March.[232] Meanwhile Resler refused to continue in the role of deputy prosecutor for the Association, since it had acted illegally towards him and he took this as a betrayal.

By *19 March* Resler had already partly come to terms with his situation. In the morning he passed by the court and asked to look at the relevant files. However, the files were not in the court office, and neither were the judges. Two hours later the judges arrived and it turned out that the files were in fact in the room, but were locked away. Resler then began to study them. The court also gave him permission to visit Frank over the following three days, in his cell A I 20, to consult with him without any officials present. Curiously, they added that "no objections shall be raised if the barrister, on Frank's request, offers him cigarettes."[233]

On *20 March* Resler delivered a request to the Bar Association for exemption from duty, with a proposal for an alternative defence lawyer: out of kindness to Resler, and in view of his health, JUDr. Jaroslav Stehlík had agreed that he would accept a court appointment to the case.[234] However, even though Resler's health was truly not in a good state, this proposal was rejected. Resler had survived tropical malaria in 1917 and in 1919 had spent five months in hospital with a gunshot wound to his thigh bone; in 1933 he had suffered a kidney infection, and in 1943 stomach ulcers. Moreover, from 1 to 10 March 1946 he had been laid low with a bad case of the flu and a high fever.

On *21 March* Resler asked the Bar Association's board once again to excuse him from the *ex officio* defence, but this was refused.[235] And so Resler began to work properly on the case. He did not let the Bar Association's malicious behaviour go, though, but simply postponed dealing with it further until he had finished a few other important cases. Once they were over, he took the matter up once again.

On *12 August* he filed a complaint with the Bar Association's disciplinary committee, against its board. With it he enclosed a proposal for measures to be taken to prevent similar incidents from happening in the future – after all, many other barristers were soon to be appointed by the courts.

231   AHMP 12, Podání s č. j. Ls IX 1524/46 [official request].
232   Podání s č. j. O 1437/46 [official request].
233   AHMP 12, Dokument s č. j. Ls IX 1527/46 [court document].
234   Podání s č. j. 1414/46 [official request].
235   AHMP 12, Rozhodnutí s č. j. O 1505/46 [official decision].

For this reason, a few months after the Frank trial had ended, on 15 August 1946, Resler proposed an alteration to the way poor individuals were represented; he extended this proposal on 11 September the same year. First of all, he thanked the Bar Association's board for their decision that while he had been working on the Frank trial, his other cases were allocated to other barristers and considered duty representation, which meant that Resler did not need to pay fees to those barristers for taking them on. At the same time, however, he emphasised his surprise that the board had deviated from the practice of appointing *ex officio* barristers in alphabetical order. He objected to this change, saying that it could lead to a situation in which a poor, ordinary citizen was not allocated a specialised barrister, but one from the alphabetical list, while a German accused of war crimes "even if it were to be, for example, an extremely clearcut case, in which everyone knows from the beginning that the accused must be and will be convicted, and that he will be sentenced to death",[236] would be allocated a first-rate, specialised defence lawyer. Resler suggested that even in peacetime legal representatives should be allocated according to the needs of each case. For this, it would first be necessary to divide the *ex officio* lawyers into various categories, according to their specialisations. His views fell on dumb ears. Then, at a meeting of the Bar Association's board on 6 September, he submitted a complaint to the disciplinary committee against the Association's procedure in selecting an *ex officio* barrister. At the meeting the President of the Association responded to the effect that Dr. Resler had performed the defence extremely well, and deserved the board's recognition and thanks for that.

On 3 October 1946 the disciplinary committee agreed to reject Resler's complaint about the board's procedure.[237] Resler complained about this decision to the Supreme Court, which was filed as file number Ds I 16/46.[238]

Dr. Gottweis of the Supreme Court, whom Resler had met at the Extraordinary People's Court in Prague, pronounced the court's decision on 19 February 1948. In its capacity as the appeal court for the Bar's disciplinary matters, it rejected Resler's complaint, stating that although there were certainly reasons for establishing the practice of alphabetical appointment, there were also cases in which such a procedure was not effective, and in which the Association's own officers could also be appointed. It concluded with the observation that "the case of the criminal defence of K. H. Frank was one such exception to the usual cases of *ex officio* representation." It explained that this exception in the Frank case was due to the Czechoslovak Republic's

---

236 AHMP 12, Podání s č. j. A 8926/46 [official request].
237 VCM, Rozhodnutí kárné rady z 3. října 1946 s č. j. Dis 113/46 [decision by the Disciplinary Board on 3 October 1946].
238 VCM and AHMP 16, Complaint against the Disciplinary Board's decision of 3 October 1946 submitted 25 October 1946.

considerable interest in the trial and the need for a high level of defence.[239] Moreover, because the Extraordinary People's Court had set the date of the main hearing for 22 March, the Association's president had to appoint a barrister quickly, and so it was no surprise that he had neglected elements of the usual procedure. The Supreme Court stated that the board's rejection of barrister JUDr. Stehlík, who had in principle agreed to take on the case in Resler's place, was acceptable as it had not been clear to the board that JUDr. Stehlík had the qualities required for Frank's defence.

Resler had a very clear opinion on the whole affair, even after the trial was over: "The complainant cannot consider the matter closed, either in itself, nor thanks to the flattering and smarmy phrases with which Mr president JUDr. Klouda and the whole of the disciplinary committee are trying to make the exceptional damage and inconvenience of defending K. H. Frank more acceptable to him, which cannot in any case change anything of the fact that Mr president JUDr. Klouda grossly breached professional law, without reason, by appointing to the official defence duties a barrister who was excused according to the usual practice from such duties for ordinary folk."[240]

REPRESENTATION BEFORE THE SPECIAL COURTS

Before the war had fully ended, the Czechoslovaks in exile and the international powers had already made plans to bring Nazi criminals and their collaborators to justice. The most significant international steps in this direction were the Moscow Declaration of 30 October 1943 on returning war criminals to the countries where they had carried out their crimes, and the agreement on the prosecution and punishment of major war criminals of the European Axis (the so-called London Agreement), issued on 8 August 1945 by the International Military Tribunal in Nuremberg; the Tribunal in Nuremberg was to try only those criminals whose crimes could not be geographically pinned down. At the Czechoslovak level, Extraordinary People's Courts were established after the war by Presidential decree no. 16/1945 Coll., on the punishment of Nazi criminals, collaborators and their accomplices and on the Extraordinary People's Courts, dated 19 June 1945, which is also known as the Great Retribution Decree. The National Court was established by decree no. 17/1945 Coll. on the same day. This was a specific court for a limited circle of top public officials. Resler had more or less no dealings relating to the so-called Small Retribution Decree no. 138/1945 Coll., on the punishment of

---

239 AHMP 16, Rozhodnutí Nejvyššího soudu Ds I 16/46 [court decision], p. 3.
240 VCM and AHMP 16, Complaint against the Disciplinary Board's decision of 3 October 1946 submitted 25 October 1946.

certain offences against national honour, which punished less serious acts with prison sentences of up to one year or fines of up to one million crowns.

The majority of Resler's criminal defence work during 1946 and 1947 had to do with retributional justice. The retribution decrees' period of validity was extended several times, in the end until 4 May 1947, after which the affected institutions became standard courts once again. When the political regime changed again in February 1948, however, the Exceptional People's Courts were renewed until the end of 1948 by act no. 33/1948 Coll., and proceedings that had been lawfully concluded could be re-opened on request from the public prosecutor. [241]

Kamill Resler defended at a number of such re-opened cases before the People's Court. According to his later accounts, he had originally resolved not to accept the role of defence lawyer for war crimes and Nazi crimes in the post-war trials. He changed his mind on this, though, when he received a request from a colleague, who was a political prisoner. This led him to take on the defence of a Czechoslovak army officer at the first division Military Court. In November 1945, the officer was acquitted on the grounds that his arrest had been an error of the revolutionary days, and received compensation for the time he had spent in custody.

During the months that followed, Resler defended a number of people, including for example Prof. Miloslav Hýsek of the Philosophical Faculty at Charles University, who was acquitted, and General Otto Bláha, who was executed.

THE EVENTS OF THE TRIAL

Given that his objections had been refused, Resler had no choice but to take on the case. He tried not to think about the fact that he was to defend a man on whose orders his own relatives and friends had been killed – people for whom he had cared deeply and whose tragic fate could no longer be reversed. Besides his personal feelings against Frank, he was naturally also very well aware of the society's hatred towards him. Resler was fully aware that there was no doubt that Frank had been destined for execution from the moment he had landed at Ruzyne airport on 3 August 1945. [242]

In the opening scenes of the film *Ex offo*, [243] the presiding judge reacts to being given Frank's case with: "Mr President, he'll swing, that's for sure. I can

---

241 For more on the Retributional Trials see Benjamin Frommer. *National Cleansing: Retribution against Nazi Collaborators in Postwar Czechoslovakia*. New York: Cambridge University Press, 2005 or Mečislav Borák. *Spravedlnost podle dekretu* [Justice by decree]. Ostrava: Tilia, 1998.

242 "Demise", p. 14.

243 *Ex offo*, directed by Jaromír Políšenský. Czech televison, 1998. The film is not available in English.

tell you that now, months before the trial has even begun! And chief prosecutor Jackson will come and watch us impartially sentence him to death! I am just praying to God that I will be able to listen to the defence at all and not only think all the while about how good his neck will look in a noose! (...) If a judge is to pass a fair sentence, he must be objective. Completely objective. And in this case that is simply not possible! One of the foundation stones of the law is the presumption of innocence. Have you tried to see Frank as an innocent man? I have, oh, all night long. And I must honestly admit that it was extremely difficult. Oh Lord. And who is going to defend him?" Although this scene was modified for the film, it well illustrates the dilemma in which those involved in K. H. Frank's trial found themselves. How then did the barrister defending Frank feel? What must he have gone through, other than the legal arguments themselves, in order to be able to say: "I fought the good fight, and upheld justice"?

Resler described his first meeting with Frank with the words: "and so I stood face to face with the man whom we all justifiably hated. I addressed him in Czech and his face fell. He did not even have good manners, but interrupted me to ask whether I speak German. I nodded, at which point his face brightened. I did not shake his hand, but sat down and started to discuss his case with him."[244] From the very start, Resler had to come to terms with the fact that Frank did not want him to represent him. On Frank's request, Resler had to write into his report for the court on 21 March that "the accused refuses to consent to being defended by the barrister who was appointed by the court, or by any other Czechoslovak citizen or Czech national."[245] Yet that situation changed the very same day; Frank accepted Resler and was satisfied with his arguments and the planned defence.

Legal questions aside, Resler also encountered other problems that he needed to solve for his client. In mid-April, during the trial, Frank lost a filling from his tooth and Resler had to look for a dentist. Frank also suffered from depression – he was bothered by the thought that millions of sudeten Germans were cursing him, and also found the separation from his family difficult. It fell to Resler to keep Frank in a suitable frame of mind such that he was able to cope with the stress of the trial and did not let go of the ability to defend himself; this was very important to the court and was in the public interest, so that the procedure looked fair to all, including international assessors. Frank had difficulty sleeping, and was already extremely exhausted by the second day of the hearing. It took Resler a great deal of effort to restore in him some self-confidence, a fighting spirit and the will to defend himself. At certain moments this became particularly difficult for Resler; he

---

244   "Demise", p. 18.
245   AHMP 12, Návrhy došlé MLS s č. j. LS IX 1527/46 [court document].

later described how awful it was to spend hours and hours with Frank in an inhospitable, cold, musty cell on beautiful spring evenings.[246]

During the three days he had for preparation, Resler did not manage to read through the whole file; this meant that he saw many things for the first time during the hearing. The atmosphere in court was agitated, and disrupted by the media, about which Resler complained: "the unusual levels of noise and disruption in the courtroom were a great bother. When I entered the courtroom with K. H. Frank, they shone three or four spotlights into our eyes, the film cameras started to whirr, and photographers jumped around us, sitting, kneeling, strutting, pointing their cameras at us and for a whole minute all you could hear was their shutters clicking. The never-ending commotion was made worse by four translators and journalists, who kept coming to ask questions. On one matter eight of them came, one after the other."[247] The entire court proceedings were translated into Russian, English and French via special headphones in the courtroom, and into German especially for Frank. The whole hearing was also broadcast live on the radio, and every evening a summary of the day's session was given.[248]

Resler gives his opening speech. (AHMP)

---

246 "Demise", pp. 19, 22 and 23.
247 "Demise", p. 20.
248 "Český národ soudí," p. 81.

Frank's trial; Resler is on the left. (AHMP)

Frank's trial. (AHMP)

Resler and his assistant Kroupa during Frank's trial. (AHMP)

Resler with Roubal, editor of *Lidová Demokracie*. (AHMP)

Frank, with interpreters' booths in the background. (AHMP)

Resler presents his proposal. (AHMP)

Resler with his assistant beside him. (AHMP)

A meeting during the trial. (AHMP)

From Frank's trial. (AHMP)

Prosecutor Drábek. (AHMP)

There was considerable media interest in the case's progress, and a number attempts were even made to influence it. Certain filmmakers, who wanted to film a scene for the USA, asked Resler whether Frank could say a particular sentence during his testimony in court. Resler responded that it would only be possible as part of an answer to a question given by the judge. Nevertheless, it seemed to him personally that this insensitive way of trying to push a man who was fighting for his life into acting was very tasteless. Resler circled this sentence in his record of the event: "I am here to defend and must protect my charge's rights."[249] Even so, he promised the cameramen that he would present their request to Frank, however little he liked it. Initially the request worried Frank, and looked up to Resler for advice. Resler told him that it was entirely his own decision. Frank then refused in his typical way, which Resler described with the words "once again an attempt not to offend, not to get into deep water, and to smooth out his relations with others. I promised him that I would convey Frank's refusal to the young men politely."

During the trial, and particularly towards the end of it, Resler also passed on various requests to Frank. These were mostly questions concerning people Frank might have known about, although it was not very likely. In some cases the questions related to other on-going trials, in which this information could have had an influence, and in other cases they came from family members who were trying to find out what they could about their relatives and shed some light on their lives under the protectorate. Some of Frank's answers were later used in other trials. This also happened to Resler, who was asked by his friend JUDr. Mellan to testify in one of his cases about information he had heard from Frank. Resler also responded to numerous letters asking him to help by asking Frank something. Resler always asked the questions, and responded to the letters. If Frank didn't answer the questions, Resler always tried to suggest what the enquirer could do next, and whom they should try to contact.

Some of Resler's duties verged even on the comic. Presiding judge JUDr. Kozák had for some reason told Frank that his lawyer would give him cigarettes, and when Resler asked what he had meant by that, Kozák replied that he was to give them to Frank himself. Frank therefore believed that one of his barrister's duties was to supply him with cigarettes. Resler wrote: "Frank smoked like a gypsy and the president's ration was not enough for him, so I, representative of the poor, had to top up the supply to honour Mr President, whether I liked it or not." This meant in practice that Frank also smoked American cigarettes sent by Resler's barrister friend Paul Edwards in New York. Resler received many packets of them; the price of all the packets he re-

---

249 AHMP 4, Kamill Resler: *K. H. Frank se hájí proti českému národu* [K. H. Frank defends himself against the Czech nation].

ceived on the black market would then have exceeded five thousand crowns. Resler was not used to this level of generosity and was therefore quite moved by Edwards' favour. In a thank you letter to him, he wrote "And as you know, it is not easy to move Dr. Resler."[250]

Once the trial was over, Resler asked the director of Pankrác prison to allow Frank to have his wedding ring and watch; he refused, for the sake of formality. Resler therefore sent his request to the Regional Criminal Court, which after consulting the Extraordinary People's Court allowed the return of Frank's wedding ring, for which Frank was very grateful to Resler. Resler's reasons for arranging this had been purely pragmatic – after the end of the trial, Frank was in mental shreds, agitated, aggressive and unable to control himself, which fatigued Resler. "I needed create some kind of shock, in order to get him into a tolerable mood so that I could carry out my remaining work without it exhausting me so much."[251] He succeeded.

Two letters addressed to Frank survived among Resler's possessions. One of them, from J. Vaněk in Sobotka, northern Bohemia, included a copy of the German magazine *Wegweiser* and wishes that Frank should find time for "the Lord Jesus Christ and not turn away from His love." This was in stark contrast to the other letter, in which an anonymous political prisoner wished Frank a pleasant Easter, with a postcard depicting a meadow on which gallows had been drawn. JUDr. Kozák had crossed them out, but they were still perfectly recognisable.[252]

On 18 May, following a request from Frank, Resler asked the International Red Cross in Geneva to negotiate with the USSR government so that Frank's second wife could be moved from Moscow into the American Zone and could live with her three small children. Frank was extremely worried for his wife. In June 1945 he wrote in one of his letters from American prison "that he was dreadfully and heartbreakingly vexed by his responsibility." Once the trial was over he complained to his family that he had suffered unspeakably during the trial, and that it had been simply a spectator sport, a show. Since all of his property had been confiscated, all he left to his children and wife was a reminder of his "rich, often difficult life as a fighter who gave himself for his German nation with heartfelt passion." He wrote that after the end of the hearing, but before the verdict had been passed.[253] In the same letter he also wrote how hard it had been for him that during his ten months of solitary confinement – before the trial – not a single person had shaken his hand. It was therefore a big moment for Frank when Resler eventually shook hands

---

250 AHMP 12 and PNP 91, Letters to Paul Edwards.
251 "Demise", p. 24.
252 AHMP 12, Postcard.
253 AHMP 12, Letter to his wife on 11 June 1945, Thoughts and records for my wife and children, especially for Harald and Gerhart.

with him at Easter. Frank wrote to his wife and children, "we must thank [Resler] for the great kindness he has shown me" and recommended that they ask Resler for a detailed description of the trial.

Throughout the trial, and in the run-up to the execution itself, Resler received many requests for tickets to watch the trial. These requests came from his own friends, such as barrister Antonín Švehla, and also from the Dean of the Business College, prof. JUDr. Richard Horn, and from a British diplomat. Altogether, Resler provided about one hundred people with access to the trial, including his own wife.

On 20 May Frank still believed that he would live out the rest of his days in a Czechoslovak prison, and asked Resler about the conditions for life prisoners. "On that day I already had a ticket to his execution in my wallet. That was not conducive to our conversation being either lively or sincere," wrote Resler.[254]

THE DEFENCE AND THE COURT PROCEEDINGS[255]

The K. H. Frank trial lasted more than two months, from the first hearing to the verdict – from 15 March until 22 May 1946. The Retribution Decree had originally set the maximum length of proceedings to three days and established that failure to keep to this deadline would result in the case passing to an ordinary court. However, an amendment to the Retribution Decree made by law no. 22/1946 Coll., which came into force a month before Frank's trial began, made it possible for such trials to continue should the public prosecutor so propose, which in Frank's case he did.

K. H. Frank was charged on ten counts (in parentheses I indicate the provisions of the Great Retribution Decree on which the charges were based):
1. Attempting to forcibly change the constitution of the Republic and to separate parts of it, including support for armed uprisings (section 1),
2. Membership in the organisations SS, FS, SdP and NSDAP (section 2),[256]
3. Publicly promoting and supporting the Nazi movement in print, radio, film or theatre (section 3),

---

254 "Demise", p. 24.
255 Unless specified otherwise, the information in this section is based on the following documents: AHMP 1, Doslovný záznam průběhu celého líčení [court record]; Karel Zajíček (ed.). *Český národ soudí K. H. Franka.* [The Czech nation tries K. H. Frank]. Prague: Ministerstvo informací, 1947, pp. 80–117.
256 Freiwilliger Schutzdienst – a semi-military Sudeten German organisation, inspired by the SA, which was involved in acts of violence in 1938. SdP – the Sudeten German Party, which merged with the NSDAP on 30 October 1938.

4. Committing many criminal acts, for example complicity in the crime of murder, complicity in the crime of treating a person as a slave and of public coercion by blackmail (section 5, para. 1, point a, para. 2, point a),
5. Commanding forced labour in conditions dangerous to the Republic's residents (section 6),
6. Giving orders resulting in the restriction of freedom, grievous bodily harm and death to a large number of people (section 7 para. 1 and 2),
7. Committing crimes against property, including arson (section 8 para. 1 point a, para. 2 point a),
8. Illegally removing property belonging to the state or an individual or legal entity (section 9),
9. Abusing others by means of duress or persecution for the purposes of self-enrichment (section 10),
10. Committing the crime of informing, as a result of which others lost freedoms or lives (section 11).

In other words, K. H. Frank was accused on almost all counts that the Retribution Decree allowed, apart from one. That was section 4, which related to disrupting the resistance movement abroad, which Frank had logically not been involved in.

If K. H. Frank had been convicted only of point no. 9 of these charges, he would have faced ten years in prison. For each of the other charges he could have been sentenced to twenty years imprisonment, or to life imprisonment, and on six of the charges he could be sentenced to death.

As early as 21 March, the day before the main hearing began, Resler submitted his first motions to the Extraordinary People's Court. In these, his argument focused in particular on Frank's membership in the National Assembly of the Czechoslovak Republic, from 1935, and went on to state that Frank was not subject to Czech law, that the trial must be held in Nuremberg, that the court was biased, and that the main hearing must be delayed on account of him not having been given enough time to prepare the defence. Frank had expressed his distaste at being sent before a Czechoslovak court to the very first American Officer who questioned him, saying: "I am ready to answer to any international tribunal, but not to be handed over to a Czech court."

Resler also read these motions to the court on the first day of the main hearing. Frank further asked Resler to raise an objection against the validity of the Retribution Decree on the grounds that it had been implemented without sufficient legislative procedure. Resler did prepare this objection, but let Frank present it to the court himself, since if he had presented it he would have overstepped the bounds of his duty as a barrister, and would have been acting in contradiction with his duties as a Czechoslovak citizen. Resler was a master at negotiating this very fine line. On the one hand, he fulfilled his task as a barrister, and on the other hand he managed not to compromise his standing as a Czechoslovak citizen, as he felt was his duty. He did not criticize the court itself, is legality or the validity of the Presidential Decrees. Yet in all questions that did not concern the existence of Czechoslovakia, his claims were uncompromising.

After hearing the objections, the court retired for a ninety-minute deliberation, after which it decided to call General JUDr. Bohuslav Ečer as an expert, as he had had a part in handing K. H. Frank over to the Czechoslovak authorities. He testified that Frank was not one of the so-called greatest criminals, in accordance with the Moscow Declaration of 30 October 1943 and Nuremberg chief prosecutor Robert Jackson's opinion. Furthermore, all the Nuremberg prosecutors explained that, like others accused, Frank need not give evidence as a witness, which was a great disappointment for Frank. Only the first Reichsprotektor, Konstantin von Neurath, asked for a statement from Frank, and then only in writing. The question of parliamentary immunity was similarly brushed aside: Frank had forfeited his parliamentary mandate on 1 October 1938 when he became a German citizen, and his mandate had officially ended on 27 October 1938 as a result of measures taken by the Permanent Committee of the National Assembly's Chamber of Deputies.

After the public prosecutor had given his opening speech, Frank made a brief response to it, which the court cut short for the sake of efficiency, and the first question of the hearing was posed: "Frank, do you feel guilty?" – "I do not feel guilty in the sense of the criminal law, but only responsible for having carried out the orders given to me" Frank responded.

The first few days of the hearing focused on supplementing the statement Frank had made before the start of the trial, in which he had (among other things) mentioned that he had attempted to find out the exiled Czechoslovak government's location in London, in order to have V1 and V2 missiles sent there. The public prosecutor presented numerous documents to show the truth about certain matters raised in Frank's statement, for example demonstrating that he had visited the Mauthausen concentration camp, which Frank denied.

After this, the longest part of the main hearing followed, which was focused on substantiation of the evidence; at this stage the witnesses were heard. The court attempted to listen to the witnesses one by one on specific questions, but it was not always possible for them to hear from the witnesses in the order that suited the court best. Indeed, the order of the witness statements at the court was determined by the theme on which they spoke, rather than who they were; this meant that witnesses from various groups – Nazis, Czech collaborators, officials and prisoners from concentration camps – were heard in random order.

The court's attention turned first to the events of 17 November 1939. During the night of 16 November university student representatives had been arrested, and some of them had then been executed. The Czech universities had been closed. The chairman of the Association of Czechoslovak University Students Ladislav Schubert was the first to testify in court to these events, and was followed by other students from the residences in question, a witness to the unjustified execution of nine students, and the German commander of the events Major General SS Bernhard Voss. Their evidence focused largely on whether Frank had personally beaten the students – which Frank denied. Most of the students responded to Resler's question by stating that they could not absolutely rule out the possibility that it had been someone else, while a few maintained that it had been Frank.

A further, though shorter topic for the witnesses was the destruction of the tomb of an unknown soldier and wreaths that had been laid on it. The German locksmith who had destroyed the tomb at first denied it, claiming he was a good Catholic and citizen of Prague, but later confessed under duress.

One of the key topics discussed during the trial was Frank's treatment of workers who were sent to Germany. Frank had often advocated for their rights, making particular efforts to ensure they were treated as equals with German workers and had access to cultural necessities, including literature. Walter Jacobi, Prague Commander of the Sicherheitsdienst, or SS intelligence service, was asked whether Frank had done this only for his own gain, and responded that sometimes it had certainly been for his own gain, but that at other times it had been of the kindness of his heart. Jacobi mentioned that, partly thanks to these efforts, Frank's colleagues had considered him a Czechophile. The fact that Frank had been against the total assimilation of the Czech nation may also have contributed to that.

Another surprisingly serious discussion focused on conditions in the concentration camps. Resler was strongly against calling witnesses on this topic, because he believed that Frank had not had any influence on how the camps were run. However, the public prosecutor's argument, which the court adopted, was that Frank had known that thousands of Czechs were being sent to the camps, and it was therefore important that he knew what conditions he was sending them to. Milada Horáková, a member of parliament later executed by the communists in 1950, gave evidence on this in court, and the chairman of the Czech Sokol Association, JUDr. Antonín Hřebík, spoke of Frank's personal attempts to destroy the Sokol.

When it came to the conditions at the concentration camp in Terezín's Small Fortress, the court heard from camp commander Heinrich Jöckel. He tried to lay as much blame as he could on Frank, and save his own name. The court, naturally, did not believe him, in particular when he maintained that he had not known anything about the torture and execution of prisoners. At one point, when he stated that a supervisor who had overseen the beating of three prisoners had himself been sent to a concentration camp for it, the presiding judge asked him in disbelief "Are you serious?." In a similar manner, Terezín doctor MUDr. Beno Kröbert also did his best to accuse others. Both testified that Frank had been directly responsible for a number of executions.

Resler also objected to the prosecution's proposal to show films from Auschwitz and other concentration camps in the courtroom, for the same reasons – Frank had not had any influence over these, and he therefore considered them irrelevant. Yet the films were permitted, as was further evidence including the presentation of tanned human skins from the Mauthausen concentration camp. Resler's role at these moments was often reduced to asking the final question to the witnesses, at which point he would ask whether the witness knew that the accused had contributed to the atrocities at the camps, or had been aware of them. The witnesses responded to this negatively. Nevertheless, Frank did admit that he had ordered the families of some exiles to be sent to the concentration camps, where many died.

The court allocated a significant amount of time to the question whether Frank had, on 28 October 1939, personally beaten some people on the street, including elderly women. The first issue was whether it had really been Frank who had beaten them, and the second whether he could have been there at all – on that afternoon he had visited President Hácha, and it was very shortly afterwards that some witnesses claimed he had been beating Czechs on the street. The witnesses' accounts varied. Because Resler was fairly sure that Frank had not beaten anyone, he stated: "Considering the witnesses' accounts (...), that the accused beat pedestrians on the streets of Prague on 28 October 1939, including an older woman, the accused points out that these people themselves or other passers-by would surely agree to give evidence, and suggests that the court call them to do so via the radio, and if they do come forward, brings proof from them." His proposal was rejected.

Naturally, the court took a similar approach to the killing in Lidice. It heard testimony from members of the Kladno Gestapo and their then commander Harald Wiesmann, and also from three female survivors. The trial's attention focused on whether Frank had been there at the time of the executions, or if not, when he had first visited Lidice. Various answers were given to these questions. The court also asked about Lidice while interrogating deputy Reichsprotektor Kurt Daluege, who did not get along with Frank. Resler did not want to allow him to attend as a witness on account of his mental condition, but this was rejected. Daluege reported that he was not suffering from any mental illness, and that he had only found out after the war that the Nazi leaders believed him to have been mentally ill between 1943 and 1945. Resler pushed Daluege harder than any other witness and accused him of lying, and Daluege often responded to Resler's questions by stating that he did not know.

Resler's behaviour towards Daluege can be contrasted with his questioning of Harald Wiesmann, who willingly responded to his questions about whether Frank had attempted to return those unfairly sent for military service to normal life, whether in the Lidice case he had held more moderate views than Hitler, whether he had refused Hitler's orders to destroy industrial sites, and whether Frank had supported Prague being declared a hospital town.

Aside from these key areas of questioning, the court also heard from JUDr. Miloš Stádník, secretary to the Prime Minister of the Protectorate Alois Eliáš, on Frank's relationship with Eliáš; Stádník reported that "General Eliáš did not hide the fact that he was physically disgusted when he had to meet K. H. Frank." On one occasion, Eliáš had apparently pretended he had a broken arm in order to avoid a meeting with Frank and a Japanese minister. Meanwhile, the court heard from the President of the Czech National Council, Albert Pražák, on his negotiations with Frank at the Prague uprising, as well as investigating the claim that members of the protectorate troops in Italy had been persecuted with Frank's consent, and looking into the demilitarisation of the Kladno police. Several of Frank's speeches were read to the court during the trial, and Frank declared that they were, indeed, sadly his. On Resler's instigation a few additional witnesses were called, including the son-in-law of a forester from the south Bohemian town of Písek, who had been granted a pardon by Frank.

Towards the end of the main hearing, a number of experts chosen by the court were also questioned. In many cases, Resler was opposed to their appointment, as he considered them biased. For example, he raised objections about a report from a political intelligence expert, which was entitled "The complex of crimes of which K. H. Frank stands accused." The court rejected Resler's objections, stating that the title only mentioned accusation and that if the report were to deviate from the permitted limits in reality, then the court would disregard it, but it would not be rendered invalid. Resler asked the experts many questions, which were designed to show his client's guilt in a more positive light. For example, for how long the SdP had acted autonomously, and whether it was true that Germany had financed the Protectorate to the tune of billions. The court only allowed him to ask a small proportion of the questions he proposed, largely for the following reasons: the questions had already been answered, were not decisive, did not relate to the case, or the court would respond to them itself. While questioning the experts, Resler's arguments also referred to the provisions of the Criminal Code, even though the Code was not applicable in proceedings brought before the Extraordinary People's Court. The court therefore concluded that the experts' reports were sufficient for the purposes of the proceedings, and that they need not meet the usual criteria, since retributional justice was not legally derived from the principles of criminal law, but from martial law.

Resler's strongest argument was his proposal to have the accused's psychological condition examined, based on his answers to questioning. This proposal was made against Frank's wishes and without his knowledge. Resler based his proposal on a number of observations, in particular that "he lacks the ability to judge the correctness, legality, and humanity of his own dealings and those of his superiors or other representatives of his nation. (...) He is unable to understand that someone could put him on trial and punish him for his actions, and claims he was following his leader's orders. (...) In short, he lacks any sense of proportion in the events of his life, whether they affect himself or others."[257]

The public prosecutor outright rejected Resler's proposal, as did the court; the court claimed that the most decisive factor in this matter was the overall personal impression the accused gave the court, which in this case utterly ruled out the possibility that the accused might be mentally ill. Moreover, no objective facts had been noted during the main hearing that would have raised doubts about the accused's sanity or mental health. On the contrary, the court was persuaded that the accused had carefully and attentively followed the progress of the hearing and that his reactions to the evidence presented, whether in person or in writing, had demonstrated perfect mental competence.

Once all the evidence had been presented, the floor was given to the public prosecutor, and then to the accused and his defence. The public prosecutor gave his reply, to which the defence reacted by closing the case. On 27 April 1946 the court adjourned the hearing without day and retired for deliberation. On 21 May 1946 a short presentation of a few documents and letters was held, at which Resler presented a number of extenuating circumstances, and a two-day announcement of the judgement followed. The main hearing was closed on 22 May 1946 at 10:30 am. It had lasted 30 days.

THE CLOSING DEFENCE SPEECH[258]

At the end of the trial, Resler delivered his closing speech, in which he once again called into question the objectivity of the proceedings as a whole and pointed out the generally unfriendly atmosphere in society and among those present at the trial, who had turned themselves into additional prosecutors. "It was after all extremely clear throughout the proceedings that there were

257 AHMP 12, Application for Frank's mental state to be examined.
258 Unless otherwise specified, the information in this section and the section that follows it is based on the previously cited work *Český národ soudí K. H. Franka* [The Czech nation tries K. H. Frank], (p. 149–231).

not only two public prosecutors here, authorized by the requisite office to carry out that role, but also numerous witnesses – largely from the educated classes, alas – who stepped over the line when giving evidence and engaged in evident prosecution.

Similarly, with the exception of the two university professors, the esteemed experts did not refrain from allowing their personal feelings to infiltrate the professional matter of their findings and reports, referring to the accused's actions directly as crimes, in one case unprecedented crimes in terms of their number and the baseness of their criminal traits and so on, or including in their reports judgements of the actions reported from the per-spective of criminal law, specifying the basis of that judgement according to the criminal code, and thus anticipating the court's judgement and condemn-ing the accused before the verdict was given by the only qualified court. (...) It is therefore impossible for any court in the Czechoslovak Republic to judge the accused, in view of section 67 of the Code of Criminal Procedure, and others, and the accused requests that the court draw its conclusions based on this directive."

That is also why Resler repeatedly reminded the court that it was acting on behalf of the International Military Tribunal in Nuremberg, which had delegated its powers to the Czech court. He did so in an attempt to call on the judges' honour, in particular the lay judges, and to persuade them to judge based on actual fault and not on their own feelings.

After this, Resler reacted to the individual elements of the prosecution.

On the preparation of the Munich Agreement and 15 March 1939, Resler stated: "The law on the protection of the Republic only considers the prepara-tory negotiations and attempts to achieve such results to constitute a crime. (...) The law does not consider at all the possibility of such acts could being successful; it works on the assumption that if such plots were to be success-ful, and thus the constitution changed, independence lost, the democratic-republican state model altered, then the resulting circumstances would be such that it would no longer be possible to prosecute for the act committed, and courts would no longer be able to try according to Czechoslovak law (...) which means that the outcome itself (...) as such, is not punishable."

Frank's defence partially acknowledged his membership in criminal or-ganisations, in as far as Frank himself admitted his membership in the SdP, NSDAP and SS, but not in the Freiwilliger Schutzdienst. He also protested the German government's criminality. His defence rested on the fact that at the beginning of the war Hitler had formally dissolved the government, and had then directly commanded the individual ministers. The government itself therefore could not be *de iure* considered a criminal organisation.

To the accusation that Frank had promoted and supported Nazism, Resler argued that it was necessary to distinguish promotion of the Nazi movement from the execution of official duties, for example issuing orders relating to language. Official duties could only be charged under sections 7 and 9 of the Decree, and not under any of its other provisions. According to the defence, Frank never promoted Nazism in films or theatres.

As regarded the charge that he had participated in the persecution of the Czech nation, Resler attempted to disprove Frank's alleged presence when people were beaten on 28 October and 17 November 1939, based on the witnesses' evidence. When it came to Lidice, he maintained that the idea had come from Hitler and that Frank had only found out about it after the Lidice men had been shot, since he had been at Heydrich's funeral in Berlin. According to the defence statement, Frank only went to Lidice later, and there observed the aftermath of the extermination. Meanwhile, Resler claimed that Ležáky had been exterminated by the Gestapo, and none of the evidence presented had shown that Frank had any part in that event. As for executions and threats of execution issued to the leaders of trades unions during strikes, he maintained the Nazi line of argumentation – these had been Hitler's orders. In the case of the concentration camps, Frank declared that he had not known how the prisoners were treated there, as he had only been to the camps on a few occasions for very short visits, and had not noticed anything.

To the charge that Frank had ordered Czech people to work for the German war effort, Frank admitted ordering Czechoslovak citizens to work in the Czech lands, but not abroad. On the contrary, he protested that he had been against ordering work abroad, and that if such a thing had happened, it was on German orders that applied across the whole of occupied Europe.

When it came to the question of whether Frank had sent Czechs to the concentration camps and signed their death warrants, Resler argued that according to the rules of German criminal procedure, death sentences were enforceable only by judicial decision, as in other countries. Frank therefore did not himself issue such sentences, but only sometimes indicated whether he did or did not recommend mercy. That could not be considered to be ratifying death sentences. Frank denied all responsibility in this matter, and denied that he had known that the Gestapo were mutilating prisoners in the concentration camps, or that they would have done so on his orders. On the other hand he admitted to having imprisoned large groups of people.

Concerning property damage caused during the extermination of Lidice, Frank confessed that he had overseen the implementation of Hitler's commands. He denied co-responsibility for the extermination of Ležáky, and similarly denied committing arson in the village of Zubří, where the owner of a wooden house was hiding five resistance fighters and, after he was found out, the Gestapo burned down the house. Resler stated that Frank had not personally started the fire, and that since the house was not of great value, the fire had not caused serious damage. Moreover, no-one had died in the fire. The defence therefore refuted the accusation of arson according to the Retribution Decree.

On the count that blamed Frank for exploiting the Czech lands, Resler summed up evidence from the trial that had shown that Czech art collections had not been looted, and that on the contrary, Frank had taken action to prevent the removal of the precious Lobkowicz collection of musical instruments. As for the other economic crimes, his defence pointed to these having been due to policy laid down by the highest German authorities, whose orders the accused was simply carrying out; at most, he was therefore guilty only of carrying out Hitler's economic orders.

When it came to the accusation that Frank had withdrawn currency from the National bank in April 1945, Resler's defence accepted that Frank had commanded that the currency be sold at the end of the war, but not to himself (as the experts claimed), rather to the Ministry of State for the purpose of protecting Germany. It was to be given to Germans as they fled the Czechoslovak Republic. He took nothing for himself, and only gave his wife 1500 Swiss Franks, for which he had paid properly. He therefore did not consider himself guilty on this count.

The defence called into question the prosecution's claims that Frank had informed; Resler stated that this had not mentioned in any case except that of the executed general Eliáš. He specified: "However, the fact that led to General Eliáš's death was reported by the Gestapo and not the accused, and Frank's letter of 26 February 1941 dates from a time after the Gestapo had been informed, (...) and is therefore not direct proof that the accused informed them himself. The accused has not therefore been proven to have informed against General Eliáš and cannot be convicted of informing."

Resler maintained that the question of intent was a very complex one for the court. In particular, it was difficult to show whether the accused could have been aware of the criminality of his actions, "while being convinced that he was carrying out his professional duty (...) and particularly when failing to carry out those duties – disobeying Hitler's orders – meant certain death for him. From this perspective the accused insists that he did not have evil intent and that he carried out his official activities under the threat of execution, that is under irresistible duress. It should be noted that section 13 of the Great Retribution Decree only rules out such duress as a reason for impunity when membership in the relevant organisation was voluntary, and not when the accused was carrying out official duties."

The defence went on to address the possibility of acquittal based on a number of facts. The first of these concerned the amnesty issued by the government on 7 October 1938, which extended to criminal acts defined in the law on the protection of the Republic and the law on national defence.

Based on this, all the accused's acts committed up until 7 October 1938 should be pardoned.

Next, Resler's argument turned to parliamentary immunity. Resler stated that the reports from experts in international law had "safely substantiated that everything that was, between 29 September 1938 and 5 May 1945 pronounced as legal by Germany or recognised as legal here, was in fact only a compilation of strictly effective, but legally irrelevant acts. The consequence of this is that, as is indeed in keeping with the prosecution's approach, the accused remained a Czechoslovak citizen, and that both the Permanent Committee's measure of 27 October 1938 Coll. no. 253 terminating German deputies' mandates and Dr Hácha's decision on the dissolution of the Czechoslovak National Assembly are worthless, and hence that the accused, though it may sound a little strange, never ceased to be a member of the Czechoslovak parliament. (...) For that reason, the court must be obliged to enforce upon the accused the protection of his parliamentary immunity, even if he has not himself claimed this, or indeed directly resists it."

The final, and principal argument of Resler's defence speech was based on the accused's psychological condition. Resler fully agreed with the court's judgement that Frank had behaved in the manner of a fully mentally capable person during the proceedings, aware of the consequences of his actions, but added: "You have failed to notice [though], that the defence has offered evidence that the accused was not of sound mind at the time when he committed the actions for which the public prosecution is now charging him, that is between 21 May 1938 and 9 May 1945.[259] (...) Come to that, you have all seen how the accused raised his arm and stared at the German flag with such a look on his face that the audience in this hall stifled a nervous laugh. Think back to that, to what went through your heads at that moment; try not to suppress the feeling and the answer will be: a ridiculous, but dangerous madman. (...) Remember (...) Hitler-god, the god-like phenomenon of the greatest politician of all time, anywhere, the sacredness of his orders, the Rausch – intoxication, and that he – without knowing its consequences – took up the mass fascination, the nation's desire for a leader and saviour, prayers for a leader for the German nation, and accepted its connection with medieval German mysticism, and even that the whole period of Hitler's dominion was a myth, a legend. All of this together and in context convinces us that the accused was suffering a mental illness during the period when the prosecuted acts took place, and taking into account this reasonable doubt as to the accused's mental health at the time of the acts, an expert's report was necessarily required."

---

259 The first Czechoslovak military mobilisation took place on 21 May 1938. The so-called time of heightened threat to the Republic is counted from this date; this was later the date from which retributional legislation could be applied.

With this point, Resler unsheathed his primary argument – the one with the greatest, if still extremely small, chance of success. Although his preceding legal arguments had been entirely appropriate, they could not have prevented Frank from being sentenced to death – Frank's own confessions were sufficient for such a sentence to be passed. Hence Resler had to dig deeper and try to find – partly non-legal – possible reasons why he should not be executed. These included the argument that Nazism was a disease that had affected the entire nation, and could not be cured by the execution of a few leaders. "Unless it is cured at a deeper level, Nazism will remain forever rooted in the soul of the German nation. Even if it may seem impossible, it is crucial to try to bring the Germans to understand what Nazism was and to realise the horrifying extent of its crimes. During this trial psychologists and psychiatrists had the first chance in the history of humankind to investigate a mental illness that affected an entire nation and plunged it into a mass delusion, like the phenomena of a thousand years ago (...) and which brought the Germans the scientifically documented 'Hitler-wahn', Hitlerian frenzy, Hitler's delusion."

Resler had opened his closing speech with a comparison with the Nuremberg Tribunal, and referred to the Tribunal once again when concluding. He left the door open, however, for the Czechoslovak court to position itself morally above the Allies' court – and thus for his client to survive: "In the Nuremberg procedure we do not get to see this evidence, because the defence lawyers are German, and lack the courage or the will to put forward such a proposal. It is possible that we have just missed a unique opportunity in human history. Yet even without the required expert's report, all those present at this trial are agreed that we have seen signs of mental illness." All his cards by now on the table, Resler had nothing left but to conclude: "In obedience to the laws of my country and of my profession, I bring this motion: Honourable Judges of the Extraordinary People's Court in Prague, I call upon you to clear the accused of the criminal charges brought against him (...) – there are insufficient grounds for prosecution according to the law and for the acts to be attributed to the accused, and so I ask you to implement measures such that the appropriate court authorities place the accused permanently in a secure institution for the mentally ill."

Once Resler had finished speaking, he wrote on a large board: "Dear Journalists! The speech is not available, and if you each ask separately, it will not be made available! Representative of the poor and defence lawyer for K. H. Frank. Pankrác, 26. IV. 1946. Questions after 1 pm." On the reverse side of this board, the journalists then signed their names or wrote messages, including for example: "I suggest that we should ask for it individually, and that way tomorrow (see pledge on the front side) there will be no speech, and our work as journalists will be much easier"; "So let us wait until tomorrow,

Journalists sitting in the front part of the hall listen to the trial. (AHMP)

With editor E. E. Kisch. (AHMP)

Kulhánek, *Zemědělské noviny*"; "The representative of the poor and defence lawyer for K. H. Frank is making a fuss. Alena Byková investigates for *Práce*"; "Maybe on Monday, but in full! *Národní shoda.*"; "That is a pity, but what can we do! *Svobodné Československo.*"; "Fiiiine, I shall send a telegraph post-haste to the great Stalin to inform him that you do nothing here even when the international press is in attendance. *Krasnaja Zvězda.*"[260]

Resler's defence speech was published in the book Český národ soudí K. H. Franka; he gave the original copy from which he delivered the speech in court to Erna Janská, to thank her for her dedicated and faithful collaboration on that foolish volume, as he described it himself.[261]

REASONS FOR CONVICTION AND ACQUITTAL

In the morning of 21 May, the day when the verdict was expected, Frank was restless and was finding it difficult to keep his temper. After a brief hearing the verdict was pronounced, and was translated for Frank by Consul Dr Jaromír Doležal. Frank took the death sentence coolly, and did not show any emotion. Given that once the verdict had been passed Frank was already dead from a judicial perspective, Resler voluntarily shook hands with him on his way out for the first time.[262] The verdict was pronounced over two days, largely because it was substantiated by lengthy explanations.

At the end of his closing speech, Resler remarked that "one day, centuries from now, our sons' sons and the sons of all the world's nations will judge us for our verdict on K. H. Frank. It is therefore crucial that each and every declaration made in the judgement and every word of its reasoning should ring sound and should certify to the Czechs' thoroughness and justice." So how did the court offset the objections raised by the defence, when it made its judgement?[263]

The defence had stated that only an *attempt* to change the constitution could be prosecuted, and not the achievement of such a change itself, since after a change of constitution has occurred it is no longer possible to penalize for it: "Since the court takes the view that there was legal continuity in both the cases of constitutional change mentioned (...) the effective impossibility in question never came to be, and in practice the situation remains as would have been the case if the attempt alone had been made and the outcome was

---

260 AHMP 12, Plakát se vzkazem [poster].

261 PNP, Frank Karl Hermann.

262 "Demise", p. 20.

263 There were many reasons for the conviction; here I focus mainly on those that were relevant to Resler's arguments, since the focus of this book is Resler rather than Frank; these were however also some of the most important reasons.

never achieved. After all, it would go against reasonable interpretation for the attempt to commit a crime to be punishable, but the achieved crime not to be."

Resler's objection that Frank was not a member of the FS was accepted, but Frank was still convicted of membership in the German government: the court considered it relevant that the government had met and executed its powers. It was concerned with the material interpretation of the organisation rather than any formal interpretation, given that after its dissolution the government as such had not existed.

The court acknowledged Resler's exceptions in the case of promotion in film and theatre. It did not, though, share Resler's view that official duties were exempt from section 3 of the Decree, since even supporting a fascist or Nazi movement was punishable and "the intrusion into various Czechoslovak freedoms by means of official orders was the very idea most supported by fascism and Nazism."

When it came to whether Frank had beaten people, the court made an odd decision: "There is no reason (...) not to believe the witnesses, whose statements complement one another as regards the particulars, even if they do not specifically agree as to the timing in relation to Frank's departure from Lány." If, according to the witness statements, Frank could not have been there at the time of the crime, it was possible that people had mistaken someone else for him, as had happened elsewhere. This charge was thus not proven beyond reasonable doubt, and from the evidence it did not necessarily follow that the act in question had taken place; whether the court decided correctly on this therefore remains a matter for discussion.

The argument that Frank had pushed for the return of a number of workers sent to Germany was not accepted as exonerating; on the contrary, the court described his motives in so doing as base – Frank had wanted the arms factories in Bohemia to function properly so that he could report strong productivity. On the basis of the evidence, the court came to the conclusion that Frank had also actively sent Czechoslovak citizens to labour abroad.

The court did, however, accept Resler's argument that Frank had not committed arson according to section 166 of act no. 117/1852 ř. z. (imperial code) on crimes, offences and violations, in the context of section 167 point a) i.e. he had not caused the death of any person, b) had not started a fire and c) had not caused substantial damage. The court also agreed that the incident in question had not involved any of the circumstances further detailed in the remaining points of section 167. Nevertheless, the court convicted Frank of "arson according to section 166 of the Criminal Code, without the circumstances or consequences of section 167." That was impossible according to section 8 of the Retribution Decree, meaning that on this point the court's decision was unlawful, as the Decree did not allow it to pass such a verdict, and the simple crime of arson without the consequences detailed in section 167 was not prosecutable at the Extraordinary People's Court.

The court agreed that "these were not exclusively the actions of the accused, but rather the planned economic policies set by the highest German authorities, which the accused was merely putting into practice. (...) It is correct that the majority of the noted acts that were damaging to the Czech economy were not carried out on the individual initiative of the accused; nevertheless it is necessary to take into consideration that the accused acted on behalf of one of the highest German authorities in the Protectorate, and as is evident for example from his dealings with the customs union (...) which he approached particularly officiously, actively broke down barriers and adopted the central German authorities' damaging approach, there can be no doubt that all the factual principles of section 9 of the Retribution Decree are attributable to the accused."

The Extraordinary People's Court accepted that since Frank had paid for the 1500 Swiss Franks he took for his wife, "he could subjectively believe that he had caused no damage." The prosecution did not prove its charge on this count.

The defence argument that General Eliáš – the only person Frank had supposedly denounced – was in fact denounced by the Gestapo was accepted by the court. Frank was therefore acquitted of this charge, too.

Next, the court responded on the amnesty of 7 October 1938. It took the view that only the President of the Republic had the right to grant an amnesty, based on the provisions of the Criminal Code and Criminal Law in connection with section 103 of the Constitution of 1920, and not the government who had actually issued the amnesty in question. Therefore the court disregarded the amnesty. On the day that the amnesty was issued, however, the Republic did not have a President; Edvard Beneš had resigned two days earlier. Section 59 of the Constitution stipulated that in such a case, "if a new President is not elected, (...) the execution of his office passes to the government." When the Constitution provides bridging arrangements for specific situations, in this case the government standing in for the President, then all the powers of the original body are transferred to the bridging body, unless established otherwise. The court could have chosen other reasons to dismiss the amnesty. Instead, it chose a formulation that did not interfere with Beneš's preferred theory that his Presidential office had continued. From a legal perspective, however, this was not a good choice.

The court also chose a strange line of argument when it came to Frank's parliamentary immunity: "Although the court accepts that the cited measures by the Permanent Committee were ineffective concerning the legal continuity between the period before Münich and the current period, it remains unquestionable that the accused was no longer a member of parliament at the time that he was brought before the court, for the simple reason that the chamber which Frank had been a member of no longer existed at that time." The non-existence of the chamber itself, however, cannot be a reason for failing to recognise immunity, as the court believed. If the Houses of Parliament had for example been burned down, as they had in Germany, and the parliament had then not been called, if some members fled abroad and others were prosecuted, it could not be inferred that the members who were caught had lost their immunity. The court needed to reflect on this point in greater depth, even though the outcome would likely not have changed.

One of Resler's arguments was that Frank had not himself put anyone to death, because death sentences could only be issued by courts. Frank could not bear responsibility for decisions that were made by a body that was not under his authority. The court responded to this by stating that – in reality – the practice had been different: "the sentences were presented to the accused Frank or to Daluege for approval, without it being evident from the verdict on whose conviction they were sentenced; the sentences were first approved by Frank or Daluege and then executed," and this applied to the period when martial law was declared. Hence Frank's dealings were considered punishable. Even in this situation, though, it is questionable whether approving the enforcement of a sentence or failing to grant mercy amounts to complicity in murder. The right to approve death sentences, to reduce them, or to grant mercy, is usually granted to the highest state officials. During the First Republic only a small proportion of death sentences were enforced, as President Masaryk amended the others to custodial sentences. Although he had this right, and used it, it would be very hard to imagine that the President could have been charged with complicity in murder in those cases to which he did not grant mercy. However perverse and inhumane the German judiciary's acts were, it is unclear whether one can entirely agree with the court's decision on this point – with difficulty, in my view.

The court had, of course, to address the defence's claim that Frank had only been following Hitler's orders and German law. On that matter, section 13 of the Retribution Decree stated specifically that actions could not be excused on these grounds, even if the offender had believed those laws to be justified. It is interesting that at this point the court spoke openly of the retroactive criminal law. Elsewhere it noted: "The defence presents the accused as a pitiful victim of mass psychosis – Nazism. Yet the documents presented to the court, in particular dating from after Heydrich's assassination, demonstrate that on the contrary this was no obedient victim, but a conspiring and enterprising accomplice, an ambitious egoist, who with substantial forethought seized the opportunity that Hitler and the Nazi world view offered, by joining them, and who then paid unusually avid attention to their aims and worked his way up the hierarchy of Nazi leaders as one of them." Thus the court also tore apart Resler's interpretation of Frank as a mentally ill man.

Frank was handed the death penalty on the grounds of particular aggravating circumstances, which the court stated were "that the accused Frank committed a whole range of crimes of various kinds, that he committed them repeatedly, that he led others to commit crimes, and that he was in many cases the instigator, accessory and leader in crimes that were committed by several individuals."

What can we conclude about the Prague Extraordinary People's Court's judgement in this case? At the time, which was not conducive to a fully objective evaluation, the court managed to put together a judgement that was satisfactory from a legal perspective, and was not afraid of acquitting the accused on several of the charges brought by the prosecution. On the other hand, the verdict is also a product of its time to some extent: it does not only take legal arguments and Frank's actions into account, but is based on a broader analysis of the historic context of the German occupation. It is not only a judgement of Frank, but in a sense also a judgement of the whole Nazi regime, through which the court came to terms with what had happened. The court conducted the proceedings appropriately, and the accused was given the opportunity to respond in detail to each of the charges. The defence lawyer carried out his task with dignity and made use of all possible legal loopholes in order to defend his client well. On most points, the court's decision was in line with the law and justice.

THE PLEA FOR MERCY

Resler attempted to persuade the court to recommend a mercy plea. He added: "Death is mysterious and incomprehensible, and the consequences of the event we know as death defy human understanding. We do not even know whether depriving someone of their life is really a punishment."[264]

After the verdict was passed, he sent a telegram to the President of the Republic, which read: "I ask you to amend Frank's death sentence into life imprisonment reasoning to follow in writing mostly acts of mass insanity six unsupported family members defence counsel Resler."[265] No reply came from the President's office until 30 December 1946, when Resler received a dry notice to the effect that the Minister of Justice had not made a positive plea for mercy, and therefore the President of the Republic's office considered the matter to be settled. The office had only addressed the issue of mercy after

---

264 "Český národ soudí," p. 233.
265 AHMP 12, Telegram to the President of the Republic.

Resler had reminded them on 7 December that his application had not yet been dealt with. What led him to return to the case more than half a year after Frank's execution we can only speculate; most likely he was bothered by it because in his previous experience pleas for mercy had always received a response, even if that had been negative. In Frank's case, which was one of the most important, he had heard nothing. Resler had also promised Frank that the plea would surely be attended to, and may thus have felt betrayed. And so, when he found he did not have other urgent matters to attend to, he wrote to the President's office.[266]

Resler had written his plea for mercy for the punishment to be reduced from death to life imprisonment even before the verdict was passed, in expectation of certain reasoning from the court. He sent the telegram mentioned on the first of the two days during which the verdict was announced, just one minute after the presiding judge had pronounced the death sentence.

Resler put together his plea for mercy along similar lines to his concluding defence speech, emphasising that the Extraordinary People's Court had judged Frank on behalf of the Nuremburg Tribunal, and thus in the name of all humankind, which gave the case extra significance. Before beginning, though, Resler had himself to come to terms with why he was requesting mercy for a man whom he himself believed deserved death. One reason was that Frank had rejected the Czech nation, Czech judge and Czech barrister, and it was thus "imperative that all the Czechoslovak officials (...) involved made utmost use of the legal means available to them." In that way, Frank was granted all possible avenues of defence and all the requirements of a fair trial were met. Hence no pretext had been given for the sentence to be called into question in the future for being unjust. Resler considered this his duty.

Resler's precise arguments were as follows. The condemned had been a close collaborator of Adolf Hitler's and "had blindly and helplessly fallen prey to his devilish influence, and been so taken in by it, that he lost all sense of the limits of his actions." Frank regarded Hitler as a god, and even saw a saviour in him, to which Resler made reference when claiming that Frank was not mentally well. He added that this fact was not fully investigated by the court, which had only judged Frank's mental health on the basis of how he had behaved in court, even though the acts for which he was tried had taken place at least ten months prior to he start of the trial. He then described the condemned's specific acts that had been significant for the Czech nation, in particular the provision of food and the rescue of 30,000 Czechs who were to be executed on Hitler's orders, as well as his contribution to the preservation of transport routes and industry in the Czech lands at the end of the war, which would have been tactically destroyed by the fleeing German forces if it

---

266 AHMP 12, Request for decision relating to mercy plea on 7 December 1946.

had not been for Frank's intervention. The condemned admitted a large part of his guilt, including those actions when he had followed Hitler's orders, from which Resler inferred that he had come to realise the German nation's culpability.

Resler did his best to plant in the President's mind the thought that it could be better for such a man to survive and come to know the full consequences of his actions. He could, for example, write down his confessions as a warning for future generations, and thus reduce the chances that similar villainy would be repeated. As a final argument, Resler put forward the argument that Frank was the head of a family of seven, which would be left without any means of support if he were executed.[267]

Nevertheless, not one of these arguments fell on fertile ground, and indeed Resler himself had not really believed that mercy might be granted. If it were granted, he believed that the President and government would have to resign.[268]

As a backup, Resler had also prepared a second telegram, in which he requested that the execution by hanging be amended to execution by firing squad, since Frank had been a high ranking politician and officer. Frank, though, did not want this change to be made. His view was that if the trial and the sentence had taken place according to Czechoslovak law, which he refused to recognise, then the execution should also take place according to Czechoslovak convention. Resler's role during K. H. Frank's final hours was described in the introduction and we will not therefore present that here.

FINANCIAL AND EMOTIONAL CONSEQUENCES OF THE DEFENCE

Defending K. H. Frank was not only a tough task in itself, for Resler, but was also a burden for him because it left him no time for the rest of his work. He was in court or with Frank from 9:00 until 19:15 Monday to Saturday, and from 20:00 until 22:30 he attempted to keep on top of the most urgent matters at his office. Although the court had originally intended the trial to last about two weeks, it ended up taking five. In one letter, Resler wrote that after just three weeks of the trial he had completely lost track of what was going on at his office and could not estimate what consequences this defence might have for his business. He worked that out later, when he submitted a report and letter to the effect that during the trial he had lost 70,000 Kčs, which was the sum of damages and missed earnings, not the cost of the *ex officio* defence itself.

---

267 AHMP 3, Request to reduce death sentence to life imprisonment.
268 "Demise", p. 28.

This difficult situation meant that shortly after the trial a bankrupcy motion against Resler's property was filed, although it apparently did not result in any action. Several clients also cancelled their contracts with Resler and commissioned other lawyers, because Resler did not have time for them. Although he was able to repeatedly withdraw large sums from restricted bank accounts[269] at the Czechoslovak National Bank (he withdrew 40,000 Kčs on 21 March and 35,000 Kčs on 18 April), this was not sufficient to cover his costs. The reasons he gave for these withdrawals were, first, the Frank defence, and second overheads and living costs.

In general, every barrister was required to complete *ex officio* duties for free, without charging a fee. They received only the real expenses they incurred while defending *ex officio*. Resler reported these to the Extraordinary People's Court in Prague as amounting to 15,771.60 Kčs. He had written out every tiny expenditure – from sending a telegram for 2.50 Kčs, up to the most expensive services, which were the salaries of his assistants, whom he paid 15 crowns per hour; the list was thirteen pages long.[270]

What fee would Resler have been entitled to, if he had not worked for free? Given that the K. H. Frank case was extremely high profile, according to the official rates of the day he would have been granted 4,500 Kčs for the first hour of the hearing, and 2,250 Kčs for each further hour. The hearing lasted 30 days, from 9 am until 4 pm, with an hour's break. Taking into account other associated tasks, Resler calculated that his total fee would have amounted to at least 500,000 Kčs.[271] In normal circumstances, he would of course never have made that much money during such a short period, but estimated that he might in the time the trial took have made a few tens of thousands of crowns. His defence of Richard Bienert, which followed immediately after Frank's case, did not help much either.[272] Thus this verse penned by Resler's long-standing friend JUDr. Antonín Švehla was rather fitting:

Ať žije slavný Kamill
na kost vyhublý jak Gandi
v procesech velký úspěch slavil
a co nejdřív z něj spadnou kšandy.[273]

---

269 It was not possible to withdraw money freely from restricted accounts; the account holder needed special permission to do so.

270 AHMP 11, Žádost o náhradu skutečných výdajů na obhajobu podle tr. ř. § 393 odst. 2 [official payment request].

271 Resler's calculations; for more detail see Jan Kober. *Advokacie v českých zemích v létech 1848–1994.* [Advocacy in the Czech lands 1848–1994]. Prague: Česká advokátní komora v Praze, 1994, p. 125.

272 AHMP 12, Resler's request delivered to the Bar Association on 23 August 1946.

273 NM, Poem entitled Employees, 18 July 1946.

Long live our famous Kamill
who looks all emaciated
his cases turned out oh so well
but soon his frame won't hold his braces.

Resler did not have a trainee while he was defending Frank, and was assisted only by his secretary Erna Jánská, who frequently helped him with
writing and formulating his speeches. At other times, he received help from
his colleagues. They did not charge him a fee for their time, and so Resler at
least urged the Bar Association to recognise their work as duty representation, so that it would count for them in the future.

While the Frank trial was ongoing, Antonín Švehla took over the supervision of Resler's practice, and nine other barristers took on a total of 38 of
Resler's court cases.[274] Several law students served Resler as "lawyerlets," as
he called them, during the trial. At the very first hearing, for which he did not
have anyone assisting him, he was accompanied by his son Kamil Resler the
younger, then a secondary school student; later, he tended to have one or two
helpers by his side. He saw them not only as workers, but as colleagues, as is
also evident from the fact that he gave some of them a copy of his book *K poctě
zbraň praporu!* (Salute the Flag!)

The most important of Resler's helpers during the Frank trial was law student Drahoslav Kroupa, who also took notes during Frank's final three hours.
Decades later, Kroupa recalled the last moments with Frank as one of the
most interesting events of his legal career. He published his memoirs in 1997
as part of an Almanach of class VIII.B of 1942 at the *Realné Gymnasium* secondary school in Třebíč. Although at the time Kroupa had no expert knowledge,
he gradually picked things up, and it was important for Resler that he could
type quickly. They remained in contact after the trial and were friends until Resler's death. As it happened, they even became relatives, as Drahoslav
Kroupa married Resler's niece. In his archive, Kamill saved an article by
Kroupa that was published *Rudé právo* in 1954, and in which Kroupa criticises
Kulaks[275]: "for years he was used to living as a parasite off others' work (...)
they are people who always lived off others' work." and the church.[276] Why did
Resler keep this article? Perhaps he wanted to have a more complete record of
Kroupa's character, perhaps it was to show what someone could be capable of
under pressure from those around him, or perhaps it had simply caught his
eye. Resler himself, though, never published any similar articles, and we may

---

274 NM, Application for adjustment of duty lawyer status on 14 July 1946.
275 Kulak was a Russian term for well-to-do peasants. In Czech, it had a pejorative connotation, and
     was used only for farmers who opposed the regime.
276 Drahoslav Kroupa. "Měsíc to zavinil" [The moon was to blame]. *Rudé právo*, Tuesday 12 October
     1954, p. 3.

suppose that he would not have agreed with its sentiment. Kroupa turned his attention to Frank once again after many years, as a practising lawyer, when he communicated with scriptwriter Janem Drbohlavý about the script for the film *Ex offo*.

For the purposes of the film's creation, Kamill Resler's daughter Blanka also described how her father had looked and behaved during the Frank trial:

"Appearance: somewhat like Prime Minister Tošovský,[277] he didn't give away his mood (...) a matter-of-fact, focused expression, (...) he was always thinking about something, and yet always interacted with those around him, he was not irritable, never shouted, he would be terser and more emphatic when he wanted to have something his way, but otherwise would simply ask in a normal voice.

He was well-mannered, dignified, at first sight perhaps rather a dry man, but very observant of his surroundings; at home he rather suppressed his sense of humour, although one was never quite sure what he was about to 'recht' to mother, for example she hated the song 'Cook is baking, her nose is running'. (...) Father wore a 'salt and pepper' suit, sort of grey, unobtrusive ties in darker colours with delicate patterns, he never wore shoulder pads, his shirts were either white or very often light blue, or a sort of washed-out yellow and grey, and he had favourite cufflinks – engraved silver; he never wore a fur coat, not even a fur collar. He smoked with a cigarette holder, and wore strong glasses, but did not appear shortsighted without them. (...) After lunch he would have a little rest on the couch with his guitar or a book, then trotted off to the office or the court. The ordinariness of everyday life escaped him, though it kept mother busy, but she brightened up the household with her sewing and beautiful crochet work (...) during the war he had to recover from a stomach ulcer. He rarely went to the cinema, only for films that really interested him.

We did not have a telephone in the flat, that came I think only after he had closed his office. No gramophone, either, only the radio, and his writing desks both at home and at work were always covered with neat piles of books and files."[278]

FRANK'S OPINION OF HIS DEFENCE

On 1 May 1946, shortly after the main hearing had closed and three weeks before his execution, K. H. Frank wrote a statement on his defence by Kamill Resler. The following is a translation of it in full.

---

277 Josef Tošovský, Czech politician and banker.
278 NM, About K. Resler – for the television adaptation *Ex offo*.

"On my defence, led by Mr J.U.Dr. K. Resler

Although I cannot agree with the Czech interpretation with which my legal representative understands 'the limits of duty', and without accepting the Czech claim that I committed, while in office as Secretary of State to the Reichsprotektor or the German Minister of State for the Protectorate of Bohemia and Moravia, evident crimes such as murder, theft, arson, and so on, and finally regardless of the exceptional trouble that Dr. Resler, as a Czech, suffered when trying to understand the case correctly as a result of his utter ignorance both of the national-socialist conception of service, and of national-socialist organisational fora, systems, promotions and suchlike (while with a German lawyer most of these difficulties would have understandably been avoided) – I can from my current position and before the verdict is pronounced observe the following:

Mr Dr. K. Resler invested the greatest of effort to defend me well and used in so doing all available means and opportunities before the Czech Extraordinary People's Court. In the short time available to him he performed a great legal and political deed. During many of our conversations, he attempted to capture and understand my German mentality. Today I can say that he largely succeeded in doing so.

Despite the inconveniences and dangers that the prejudiced and biased threats of the Czech public must have caused to 'my lawyer', he led the defence boldly, fearlessly and objectively, and most likely he has been able to break some ice by so doing.

After the end of the hearing, I realised that in the whole of my defence three fundamental extenuating circumstances could, in my view, have been better developed and repeatedly emphasised – that is, the following three positive actions:

1) My constant efforts to secure the Protectorate's food supplies.
2) The rescue of 30,000 Czechs from execution by firing squad.
3) My agreement with Malzacher against destructive orders in the Protectorate.

Over time, as I discussed with Dr. Resler, I came to trust him more and more, to the extent that I revealed my soul to him and shared my true thoughts with him in a way I have not ever shared them with any other person, even though in my already painful situation in custody he often made me sad and angry, and even depressed me with his utter ruthlessness and criticism of German actions, mistakes and failings.

His defence speech was, in my view, legally, politically and generally humanly outstanding. I hope that it will receive an appropriate response and result in the desired outcome.

My heartfelt thanks to him for his great, selfless effort and work.

K. H. Frank." [279]

---

279 AHMP 12, Frank's reaction to Dr. K. Resler's defence. The original German was translated into Czech by Mgr. Lenka Pecharová, to whom I thank for it.

THE SIGNIFICANCE OF RESLER'S DEFENCE AND REACTIONS TO IT

When the main hearing in Frank's trial finished on Saturday 27 April 1946, Resler did not get much of a breather, since the very next Monday at nine o'clock in the morning he began the main hearing in a trial with the Protectorate government, in which he took on the defence of the Ministry of the Interior and last Protectorate Prime Minister Rudolf Bienert. As a result, Resler ended up spending an uninterrupted three and a half months in the Pankrác courtroom.

After this long ordeal was finally over, he wanted to relax in the countryside where he had grown up, where everyone he met was either a friend or a relative. He set aside eight days for this break. On the last day, though, a distant relative of his, who was a well-known local official, asked him whether he might be able to come to the Sokol in the evening and say a few words about the Frank trial; he accepted. After this first talk in Nasavrky on 12 July 1946 many others followed; interest in the case peaked at the end of the '50s, when Resler spoke in Jihlava, Čáslav and Prague, among other places.[280]

During these talks he explained his opinions of Frank and some of the things that had surprised him, for example that Frank was not convicted of the Ležáky extermination, or Frank's aversion to being given an electric heater in mid-December to heat up his cold, damp cell. He spoke only positively of his dealings with Frank, stating that in his opinion the Czechoslovak authorities had fulfilled their duty and "tried K. H. Frank with the dignity worthy of an educated nation." Foreign dignitaries and soldiers were also frequently convinced of this. Resler went on to describe the details of the trial, with which we are already familiar, and concluded his lectures with the words: "With Frank, we executed a horrible enemy to the Czech nation. A nation of seventy million produces hundreds of those enemies. We must think to the future. We must bring up our nation such that our sons will one day know how to face the dangers that these opponents bring. Remember that, and educate your sons so that they know how to defend and protect the freedom and independence of the Czechs and Slovaks."[281]

After taking on Bienert's defence, Resler had to decide what his role in the case was to be, and what he would try to achieve. Deep down, he set himself the personal goal to "defend this man fairly and thoroughly, for the love of personal freedom, for the freedom of the Czechs and Slovaks, and for the freedom of all people." He suggested to Bienert that he would hand his defence to someone else, because the smallest slip during Frank's trial could have been damaging both for him and for Bienert, but Bienert was not persuaded.

280 AHMP 4, Invitations to talks.
281 "Demise", pp. 15 and 41.

In his lecture *Zaniknutí K. H. Franka* (The Demise of K. H. Frank) Resler explains his view of the defence lawyer's task: "Human society gives this person to the accused as a final helper and friend, and the defence lawyer is duty-bound to serve the accused fairly and faithfully. Were he to fail to fulfil that duty, the Bar Association would punish him severely, possibly even removing him from the profession. The barrister must therefore forget his own feelings and attitudes, give up his own character and, however hard it might be, carry out his duty thoroughly. (...) It was therefore necessary to defend K. H. Frank with utter fairness using every available means, and pursue those to the bitter end even though it was clear that the Extraordinary People's Court would be forced to find a way to overturn every one of those means, even the most serious."[282]

He expressed a similar opinion in a letter to the editor of the Czechoslovakian Radio, who had reacted to his defence extremely positively; Resler thanked him for that, as it was a great service to the Czech Bar. Another similar favour for the bar came from *Svobodné slovo*, which published an article discussing the trial of fifteen Sudeten German members of parliament. The article's author expressed the view that the fact that those people were allocated a barrister *ex officio*, who then defended them, was not just a redundant formality. He presented it as one of Czechoslovakia's strengths as a country dedicated to defending justice at all times: "Those defence lawyers were Czechs who were ordered to do the job and had to carry it through with the greatest self negation and against their own convictions. Despite that, they carried out their task selflessly, sovereignly and conscientiously – and took pride in so doing! (...) We must appreciate their work. For only we know how much self negation was necessary in order to do that."[283]

After the Frank trial, Resler received several letters[284] expressing support and thanks for his defence, admiring his courage, his humane approach to Frank, and the amount of time he had spent with him. One lady wrote, for example: "It was a beautiful and generous defence, which did not get caught up with prejudice because the accused was a German and thus one of our nation's arch-enemies." Another writer, who was a retired political clerk, reacted similarly: "Forgive this old man if he takes the liberty of saying that you have given a brilliant example of how human, national and professional duties should be carried out." Needless to say, Resler also received letters expressing the opposite opinion, including the letter from Sekora that we mentioned earlier.

Some of these messages encouraged Resler to continue in his work. In a letter dated 6 May 1946, i.e. after the main hearing had closed, but before the verdict had been pronounced, Resler wrote to his friend Alois Dyk: "When you

---

282   "Demise", pp. 18–19.
283   *Svobodné slovo*, no. 4, 17 January 1947, p. 1.
284   AHMP 4, Letters.

have heard that in Záběhlice there is a sign reading *Away with traitors' counsels* and that a certain party carried it through the streets, you are cheered when someone so much as shakes your hand, looks you straight in the eye, and says wordlessly 'I know you are a fair chap.' You have done much more. (...) Even a thick-skinned lawyer defending murders, adultery and arson, war crimes and treason eventually surrenders to a certain emotion."[285]

To his friend and colleague Paul Edwards, an attorney in New York, Resler described his conscientious defence and perception of the political context as being like balancing on a knife edge: "The only success was that the court did not convict Frank for the dirty crimes of informing and currency extortion from the National Bank and that Frank therefore died, even according to the Czechoslovak court, a political criminal and not a dirty criminal." He learned from Edwards that his defence of both K. H. Frank and Richard Bienert had attracted great attention and approval in the Czech papers in New York, "as you [carried out] the difficult task entrusted to you effectively and with great legal eruditon. I can fully appreciate that it must have been an enormously hard task."[286]

Resler's assistant Kroupa evaluated his performance as follows, when writing up his memoirs in 1997: "Dr. Resler handled his extremely difficult task brilliantly, and the views from abroad were also that he deserved 'full marks and a gold star'".[287]

It appears that Robert Jackson, a judge from the Supreme Court of the United States of America and the General Prosecutor at the International Military Tribunal in Nuremberg, who attended the hearing at the Extraordinary People's Court in Prague, also felt similarly about Resler's work. He declared that he would have no hesitation about entrusting the Nuremberg process to the court that he had seen in Prague. This was undoubtedly also credit to Resler.[288]

Praise even reached him from the opposite camp – the communists. In a letter to Zdeněk Kratochvíl in 1959 Resler mentioned that he had heard that "President Gottwald spoke of my work with appreciation."

Nevertheless despite all the recognition he received, it is clear that Resler bore his fate heavily. On 7 June 1946, he wrote to his friend František Hrbek: "As you guessed, life is hard, monastically severe; at work I bear others' pain and suffering."

---

285 NM, Letter to Alois Dyk on 6 May 1946.
286 AHMP 12 and PNP 91, Letters between Resler and Paul Edwards.
287 NM 214/168, Drahoslav Kroupa. *Poslední dny a chvíle K. H. Franka* [K. H. Frank's final days and moments], *Almanach VIII. B, maturitního ročníku 1942 reálného gymnázia v Třebíči* [Class VIII B final year almanach, 1942, Reálné gymnázium in Třebíč], 1997, p. 34.
288 NM, Transcript of the programme "Advokát, který měl rád knížky" [A barrister who liked books], produced by Pavel Kosatík, Český rozhlas Vltava, broadcast on 18 June 1995 at 8:00 pm, p. 19.

THE MEDIA'S ATTITUDE TO THE TRIAL, AND RESLER'S LATER TALKS ON THE TRIAL

Resler spent a lot of his time reading the papers, and kept cuttings from interesting periods (before and after the war), in particular relating to his cases. His own contributions to the papers most often took the form of corrections, but he also sometimes wrote short comments on social topics, for example on the unconvincing beginnings of the Nazi anti-Soviet movement Česká liga proti bolševismu (Czech League against Bolshevism) and on the curious reasons why in 1944, when the organisation was founded, many intellectuals refused to join it.[289]

The Frank trial was on the front pages of the papers almost constantly, and on the rare occasions when it did not occupy this position, a large part of one of the inner pages was given over to it. In the first week of the trial, it competed with news of a visit from Yugoslavian Prime Minister Josip Tito.

It is interesting that Resler was not depicted in a negative light by the papers, during the Frank trial. On the contrary, even in the brochure *K. H. Frank, vrah českého národa, před soudem lidu* (K. H. Frank, slayer of the Czech nation, before the People's Court)[290] which took an extremely hateful view of Frank, a page is dedicated to his defence, expressing the view that justice claims its own ("Every person accused of a crime must be given the full opportunity to defend their case") and that the lawyer's task in this case was not to be envied. For example, when the defence claimed Frank's parliamentary immunity, the brochure's authors focused only on Frank himself, and did not depict Resler negatively or criticize him at all. It is surprising how capable the journalists were in 1946 of separating the defence arguments themselves from the lawyers presenting them.

Aside from the newspapers, which were rather factual, Resler also enjoyed reading what the satirical magazines had written, most of all *Dikobraz*. For example, on the question of trials before the National Court it responded with the question: "How much will Raw get, if Baked got 5 years?"[291]

Resler also wrote down a few other anecdotes from this magazine related to Frank: "Judge: K. H. Frank, you surely must have seen with your own eyes

---

289 *Dnešek* II, no. 9, pp. 140–141.

290 AHMP 15, "K. H. Frank, vrah Českého národa před soudem lidu, proces a rozsudek nad K. H. Frankem [K. H. Frank, murderer of the Czech people before the People's Court, the Trial and judgement of K. H. Frank]," *Pravda* (1946/7), Žilina.

291 Karel Pečený ("Charles Baked") was the owner of a film company that had collaborated with the Germans. General Jan Syrový ("John Raw") was Prime Minister in autumn 1938 and Minister of Defence from March 1939. After the war he was sentenced to twenty years imprisonment for treason.

what was in the concentration camps? K. H. Frank: *Jawohl*, but I always closed one eye and I couldn't see anything out of the glass eye."

"Frank stands under the gallows and the executioner asks him: Your final wish, please? Please hang me by the waist, I am very ticklish around the neck."[292]

In another anecdote, this time in a cartoon from the *Svět Práce* paper, Frank stands beneath a statue of K. H. Mácha, and says to him: "*Jawohl*, I'm K. H. too, and *meiner Erinnerung nach* [as far as I can recall], I also made sure that the Czechs would never forget May, but now it doesn't look like I will be getting a statue for it like you."[293]

Resler corresponded with the editors of *Dikobraz* about various of the jokes and caricatures they printed about the trial, and even sent them some letters that he had received in connection with the Frank case.

In one illustration, Ondřej Sekora depicted him as a hunched figure sitting on a chair with his head in his hands, with the caption: "K. H. Frank's last victim. His duty barrister Dr. K. Resler: "I didn't want the case!"[294] Resler wrote to Sekora that it was a pity he had not drawn him like Ferda Mravenec and that he shouldn't have given him so little hair.[295] Sekora replied with a spiteful letter, which concluded with the words "I would rather have lost my doctorate and committed suicide than deliver a defence speech for that kind of murderer." He did, though, send Resler the original drawing, for which Resler thanked him kindly, as it helped him to solve a difficult professional matter with detachment and humour.[296]

In addition to paper cuttings and jokes, Resler also kept photographs. Many unique photographs of the trial only survive today thanks to his collections. Resler had ordered all the available photographs from the trial from Jan Kaplický, photographer for the *Práce* daily, and there were several hundred of them. These included, for example, photos of Frank's second wife beating carpets in the Pankrác prison.

Resler was also given a literary reminder of the trial by his artist friends, in the form of a special bookplate; it depicts a paragraph symbol whose shape is reminiscent of a swastika.

---

292 *Dikobraz* II, nos. 16 and 18, 17 April 1946 and 30 April 1946.

293 Karel Hynek Mácha was a Czech poet whose most famous poem is called "May". *Svět práce*, 8 May 1946.

294 *Práce* no. 70, 23 March 1946, p. 3.

295 Ferda Mravenec is a cute ant character who appeared in Ondřej Sekora's comics and other books. Although his stories were originally intended for adults, they later became particularly popular with children.

296 AHMP 4, Letters between Resler and Sekora.

VISITING PRESIDENT BENEŠ

When barrister Kamil Rösler of Zbraslav[297] received an invitation in early 1947 to visit the President at Prague Castle, it was no surprise to him. It often happened that he would receive documents intended for Kamill Resler, including files from the Extraordinary People's Court in Prague. Like the others, he sent this invitation on to its true addressee.

Kamill Resler was invited to visit the President at Prague Castle on 28 October 1947 at noon.[298] Resler held Beneš in high esteem, and after their meeting he described him as the embodiment of a quarter century of Czechoslovak efforts for independence.

Resler began the conversation by telling Beneš that Frank had left him one document, marked *J. D.*, which he had described as containing state secrets of international importance, and which Resler had preserved in top secrecy. To demonstrate its authenticity, Resler presented Frank's text *Some notes on my defence*, from which Resler believed it should be possible to judge whether the *J. D.* document was real or just a trick.

The document concerned James Dickson, which was the cover name used by a negotiator between the British and the Swedes. Beneš's interpretation of the document's contents was as follows: "If the Germans had reduced production at the Škoda factory to 25%, the British and Americans would not have bombed the Škoda factory or the Protectorate, because they wanted to retain some sort of weapons base in case of a future war with Russia. I did not know anything about that. That was in 1943/4. Back then, not even conservatives in the English circles were thinking about a war with Russia, in my view. Maybe some outlying group, I can't rule that out. (...) I think that this was a trick, and that Hitler was right to see it and dismiss it." In Resler's view, Frank had also viewed the offer with mistrust, but believed that it was Germany's last chance of survival, and therefore considered Dickson's offer important.

After that, Resler discussed the Frank trial with Beneš. Resler began with his own defence – explaining to the President that he had not met Frank before being allocated the case, and that from the way in which the defence was allocated and carried out it was clear that he had not overstepped his role as representative of the poor and duty counsel.

Beneš asked him whether Frank had really believed what he had said in his final months. Resler replied that he believed Frank had written his text about the defence at a time when all that was left of him was a "bare man, tormented by the thought that millions of Sudeten Germans were cursing him, by worries about his family, and by the excruciating memory of the collapse

---

297 A town on the Southern edge of Prague, nowadays officially part of Prague.
298 AHMP 4, Dr. Resler's meeting with President Beneš.

of the German forces, which he had seen on his way from Prague to Plzeň. He had only one desire, which was to be able to live in peace with his family." His elder son from his first marriage had been injured on the Slovak river Hron and was hospitalised with only one leg in Vimperk (South Western Bohemia), where his younger brother also lived. At the end of the war they both left for Bavaria, but Frank did not know what had happened to them after they left Vimperk. He had last seen his second wife and their three children before being taken to the West Bohemian town of Plzeň by an American officer. A few months later she had disappeared from Prague and only in May 1946 did the Russians ask the Czechs whether they needed her for Frank's trial. When the answer was negative, she remained in Moscow until 1955, while the children were brought up at an American children's home in Frankfurt am Main.[299]

Resler believed that Frank had regretted his actions, and for example considered the extermination at Lidice to have been criminal, with hindsight. Behind his soldierly facade, Frank was really a weak man. That was evident, too, from the fact that he avoided direct responsibility. For example, he ordered the arrest of 150 people, but then did not oversee it, and did not want to supervise how the Gestapo treated them. After the war he let all the responsibility for this episode fall to the Gestapo. Resler noted on this point that: "our regular disagreement was over how far obedience goes and where it ends, because conscience and humaneness prevent us from crossing certain boundaries, so that following orders does not turn into committing a crime." Resler demonstrated the possible solutions to Frank's then situation using an example of his own. When Resler had arrived in Albania during the First World War, he had found out that his regiment was executing Albanian insurgents. He speculated that if he had been given orders to execute someone, he would have asked his regimental commander to excuse him of that duty. If he had refused to do so, he would have asked once more. If he had still refused, then he would have handed over his weapon and asked to be arrested, because he refused to obey military orders. He was not willing to break his commitment to personal honour and humanity against his conscience.

Resler's discussion with Beneš continued on topics including Frank's education and his attitude to the Czech nation, and – although it is not clear why – Resler also mentioned that in 1939 he had tried to put in a good word for MUDr. Jiří Scheiner, his long-term friend and the son of Resler's legal mentor and head of the Prague Sokol Josef Scheiner the elder.[300]

---

299 "Demise", p. 13.
300 The son was imprisoned during the Second World War, while the father had been imprisoned during the First World War: Josef Scheiner was arrested on 21 May 1915 together with Karel Kramář. *Národní listy, Večerník*, 11 January 1932, p. 1. Available online at kramerius.nkp.cz.

Resler also told Beneš about the conditions in the Pankrác prison. Frank was apparently never beaten while in prison, but an incident when two Czech inmates had wanted to show him what Czech Christmas, the feast of peace and quiet, was about – by pushing a basket of bread into his cell – had made a horrible impression on him. The prison wardens had found Frank sitting at the table, hunched in tears over the Christmas present. He was fully prepared for anger and hatred, and could have put up with these – it would have been easier for him. But it was very difficult for him to receive love from the nation he had so long fought against.

Frank had always been convinced that the court would not condemn him to death, but he suffered from doubts and sometimes asked Resler whether some of his proposals weren't just delaying tactics, as it struck him that he would be condemned to death.

Resler also spoke about Frank's behaviour towards him. To begin with, Frank was cautious, but later showed him greater and greater trust, once he had seen that he was doing his job as defence counsel properly. Socially, Resler had kept his distance, and never shaken hands with Frank on arrival or departure, even though Frank wanted him to. Only at Easter, when Resler had obtained the court's permission to take him a red egg, did he behave differently. When Frank saw the egg, he expressed great joy and went to shake his hand. Resler described the situation to Beneš thus: "so as not to spoil what I had had in mind, I had to shake his hand (...). He was overjoyed when he discovered that he could keep the egg in prison, and that he could do whatever he wanted with it. (...) I saw him differently from you, I saw the rebel in him. As his defence counsel I had to find a human approach to him, because I had to live and work with him."

Resler quoted some of Frank's ideas to Beneš, including for example that if at the turn of 1941–1942 the Czechs had announced a general strike, the Reich would have been fatally wounded. In the end, he also added Frank's view on Beneš: "Beneš is an extremely skilful diplomat. He has created a political masterpiece that can never be repeated. It is after all bizarre and impressive that a politician should flee abroad twice, and twice return to bring his country freedom within his lifetime. That is a great display of statesmanship."

It is typical of Resler that he does not mention himself at all in his notes of the meeting, but writes only about Beneš and Frank. It is hard to imagine that Beneš would not have mentioned his gratitude for Resler's work, or at least commented on it in some way – yet out of self-modesty, Resler did not record this. Nor did he mention anywhere, even in later letters, that he had met the President. Most likely, he would have considered that inappropriate boasting.

RESLER'S INTENTION TO PUBLISH A BOOK

After the trial was over, Resler had intended to write a book about his experience with Frank. It was largely to be a personal reflection on his character and behaviour, rather than a description of the defence and judicial procedures. One of the reasons why Resler attended several other German leaders' executions was so that he could compare their last words with Frank's. He mentions nearly ten such cases in a letter to the presiding judge of the Extraordinary People's Court, JUDr. Vladimír Kozák, who had judged K. H. Frank. In first place, he notes Frank's statement: "Germany must live, even if we must die! Long live Germany! Long live the German spirit!"[301]

Although Resler did in the end manage to gather a lot of material, he never wrote the book. He did, though, contribute to the book Český národ soudí K. H. Franka (The Czech Nation Tries K. H. Frank), which was published seven months after the end of the trial by the Orbis publishing house. He provided them with the text of his defence speech and a translation of K. H. Frank's own speech, and for these was paid an author's honorarium of 7,185 Kčs. In addition, he read the whole draft of the book and gave the author JUDr. Karel Zajíček various pieces of advice and ideas for the book's design.

Resler liked the book a lot, and referred to it as a work deserving respect. He was convinced that the print run of 5,500 copies was small and would be sold out within a few hours, even though people did not have much spare money at the time. Whether this was indeed the case, though, we do not know.

Resler also retained a number of other unique documents relating to Frank's case in his own archive. Apart from the photographs we have mentioned, these included the originals of K. H. Frank's death certificate and coroner's certificate.[302]

Resler also had plans to produce other legal publications. In early 1948 he signed a contract with publisher Vladimír Žikeš to put together a book entitled Rozsudky národního soudu (National Court Judgements). The book was to contain all the judgements made by the National Court, with a short introduction and afterword. Unfortunately, we do not know why but the book was never published.[303]

---

301 AHMP 4, Letter to JUDr. Vladimír Kozák on 1 October 1947.
302 AHMP 12, Coroner's report.
303 PNP 111, Letter to Resler on 4 February 1948.

5. 1946–1948: ENTERING THE TWILIGHT

DEFENCE OF RICHARD BIENERT

Immediately the main hearing was over in K. H. Frank's trial, during the three week wait for a the verdict to be pronounced, Resler began to defend the last Prime Minister of the Protectorate and former Minister of the Interior of the Protectorate Richard Bienert. His trial, with four other Protectorate ministers, is generally known as the Protectorate Government trial, even though other government ministers were judged before the National Court separately.

Bienert's defence, like Frank's, was none too easy for Resler. The situation became particularly tough when his two clients – Bienert and Frank – met in court, Bienert as a witness and Frank as the accused. They did not agree over Bienert's view that Frank had taken a leading role in persecuting the Czech nation.[304]

During Bienert's trial, Resler wrote to a friend: "It is not good to see Richard Bienert turn round with a sour face and hear him say 'coward!' when he hears the court read out a statement from a witness who was his close friend." Bienert considered himself an upstanding Czech. In his closing speech before the National Court, he said that he had taken the German violence just as hard as any other Czech. Meanwhile, he emphasised numerous good deeds that he claimed to have done for the nation as head of the regional authorities, adding: "I believed that the great efforts of our fellows abroad, who were free men, and our efforts resisting servitude here, would in the end lead to success in the Czech cause."[305]

The main charges in the trial were that Bienert and the four other ministers had supported the Nazi movement, approved and supported a foreign occupational power on the Republic's territory, organised *Totaleinsatz* (forced labour in Germany) during the war, and helped to steal property from the Czechoslovak state.[306]

---

304 *Muchka*, p. 40.
305 PNP, Richard Bienert. Closing Speech.
306 Benjamin Frommer. *National Cleansing: Retribution against Nazi Collaborators in Postwar Czechoslovakia*. New York: Cambridge University Press, 2005, chapter 7.

Resler began his closing speech by describing the mood of the nation, which was waiting for the National Court to "answer the basic question of why it is that if two different people do the same thing, it is not the same thing." Who was acting in the Republic's interest, and who was a true traitor? According to Resler's closing speech – which cannot be assumed to represent his personal views – a nation needed two types of politicians: one lot to represent the nation's permanent ideas, and a second lot to represent its temporary interests and needs. This worked in the example of Chamberlain and Churchill, or could be seen in the USSR's negotiation of the Molotov-Ribbentrop pact, which Resler explained was an absolute necessity, although the Soviet voice had never abandoned its principle of freeing the nations from the East.[307] He compared his idea to the "Young Czech" and "Old Czech" movements in Czech history.[308] He described Richard Bienert's policy as the second type, protecting the nation's existence by attempting to avert total Germanisation. After a long speech on the o frightful extermination at Lidice, he added: "Every act of resistance, every expression of protest put vast swathes of the Czech nation in danger. The fierce Germans had to be tamed and calmed down, asked for relief and more moderate consequences, and for that it was necessary to feign a positive understanding of the 'Reich', make speeches, and so on. Someone had to do this, even if it was a sorry task. It was necessary, after each and every blow, to calm the Czech people down so that they did not despair and lose hope and so that they did not commit the imprudent acts that the Germans were waiting for, even intentionally provoking, in order to be able to show off their power, harass even more Czechs, and turn them into a helpless, confused herd. That was Richard Bienert's task." Not only did Bienert, according to his defence, fulfil the same role as Generál Eliáš, but shortly before his own arrest Eliáš had in fact entrusted him with a task that he had carried out himself until that point, asking him to continue in his place. "We can therefore criticize Bienert for having chosen a soft route, a route of subterfuge and subversion, for having humiliated himself (...). He too sacrificed his human dignity, his past as a subversive traitor to Austria, in order to save whatever he could from the burning building his country had become. Did he also sacrifice his public popularity? Not at all! There was not a single person who believed he was giving the Czech nation up to the Germans. All strongly believed that he had joined the government not in order to support the oc-

---

307 In his speech Resler spoke of the USSR as a country that "today promotes the idea of renewing humankind in a new societal order (...) in Autumn 1939 (...) it was forced to negotiate a truce with Nazi Germany." I do not believe this was really Resler's view – his previous statements, in particular in 1938, did not suggest this.

308 The "Old Czech" movement practised passive resistance in the second half of the 19th century – refusing to attend parliamentary sessions. The "Young Czech" movement put an end to this and actively attended meetings of the Austrian Imperial Council.

cupation, but in order to personally keep the German onslaught and violence at bay, to serve Czech interests, and only to pretend to help the Germans. A slave's only weapon is betrayal, his only pride is in keeping quiet. For his people, Bienert was willing to give up even the second of these – his personal pride."[309]

Resler wrote his closing speech with his secretary Erna Jánská during the night of 3 July 1946. He gave Jánská the original copy of the speech, with thanks for a "night of hard and tiring work (...) contributing to the fight for clarity in the life of the Czech nation."[310]

Resler also kept a second defence speech in his files, which he had written on 28 June 1946, but never used. He gave that, too, to Erna Jánská. It was probably she who had provided this section addressing the judges: "The State Prosecutor's voice reached the ears of seven million Czechs. Richard Bienert's pained voice and my own voice were confined to this room. Your voice will be heard for centuries."[311]

The outcome of the trial was not decided for a long time, because the government – in particular the communists – intervened in the decision. Supported by Soviet advisors, they wanted to put three of the five ministers on trial to death. At first, the government agreed to this, but after six weeks of the trial the prosecutor advised handing out only two death sentences – saving Bienert. The communist ministers, who had appointed and instructed the lay judges from their party, wanted the others to instruct "their" lay judges too. When the presiding judge Dr. Tomsa found out about this, he immediately handed in his resignation, although it was not accepted.

While the government was still in discussion, however, the National Court made its decision and did not impose the death penalty on any of the ministers. The political leaders were not willing to accept the judgement, and so searched the Nazi archives, in particular the Štěchovice archive, in case evidence from them could have enabled the case to be reopened and the prosecution extended.[312] However, after ten days they had not managed to find anything, or to persuade the court to change its mind, and so the verdict was pronounced in the presence of 300 members of the SNB (the National Security Corps). Richard Bienert was sentenced to three years of hard labour, and was released from prison in 1947.[313] He died on 3 February 1949.[314]

---

309 PNP, Richard Bienert. Closing Speech.
310 PNP, Richard Bienert, Closing Speech written on 3 July 1946.
311 PNP, Richard Bienert. Closing Speech written on 28 June 1946.
312 Dušan Tomášek,and Robert Kvaček. *Obžalována je vláda*. [The government is prosecuted]. Ed. 1. Prague: Themis, 1999, pp. 175–181.
313 *Richard Bienert*. [online]. [accessed 2013-10-29]. Available at: http://www.vlada.cz/cz/clenove-vlady/historie-minulych-vlad/rejstrik-predsedu-vlad/richard-bienert-440/.
314 See also Benjamin Frommer. *National Cleansing: Retribution against Nazi Collaborators in Postwar Czechoslovakia*. New York: Cambridge University Press, 2005, chapter 7; Mečislav

Resler also defended a number of other ministers of the Protectorate government before the National Court. These included JUDr. Jiří Havelka, who had worked with Emil Hácha as minister without portfolio until April 1939 and subsequently as Minister of Transport until 1941. He had kept in contact with the resistance at home and abroad, much like the then Prime Minister Eliáš. While Generál Eliáš had been executed, Havelka had only been placed under house arrest until the end of the war. The National Court acquitted him. Another of Resler's clients, historian and lawyer Professor Jan Kapras, who had been Minister of Education from 1939–1942, was also freed, and his contribution to the home resistance movement was recognised. Kapras died a month after his acquittal.

THE NATIONAL COURT

The National Court in Prague, at which Bienert was tried, was established by Presidential Decree no. 17/1945 Coll. on 19 June 1945. It was a special court for a circle of well-known people, although the exact extent of that circle could be interpreted more or less restrictively by the State Prosecutor. The decree applied specifically to crimes defined in the Great Retribution Decree that were committed by the State President of the Protectorate, members of the Protectorate government, the top leaders of the *Vlajka* organisation, members of institutions and unions established by law, or journalists who had contributed to propaganda under the occupation, as well as other leading individuals in politics and business who should have set an example to their fellow citizens.

The court operated both as a criminal court and as a court of honour, and therefore judged not only crimes but also behaviour that did not correspond to that expected of a loyal and brave Czechoslovak citizen. Such cases could be punished with sanctions that restricted civil liberties. Unlike the Extraordinary People's Courts, the National Court's proceedings were not run on the basis of martial law, but according to the general provisions of the Criminal Code. One could say, therefore, that the proceedings at the National Court were fairer, allowed greater room for defence, and were more orderly, as in ordinary courts.[315]

Borák. *Spravedlnost podle dekretu: retribuční soudnictví v ČSR a Mimořádný lidový soud v Ostravě (1945–1948).* [Justice by decree: retributional justice in the Czechoslovak Republic and the extraordinary people's court in Ostrava (1945–1948)]. Ed. 1. Ostrava: Tilia, 1998, p. 183 ff.; Dušan Tomášek, and Robert Kvaček. *Obžalována je vláda.* [The government is prosecuted]. Ed. 1. Prague: Themis, 1999.

315   Kamill Resler. "Obnova lidového soudnictví v Českých zemích. [The renewal of people's justice in the Czech lands]." *Právní praxe* XII (1948), p. 60.

In total, 80 people were tried before the National Court, of whom Kamill Resler defended at least six. He achieved two acquittals, one three-year prison sentence, two life sentences and one death sentence. Of all the National Court's judgements, 15 resulted in full acquittal, 4 in charges being dropped, 35 in prison sentences with an average length of nine and a half years, 8 in life sentences and 18 in death sentences.

The National Court was located in the Criminal Court building at Karlovo náměstí, in the centre of Prague and close to Resler's office. The prisoners were held at Pankrác prison, which is next door to the building that previously housed the Extraordinary People's Court and is now the High Court in Prague.

Resler knew the President of the National Court, JUDr. Jaroslav Křižan, very well. He had met him as a young judge at court in the Central Bohemian town of Beroun, and had noted that he dealt with cases quickly, astutely and utterly impartially, which had made an impression on Resler. Resler recalled that as Křižan had questioned a witness at one divorce hearing before the Regional Court in Prague, Resler's old friend Dr. Dukát had whispered to him that Resler would have questioned him in the same way if he were a judge. Křižan and Resler were very similar not only in character but also in looks, and were sometimes mistaken for one another. Resler deeply respected Křižan. In one letter he remembered him as a man "who, in that hotbed of hatred and quagmire of malice, remained humanly simple and genuine, and did not realise that he was wading into deep waters." As for the fact that people had addressed him in the corridors as Dr. Resler, Resler wrote to him: "Something about our looks and way of thinking is certainly similar, but the mistake is that you do not know how to be as tough as me.[316]

Resler took on his first case before the National Court in Prague on the insistence of a barrister friend of his, who was a political prisoner. It was the defence of Police General Otto Bláha in the National Court's very first criminal case. Otto Bláha had been the chairman of the Český svaz válečníků (Czech Union of Warriors), an organisation originally formed to bring together veterans of the First World War, but which later participated in the Aryan campaign and collaborated with the occupying powers. He was accused together with the union's second chairman, Divisional General Robert Rychtrmoc and the chief editor of the pro-German magazine *Kamarádství*, Major Gustav Mohapel.[317]

---

316   PNP 111, Letters to Jaroslav Křižan on 16 June 1951 and 7 December 1951.
317   See also e.g. Ivo Pejčoch. *Osud generála, který se v osudných chvílích přidal na špatnou stranu.* [The fate of a general who in fateful moments took the wrong side]. [online]. 2012 [accessed 2017-11-28]. Available at: http://www.vhu.cz/osud-generala-ktery-se-v-osudnych-chvilich-pridal-na-spatnou-stranu/.

On the first day of the trial, 15 January 1946, Resler attempted to have the case transferred from the National Court (under judge Dr. Tomsa) to the Extraordinary People's Court, on the grounds that Bláha had not occupied a particularly important position either professionally or in public life. After the second day of the defence, Bláha attempted to commit suicide, but unsuccessfully; he said he had not had the nerve. Resler wanted to call Frank as a witness, but this never took place. On the fourth day of the trial Resler delivered his closing speech, in which he tried to reduce the bad impression Bláha had given by making him appear politically illiterate, and to show that Bláha had had no choice than to be a two-faced politician. On the fifth and final day of the trial, 21 January 1946, the State Prosecutor agreed in his reply that Bláha had played a two-faced politician, but claimed that he had done so in order to provide for himself financially.[318] Responding to that, Resler delivered his shortest ever defence speech: "No comment." Not long after that his client also fell silent – Resler accompanied him to his execution. He asked for the execution to be postponed for three hours, but his request was denied.[319] He spent the next few days in an unsuccessful attempt to have the body buried according to the family's wishes.[320] Later, in 1948, he pointed out that after the trial the KSČ's Iˢᵗ region legal commission had come to the view that although he had defended his client extremely strongly his defence had not breached loyalty to the Czechoslovak state.

DEFENCE OF JIŘÍ STŘÍBRNÝ

One day, when Resler went to the Pankrác prison hospital to visit his clients, he saw prisoners walking about and spending time in the small garden, and thought what a change there had been since the time of the Protectorate. One prisoner in particular caught his eye – he thought he had seen him somewhere before. He then realised that it was Jiří Stříbrný – "Every defence counsel sympathises with prisoners, that is part of his calling, because he is always on their side, and so – as I walked past Jiří Stříbrný, I dipped my head slightly in greeting. At that point all the prisoners knew me, as I had been a daily guest at the prison for the past six weeks. So for sure Jiří Stříbrný also knew me, but he did not realise that I knew him. It evidently pleased him that I had recognised him, and he returned the greeting. Bienert was sitting sombrely on his stool by the hospital wall. His head was leant on the wall and

---

318   *Svobodné slovo*, 16 January 1946, p. 2; *Rudé právo* 18 January 1946; *Rudé Právo* 19 January 1946, p. 2; *Rudé Právo* 22 January 1946.
319   Poem enclosed with letter to Alois Dyk on 6 May 1946, NM; *Svobodné noviny*, 22 January 1946, p. 2.
320   PNP 78, Letter to Jiří Karásek ze Lvovic on 1 February 1946.

he was staring stiffly ahead of him, without moving. We greeted one another, and I wanted to stay out in the sun with him so that he did not lose out on his chance to recuperate, but the prisoners' recreation was already coming to an end. So on his suggestion we went to sit in one of the rooms in the pleasant hospital for our meeting." [321]

Jiří Stříbrný, a politician of the First Republic with fascist tendencies, who had been a leader of the National Socialist Party in the '20s, also later became Resler's client. Before his trial began, the Eastern Bohemian edition of the paper *Svobodné slovo* published a piece about Resler on its final page on 6 January 1947, headlined: "Also from Pardubice." It informed readers that while listening to his defence they should be aware that the defence counsel was friends with many artists and had an enormous collection of books about magic. He was known to treat anyone from Pardubice well. From this it is clear that the paper was trying to show Resler's human side, and that the defence counsel was to be viewed separately from the man he was defending.

Jiří Stříbrný mistook Resler's name and refers to him throughout his memoirs as Karel Resler. Resler was optimistic about his defence, because Stříbrný was not interrogated for long and had not been told what he was charged with. They were only handed the charges on the evening before the trial began and supposed that this was because there was little evidence. This was quite clear from the fact that of the fifty pages of charges only thirteen addressed the key time period for the trial; the rest of the text was dedicated to things Stříbrný had done before that time.

Stříbrný was charged on two main counts: with supporting and promoting the Nazi movement, and with the crime of informing. In the end, he was only found guilty on the first count, for which he was sentenced to life imprisonment. This verdict was, and remains, rather questionable. Stříbrný had only been active in journalism until August 1939, at which time he had also written against Beneš. The prosecution deduced from this that "the accused, an experienced politician who had been part of the fight for freedom in the First World War and had experienced Masaryk and Beneš' roles, could not have doubted even for a moment that the departure of Dr. Beneš and his companions abroad meant that a new fight for freedom had begun, and that the fate of our independence lay in his hands. The accused's diatribes against him were therefore a conscious attack against our freedom, and endorsed the occupation." [322]

---

321   AHMP 4, Own description of the situation.

322   Libor Vykoupil. *Jiří Stříbrný: portrét politika*. [Jiří Stříbrný: Portrait of a politician]. Ed. 1. Brno: Masarykova univerzita, 2003, p. 220 ff. Available online at: http://digilib.phil.muni.cz/han-dle/11222.digilib/103757. Further quotations regarding Jiřího Stříbrný are also taken from this source.

Stříbrný's defence was that during the '30s he had been targeted by Nazi contacts and had been offered money. He had not, though, joined any collaborationist organisations, and, in his words from the closing speech had "refused to make speeches or write articles for the Germans and against emigration (...), no one can demonstrate that I defended the German government in Czechoslovakia in any speech, article or activity. Despite my opposing views, I always had a good relationship with the Czechoslovak army. I behaved entirely properly from a national perspective all my life, and at least with dignity during the occupation."

The verdict was criticised by many, even Stříbrný's opponents, for being too strict. Philosopher and writer Václav Černý wrote in his memoirs: "Beneš [the President] had my right-wing rivals of the last pre-war years mercilessly trampled down, in a mixture of injustice and lack of foresight or democracy. Jiří Stříbrný, Rudolf Beran and Radola Gajda were trivial, low calibre politicians who did not deserve life imprisonment, which they were given not for any alleged national treason but for old instigation to anti-Benešism; in Stříbrný's case, he had already repented."

The professional judges were also aware of this and so, when Stříbrný submitted a plea for mercy at the end of 1947, the Regional Criminal Court in Prague recommended that it should be accepted and the punishment reduced or revoked, because the convicted individual had behaved soundly during the occupation. The lay judges at the National Court, who included the editor of *Rudé právo* and the daughter of Zdeněk Nejedlý, a long-time communist minister after the war, reacted to this by writing to the President to object. Beneš responded to their letter saying that their role had expired with the end of the retributional judiciary on 4 May 1947, and he would therefore not take their view into account. He did not react to the plea for mercy, nor to the court's letter. Jiří Stříbrný died on 21 January 1955 in Valdice, one of the oldest prisons in Bohemia.

Resler's work was hardly ever over with the court's decision, or in other cases the execution. On Christmas Eve 1947, Resler asked permission to visit a number of prisoners in the Plzeň-Bory prison, to discuss applying for mercy on their behalves to the President.[323]

Another client whom Resler defended before the National Court was Václav Crha, who had been the chief editor of magazines *Národní politika*, *České slovo* and *Zteč* during the war. He was also sentenced to life imprisonment for promoting and defending the Nazi movement, among a few other crimes. His wife submitted a plea for mercy through Resler. Her argument rested on the fact that the retributional courts had initially handed out harder punishments than they did later on, and that it would therefore be fair to shorten

---

323 PNP 78, Application for exceptional visits to criminals.

her husband's punishment.[324] In her plea, she mentioned nine other journalists who had been given lesser sentences for similar crimes. Similarly, in another trial brought by the public prosecutors at the new people's courts, two journalists were given lesser sentences than Crha, although stricter than those given in the people's courts' previous period of activity. And yet the plea for mercy was rejected on 20 December 1948. Resler wrote with this sad news to Crha's wife Jindřiška Crhová on 31 December 1948, which turned out to be a significant day in his legal career.[325]

CASES BEFORE AND AFTER THE RENEWAL
OF THE EXTRAORDINARY PEOPLE'S COURTS

After the Second World War, 24 Extraordinary People's Courts were established by Presidential Decree no. 16/1945 Coll. and housed in Regional Court buildings (sec. 22). Each court chamber was composed of one professional judge and four lay judges. These post-war retributional courts ceased to function on 4 May 1947 – two years after the Prague Uprising. Nevertheless, after the communists came to power these courts were re-opened for a further period of eight months, until the end of 1948. Their purpose was both to try cases that the communists considered to have failed to achieve their retributional purpose, and to re-try cases that had resulted in acquittal or a punishment that the communists considered too lenient.

It was usual at the time that barristers would recommend clients to one another; in particular, if they could not take on new clients at the time or the new clients were not from the town where the barrister was based, they would pass them on to their colleagues. Hence Resler recommended five clients for defence before the Extraordinary People's Court to his barrister friend Josef Doležal. In recognition, Doležal gave Resler 30% of the fees he received, and all five were acquitted. Resler thanked him for helping him at the most difficult time in his career, expressed his admiration for him as a colleague, and apologised for refusing to accept the money. He explained that he had in the past brought other similar deals to disciplinary proceedings for contravening the Bar's behavioural code, and so he could not accept his kind offer.

In Resler's records, a good number of documents survived on some of his trials in the post-war period; we now take a closer look at some of the information these give us about Resler.

---

324 A similar situation arose at the Exceptional People's Courts, see also Benjamin Frommer. *National Cleansing: Retribution against Nazi Collaborators in Postwar Czechoslovakia*. New York: Cambridge University Press, 2005, chapter 3.
325 PNP 69, Letter to Jindřiška Crhová.

KELEMEN ALEXANDER[326]

The Government Commissar for the Western Bohemian town of Domažlice, Alexander Kelemen, was found guilty before the Extraordinary People's Court in Plzeň and sentenced to life imprisonment, the loss of his civic honour and the loss of all his assets. However, the most interesting thing about this case for us (and for Resler) was not the person convicted, but his defence counsels and their approaches.

Kamill Resler was the first to defend Dr. Kelemen, since he was being held in custody in Prague. In one letter, Resler wrote that Kelemen had been imprisoned once previously, but had been discharged. However, he had begun to claim his furniture back and so someone had probably wanted him to end up in prison again. Since the proceedings were to take place in Plzeň, Resler agreed with JUDr. Luděk Bezděk, a barrister based there that they would work together, and later that Bezděk would take over the whole case as Resler's substitute. He succeeded in avoiding a death sentence, on the basis of sec. 29 of the Retribution Decree, which ordered that death sentences be converted into prison sentences of 20 years or life if the death sentence would be disproportionately harsh, or if it had been passed by only three of the five judges. This was the first time that this section had been invoked before the Extraordinary People's Court in Plzeň – and it came less than a month before the two-year existence of the Extraordinary People's Courts was due to end.[327] Dr. Kelemen thanked his defence counsel very much, as the public had been so sure he would be handed a death sentence that the executioner had even been waiting in the courtroom.

All that remained was to settle the costs of the legal representation. Dr. Bezděk gave Resler a friendly substitution discount of one third of his usual rate, with the explanation: "Sometimes I give even bigger discounts, but this case was really not very easy." Resler then asked Kelemen's wife and father-in-law, writer Karel Horký, to pay the dues amounting to 7,412 Kč, since he had taken on the defence at their request. Horký responded directly to Bezděk, complaining that the bill was not itemised and was extremely unreasonable. Bezděk responded stating: "you will find that it is calculated according to the standard rates, or rather much less." He added a note on his personal experience of the defence: "Personally, I must admit that your letter hurt me a lot. I suppose you do not realise that during the past three months we – there are only 24 of us *ex officio* counsels – have worked harder than anyone in the

---

326 PNP, Kelemen Alexander, inv. no. 2849–2890.

327 The Extraordinary People's Court in Plzeň was active between 18 September 1945 and 4 May 1947 – Jana Žamberská. *Retribuční soudnictví – Mimořádný lidový soud v Plzni.* [Retributional justice – The extraordinary people's court in Pilsen]. Dissertation. Pilsen: Západočeská univerzita v Plzni. Fakulta filozofická, 2010.

Republic. We had up to three cases per week. We have spent countless hours in prisons, and countless days at hearings non-stop from 8 in the morning until late into the evening; and there was no rest, since it was almost always a question of life or death. We spent countless nights studying court documents and preparing. In all that time I had just one paid case, which brought me 700 Kčs. And then I took on two paid substitutions from Dr. Ressler, of which Mr Kelemen's was one. I surely do not need to tell you how many offensive things we heard in court, on the streets and in the papers. For each "paid" case we were rewarded with another, tougher case on the side. We have had no time in the past three months to attend to our usual work. No one stopped to consider how we and our families would survive when all our life savings, whether deposits or investments, have been blocked. (…) And now you say that my bill is unreasonable. An almost unbelievable thing took place: an executioner and his entourage attended the sentencing of a man who was not handed over to them. I had better finish, lest I become bitter. To the point: I am not money-grubbing, nor do I wish to make my fortune from another's loss. Please discuss the matter with Dr. Ressler. If he decides that my bill should be cancelled or reduced to be more acceptable to you, so be it. Yours respectfully, Bezděk."

He then left it up to Resler whether to send the letter on to Horký; he decided instead to copy a large part of it into a letter of his own. Resler briefly explained why the bill should have been much higher, and that it was in fact only as low as it was out of kindness towards both Horký and himself. He ended his letter with the words: "If you are as I remember you, Mr Horký, I can finish there. I made arrangements with Mr JUDr. Bezděk myself, and am indebted to him. Please do not write to him, but negotiate the matter with me. A reduction to the bill cannot be considered (…) we may discuss payment in instalments. (…) I will pay JUDr. Bezděk myself, as soon as I am able, so that he can put the matter behind himself and does not have to return to such painful matters."

Resler sent a copy of this letter to Bezděk, and advised him to forward any further letters he might receive to him. He apologised for not having paid within three days, as had been his habit for the past twenty years, and explained that he too was struggling with the current financial situation. Although he had been putting on a brave face, he hadn't managed to smile three weeks earlier, when the tax collectors had demanded 15,000 Kčs and left Resler with just 200 Kčs. He therefore asked Bezděk to give him six weeks – noting that if he desperately needed the money sooner, he promised to find a way of raising it.

Over the next few months, Resler sent on the instalments he received from Karel Horký. However, Horký only paid Resler three fifths of the amount he owed in total. Dr. Bezděk's penultimate letter reveals his charitable character:

"As for my bill for the substitution, I meant it when I said that if he cannot pay it, I am willing to write it off. Thank you kindly for your efforts, but I really would not want anyone to become destitute as a result of paying for my services. I will get by somehow." Why Horký failed to pay his debts we do not know.

Resler had met JUDr. Karel Horký prior to this case. In April 1939, Hácha had told Horký, who was then a journalist and had been an opposition politician during the First Republic, about the events of 14 and 15 March 1939. Horký mentions this in his detailed notes, which he gave to Kamill Resler after the war, but which are not to be found in Resler's archives today.

PROF. MILOSLAV HÝSEK[328]

Resler's representation of Miloslav Hýsek, a professor of Czech History at the Philosophical Faculty of Charles University, was a defence of a completely different kind – that is, one that did not cause Resler any concern, either morally or in terms of public opinion. Hýsek had been chairman of the Protectorate's Cultural Council, which had been established as early as December 1938 with the aim of contributing to the development of Czech culture without any ideological, philosophical or political views. On 28 June 1945, 29 professors had signed a declaration in response to his having been taken into custody, defending his genuine Czech attitudes and his pro-Czech efforts during the war. Three weeks later, following a petition from his wife too, he was released. The State Prosecutor first brought his case before the National Court in Prague as case number 167/46, but after a thorough investigation he decided to call off the proceedings. The papers reported this event with the headline: "Dr. Hýsek's trial suspended."[329]

The State Prosecutor announced (possibly by mistake) that he did not consider himself to be the appropriate person for the case, and handed the files over to the Public Prosecutor at the Extraordinary People's Court in Prague, who charged Hýsek on 26 March 1947 with having been a member of the board of the League Against Bolshevism and having supported the Nazi movement. The main hearing was scheduled for 18 April 1947, but on 16 April the Public Prosecutor requested the files for the Ministry of Justice, and so it was not possible to hold the hearing.

When Resler called upon the Ministry of Justice to return the files so that the court could make its decision he understood from their unwillingness to do so that they were preparing to order the trial be called off. Over the phone, they informed Resler: "We cannot let you have this victory." He emphatically

---

328 PNP, Hýsek Miloslav, inv. no. 1722–1726, 1727–1768.
329 *Svobodné slovo*, 19 April 1947.

demanded that the ministry drop this plan and allow Hýsek to clear his name in court, but received an evasive reply and on 3 May 1947 the Public Prosecutor eventually withdrew his charges. A month later, the Regional Criminal Court in Prague officially cancelled the proceedings; the Extraordinary People's Court had already ceased to function on 4 May. Resler had already prepared part of his closing speech, in which he referred to Hýsek as follows: "In him you are judging one of the top spiritual leaders and educators of our nation, a man who was obliged more than anyone else, during the tough times of the German occupation, to be an example to his fellow citizens of how to fulfil their national duties (...) his lectures strengthened Czech national knowledge, strengthened the nation's confidence in their future and in eventual victory for the Czech national cause."

The National Front's Action Committee at the Philosophical Faculty excluded Profesor Hýsek from the university on 10 March 1948. The reason they gave was his supposed membership on the board of the League Against Bolshevism and his position as chairman of the Cultural Council, which E. Beneš had declared an enemy and betrayer of the Czech nation. Hýsek appealed against this decision – he had not been a member of the League Against Bolshevism, while the work of the Cultural Council had been to support Czech artists, and he had done his best to prevent it from Nazification. He denied behaving accommodatingly towards the Nazis, and stated that on the contrary the Gestapo had mistrusted him and suspected him of committing acts against the Reich. That was also evident from the fact that *Vlajka* had criticized him for failing to salute with his right arm raised, and for being a "Masonic admirer of Beneš." Furthermore, the Action Committee's argument was flawed. President Beneš had not been removed by the Cultural Council but by the National Council. Based on these statements, he demanded that the decision to bar him from his work as a professor be retracted. He hoped that the Action Committee's words "we do not wish to claim that we are infallible" were meant seriously. The outcome of the dispute is unknown, but it is clear that he never resumed his public function after 1948, and we may assume that this is because his appeal was unsuccessful.[330]

A number of well-known figures of public and cultural life also came forward in Hýsek's defence, including Rafael Kubelík, an acclaimed Czech conductor. He wrote that throughout the occupation Hýsek "did not hide his hatred for the Germans from me, was constantly on the lookout for ways to ideologically sabotage Germanness, and advised how to avoid pressure from the occupiers. In Prof. Hýsek I saw a champion of Czechness, and was never in any doubt about his patriotic feelings; only those who experienced ser-

---

330 For more on Miloslav Hýsek: Jan Chodějovský. *Miloslav Hýsek.* [online]. 2012 [accessed 2017-11-28]. Available at: http://abicko.avcr.cz/archiv/2007/3/07/.

vitude under the so-called Protectorate can appreciate his attitude to Czech musical culture, in as far as it was able to survive here after 15 March 1939."

Petr Bezruč, who had known Hýsek for forty years, also expressed his appreciation of his character: "he has an impeccable character, and never doubted that the sacred cause would be victorious; he did what he had to do."[331]

ZLATKO BILIAN[332]

Resler defended Zlatko Bilian before the Extraordinary People's Court in Prague. Bilian was the director of the agricultural educational establishment in Prague-Uhříněves, and was accused of supporting the Nazi movement. Resler demonstrated that far from being criticized in court he should be honoured for having supported his nation through difficult times. The proceedings against Zlatko Bilian were called off. Naturally, that did not prevent the paper *Rudé právo* from responding to the case in its own way. The headline alone of the article it published on 6 November 1945 is telling: "A camel would more likely pass through the eye of a needle than a collaborator cross the prison threshold."

HUGO SONNENSCHEIN-SONKA

Several of Resler's colleagues weren't so lucky – for example, poet Hugo Sonnenschein-Sonka, who had built the first Communist cells in the Czechoslovak Republic.[333] Resler only got to know him later, when he was accused of collaborating with the Gestapo, but his experience with him was good, and they got along extremely well. Sonka was happy with Resler's defence work for him even though the outcome of the trial was very bleak: he was sentenced to fifteen years in prison for informing. According to Resler, his case was inexplicable in a way that only the fates of certain people under

---

331   However, based on the materials that survived in Resler's archives, Bezruč also had other opinions. For example, in a short letter from Bezruč to Resler in 1947, aside from settling some old accounts for Resler's legal work, Bezruč also writes: "But I think the matter will turn out well. The fact that someone turned against the Jews – they were always our enemies after all, which we felt in particular in Moravia and Silesia! They got what they deserved. Hitler didn't impose antisemitism – he lived among the German youth sixty years ago, I was among them too – Brno was German." (PNP Hýsek Miloslav inv. no. 1722–1726, 1727–1768). Bezruč's view was therefore directly opposed to Resler's. It's interesting to compare this with Resler's view – also in 1947 – on a certain book by Salač, that was antisemitic: "I have everything ready so as to be able to intervene if he tries to continue with the publication. Public opinion is clearly against Jews, but the Jews are influential enough to prevent the publication of such works."

332   PNP, Bilian Zlatko, inv. no. 45–82.

333   AHMP 14, point 44, Rozklad proti rozhodnutí Akčního výboru Advokátní komory pro Čechy [appeal].

German rule could be.[334] Apart from his prison sentence, Sonka also owed 17,055.30 Kčs for his legal representation; the final 660 Kčs of this debt was only claimed during the execution of Sonka's inheritance after his death 1953. His son, ing. arch. Ivan Sova, who had originally asked Resler to represent his father, was guarantor, but not even he had the money to pay the outstanding debt. Although he had taken care of his father during the trial and had taken a keen interest in the defence, he had turned his back on paying the fees afterwards.[335] Despite that, and despite no longer having any interest in he case, Resler requested the Ministry of Justice to grant Sonka mercy after 1948, as he thought the punishment too high relative to the case's importance.[336] He did not succeed.

MARTA BIDLOVÁ[337]

While representing Marta Bidlová before the Extraordinary People's Court in Prague, Resler interceded on her behalf with JUDr. Jaroslav Drábek, the general prosecutor at the court, asking him to process the case especially quickly on account of Bidlová's mental state.[338] Marta Bidlová was accused of denouncing people for listening to foreign radio broadcasts, and for threatening that they would be imprisoned by the Gestapo. Her defence argument was that the letter in question had been dictated by her mentally ill spouse; those it denounced were his superiors, who were behaving unkindly to him and at the time of writing the letter had driven him into a frenzy. She claimed that while in that state he had forced her to write the denunciation letter. The court did not accept this argument, and sentenced Marta Bidlová to three years of hard labour. Resler continued to deal with her situation during her incarceration; he asked the court to allocate her lighter work, for health reasons, and later to release her from the remainder of her punishment on the grounds of serious illness. The Public Prosecutor disagreed, on the grounds of a favourable health review, and the court refused to grant Resler's request as it did not find evidence of a state of health that would have ruled out the enforcement of the punishment. Resler therefore sent a plea for mercy to the President of the Republic, which the Regional Court rejected, because it could not find any serious reason to pass the plea to the higher court, which would in turn then have passed it to the Ministry of Justice for approval. Marta Bidlová wrote to Resler every two weeks to ask him to send money and parcels.

---

334 NM, Letter to Kristian Fanta on 5 December 1952.
335 PNP 29, Letters to the notary public and to Ivan Sova.
336 PNP 29, Request for mercy to be considered.
337 PNP, Marta Bidlová.
338 For more on his character see Jitka Melšová. *Ústecké kalendárium – květen 2011.* [online]. [accessed 2017-11-28]. Available at: http://www.zpravodaj.probit.cz/2011/UOkalend_5_11.htm.

Unfortunately, we do not know how Resler responded and whether he helped her in these matters.

KAREL KRÁLOVEC

Karel Královec was a contributor to the magazine *Arijský boj* until 1943, when he was sent to the Reich for forced labour. His case was decided five days after the renewal of the people's justice, and two days after the Extraordinary People's Court started its work (again) – on 10 April 1948. Královec was sentenced to ten years of hard labour, the loss of his honour for life, and the loss of all his assets. This was the hardest possible punishment the court could give him, in the circumstances. Resler was not able to defend him at the time, but he was allocated an *ex officio* barrister, who did all that was necessary. In a letter to Královec's wife Resler mentioned that he believed he had only been given such a hard punishment because the court had just been re-opened. If he had been tried before an ordinary court, Resler reckoned that his punishment would have been in the region of four to six years – and if he had been tried in the new people's court later on, after their "run-in," then he might have expected six to eight years. As it was, though, he was stuck with the highest possible sentence.[339]

FRANTIŠEK VALACH[340]

In 1947 and 1948, Resler defended the wartime director of the *Národohospodářský svaz* (Economic Union) in Brno, František Valach. In 1945, Valach had been tortured and taken to the concentration camp in Mirošov, but had behaved perfectly and like a good Czech, i.e. without moral fault, throughout his time there. His health was so poor that Resler had to ask for the proceedings to be transferred to the Regional Criminal Court in Prague, which was nearer to Valach's home. František Valach died on 15 October 1948, most likely before the case had been settled.

KEY EVENTS OF 1946 AND 1947 AND RESLER'S EVERYDAY WORK

At the end of each year after the war, the newspaper *Právo lidu* asked celebrities which events of the past year they considered the most important in the life of the Republic. In 1946, Kamill Resler replied: "1. The expulsion of

---

339   PNP 75, Letter to Jaroslava Královcová (sic) on 13 April 1948.
340   PNP 6166–6178.

the Germans from the Czechoslovak Republic, by which the Czechoslovak politicians, who had never claimed their right to retaliation, inflicted on the Germans the consequences of Hitler's teaching about the national living space, which the Germans had willingly accepted, never once thinking that this right they had reserved for themselves could one day be applied against them. 2. The fact that the Czech people survived the effects of six years of German occupation in such a state that they were able to launch themselves quickly into peacetime work. 3. The fact that the Czech and Slovak nations also weathered the effects of the liberation and that citizens of the Czechoslovak Republic have proven their honour in the unfair battle over the administration of property taxes."[341]

In 1947, his response was: "1. The end of special justice at the National Court and Extraordinary People's Courts in the Czech lands. 2. The fact that the so-called President of the Slovak State was condemned to death. 3. The declaration by the presidium of the ÚRO [Ústřední rada odborů, Central Council of Trade Unions] that its undisciplined members would be sent to the mines. 4. Various political parties' attempts to pass off their party interests as the interests of the Czechoslovak Republic. 5. Clarity on the question of extraditing political exiles. 6. Certain Slovak groups' plots against the unity and integrity of the state."[342]

In a letter to Paul Edwards in 1946, he wrote: "Things are different today, we are taking a slightly unusual route, courageous as ever, towards the distant future of humanity, but it is the right route, even if it may be painful for a short time. It will enable our descendants to live. Despite the difficult postwar conditions, our country is working hard and pulling itself up quickly. Supplies are improving day by day. We now leave our tables feeling satisfied, and the quality of food is constantly improving. Great credit for that goes to UNRRA;[343] the cleanliness, orderliness, and perfect effectiveness of its military food rations, and the quality of the American products, is impressive. Times are very hard for making a living in law, as the people have little money, and many of our profession have had to take out loans to keep their practices running. Our rates are now two or three times higher than those you will remember, but as you know, barristers always receive their fees only after some time."[344]

341 *Právo lidu*, no. 295, 25 December 1946, p. 7. On the expulsion, see Zdeněk Radvanovský. "The Transfer of Czechoslovakia's Germans and its Impact in the Border Region after the Second World War." In Mark Cornwall, and R. J. W. Evans, (eds.) *Czechoslovakia in a Nationalist and Fascist Europe, 1918–1948*. Oxford: Oxford University Press and British Academy, 2007.

342 *Právo lidu*, 25 December 1947, p. 4.

343 The United Nations Relief and Rehabilitation Administration.

344 PNP 91, Letter to Paul Edwards on 24 June 1946.

His post-war defence work at the Extraordinary People's Courts had placed Resler under significant financial strain. In 1947 he had made just 33,988 Kčs, with income of 257,756.30 Kčs and outgoings of 223,768.30.[345] Despite this tough situation, he still tried to help his friends who had got themselves into financial difficulties, sometimes by finding them jobs.[346] Besides his special cases, Resler also of course had many standard cases to deal with during the post-war years, some of which we now present briefly.

On 20 February 1947 Antonín Bouček, co-founder and editor of the communist daily paper *Rudé právo*, died. His wife entrusted Resler to deal with his estate, as his longstanding friend and lawyer. Resler conducted the inheritance proceedings, including disputes with the financial authorities and courts, without asking her for any fee, even though the proceedings lasted until 1949. The *Rudé právo* editorial board paid for Bouček's funeral, which cost 7,328 Kčs.[347]

Resler also had a hand in Jan Karsten-Klepentář's fate, as his legal representative. Karsten-Klepentář was convicted of complicity in murder, along with a few other crimes, in 1928. He claimed never to have committed the crimes. After the war, in his forties, he decided that he wanted to study Law at Charles University, which he began and passed a number of exams. Later, though, the faculty informed him that although it would allow him to continue to study, and to take exams, he would not be allowed to graduate with the degree of Doctor of Law, because of his criminal record. The faculty grounded its decision on a decree dated 23 March 1791.[348]

At this point, Kamill Resler took up the case. During verbal negotiations with Resler Prof. Saturník, the Dean of the Law Faculty, told him that even if he managed to have the convictions annulled the university would not be able to change its mind. Resler himself agreed with this – his client was strongly tainted by his convictions. In relation to others graduating from the faculty, Resler wrote: "I know that the university admits half-wits and dunces to the doctorate, who have only superficial knowledge and who only need it in order to establish themselves in influential, lucrative positions, people without honour, without so much as a crumb of the value that you will always have, even if overshadowed by your criminal convictions."

Karsten was still determined to achieve his position at the faculty, even after the university had permanently excluded him in 1947. An amnesty in administrative criminal matters on 18 June 1948 and the President of the Republic's mercy granted on 9 September 1948, which wiped all his offences

345 NM, Letter to Antonín Švehla on 7 March 1951.
346 NM, Letter to Jožo David, president of the Czechoslovak Constitutional National Assembly, on 18 August 1947.
347 PNP, Bouček Antonín, inv. no. 83–155.
348 Directive PGS Bd 2. S 114 No. 46.

from his criminal record, helped a lot with this. Because he had been granted mercy, the Academic Senate of Charles University cancelled Karsten's expulsion in December 1948 and he was able to continue with his studies.[349]

Nor did Resler manage to avoid cases caught up in the disputes between the West and the East. In late 1947 he defended Major Richard Pollak, a member of the British Council in Prague, who was accused of military espionage. The police held Pollak for twice the permitted time – 4 days instead of 48 hours – before handing him over to the court, to which Resler objected. Pollak was then released from prison with the Public Prosecutor's consent.[350] The *Partyzán* magazine published a piece on 2 January 1948 accusing Pollak of espionage and Resler of expressing sympathy with the Western powers; this reportedly made Resler rather cross, and they both decided to sue the magazine. However, Major Pollak then commit suicide, and Resler retracted his lawsuit. The *Partyzán* magazine was represented by JUDr. Zikmund Stein who was frequently Resler's opponent in similar cases.[351]

ZIKMUND STEIN

JUDr. Zikmund Stein was a barrister colleague of Resler's. In March 1939, before Stein left for Russia, he praised Resler for having behaved splendidly amicably towards their Jewish colleagues. On his return after the war the two of them became friends, and from 1945 onwards they also worked together in the leadership of the Bar Association: Resler was the Association's deputy prosecutor, and Stein was a member of the Board and a disciplinary judge at the Supreme Court.[352] During a court hearing early in 1948, however, Resler approached a group of barristers including Dr. Stein, to greet them. As he then wrote in a letter to Stein, "I turned to you first, and when I greeted you and offered my hand, you stuffed your hands into your pockets and refused to shake hands with me. Both the other gentlemen present noticed. I am not aware of having personally insulted you, and cannot comprehend your behaviour. Naturally, you will understand if in future I avoid social contact with you." This was followed by Resler's typical closing phrase: "Yours most respectfully."

Half a year later, when Stein of his own accord requested 310 Kčs less in charges for legal representation than the court had awarded him, Resler wrote to him: "Thank you for adjusting your award. I knew that you would not allow your office's oversight to slip through."[353]

349 PNP, Karsten-Klepentář Jan, inv. no. 2585–2588.
350 PNP 78, Editors' response to request for corrections to the article "Tvrdá fakta."
351 PNP 78, Letter to Zikmund Stein on 10 March 1948.
352 Stanislav Balík. *Dějiny advokacie v Čechách, na Moravě a ve Slezsku* [A History of Advocacy in Bohemia, Moravia and Silesia]. Prague: Česká advokátní komora in co-operation with Národní galerie, 2009.
353 PNP, Mareš Michal, inv. no. 3285–3322.

It remains unclear whether Stein had turned away from Resler because he thought his behaviour dishonest, or because he thought that the times required him to – JUDr. Stein went on to become president of the Action Committee of the Bohemian Bar Association, and in early 1949 chairman of the executive committee of the Ústřední sdružení advokátů (Central Association of Barristers). Repressive events quickly turned against him, however: in December 1949 he was dismissed from these roles, and in 1954 was convicted for aiding and abetting a former class enemy with high treason and sentenced to 12 years in prison.[354]

ONE INSIGNIFICANT CASE

Some cases were risky for Resler's professional legal practice, whether as a result of the stress they caused him, or from a political perspective – but Resler was certainly not expecting the latter to apply to a dispute between small potato farmers in Eastern Bohemia. Even today, the case sounds unimportant, but it turned out to influence Resler's future. Resler was involved as legal representative for Ing. Stanislav Horčička, director of the Sativa company; Horčička had attempted to keep the company going during the war and this had meant he had to collaborate to a certain extent. Resler defended him between 1946 and 1948, and also became personally involved in the case himself, privately suing two journalists from the paper *Rudé právo*, Oldřich Švestka and Vojtěch Dolejší.[355] These journalists had jointly written an article reporting that Resler had succeeded in having several lay judges on the Horčička case replaced[356] by judges who were more favourable to his client. The article claimed that he had openly admitted doing so.

Resler did not deny that had asked for the judges to be replaced, but said that it had been for a different reason – four of the five lay judges were members of the communist party, and the fifth was a candidate for the same party in the elections to the Local National Committee. Resler considered that this damaged the court's impartiality. Although it was not an important case, the exchange of the lay judges led to the Minister of Justice being questioned by members of parliament.[357] Minister Drtina stated in response that "the counsel's objection was justified."[358]

---

354 J. Kober, *Advokacie v českých zemích v létech 1848–1994* [Advocacy in the Czech Lands 1848–1994], Prague: Česká advokátní komora, 1994, p. 130.

355 ČAK, Soukromá obžaloba, č.j. Tk XIX 3487/47 [lawsuit].

356 File no. Ls 381/46.

357 ČAK, "Poslanci KSČ interpelují ministra spravedlnosti ve věci Ing. Horčičky z Havlíčkova Brodu [Deputies of the Communist Party question the Minister of Justice in relation to the case of Ing. Horčička of Havlíčkův Brod]." [Article].

358 "Odpověď ministra spravedlnosti na interpelaci poslanců Paška, Pešáka, V. Davida a Koštejna (tisk 485) ve věci protiprávního postupu krajského soudu v Kutné Hoře. [Response from the

Kamill Resler retracted his accusation against the journalists in 1948, before the court's deliberations, and had to pay legal costs of 3,580 crowns to the journalists' counsel, JUDr. Zikmund Stein.[359] He thought this would be the end of the matter but, as we shall see, that was not to be.

As for Stanislav Horčička, he was acquitted on eight counts and convicted on three, in particular supporting and promoting the Nazi movement, for which he was sentenced to one year in prison, although he had already served this time. He remained in contact with Resler until 1960, despite living in Brazil. The letters were addressed to Resler alone, and Horčička specifically asked Resler not to inform his family (who had apparently stayed in Czechoslovakia) about the matters they discussed. In 1959, eleven years after his case had closed, Horčička sent Resler 50 dollars to thank him for his defence.

THE END OF RESLER'S CAREER AS A BARRISTER[360]

After the communists came to power in February 1948, many things changed.[361] The Action Committees of the National Front, which were formed without any legal basis and retrospectively legalised by act no. 213/1948 Coll. on 21 July 1948, played a key role in the changes.[362] On 3 March 1948 Resler obtained confirmation from the Action Committee of the Bar Association in Prague that he was "for the time being authorised to practise as a barrister and to represent parties before the courts and authorities." What it was that made him request this we do not know. Perhaps he was unsure what would follow in the turbulent times, and wanted to take precautions.

Nevertheless very shortly afterwards, on 10 March 1948, he discovered from the newspapers that only barristers who obtained an authorisation to continue to practise would, from then onwards, have the right to represent before the courts and authorities. Resler was not given that authorisation, and so had to arrange for a deputy.

Minister of Justice to the questions by Deputies Pašek, Pešák, V. David and Koštejn (print 485) relating to unlawful action by the Regional Court in Kutná Hora]." [online]. [accessed 2017-11-28]. Available at: http://www.psp.cz/eknih/1946uns/tisky/t0634_00.htm.

359 AHMP 14, Decision on 3 April 1948.

360 Unless otherwise stated, the information in this section is based on materials from ČAK.

361 See Jiří Pernes. "Establishment and First Crisis of the Communist Regime in Czechoslovakia (1948–1958)." In Jaroslav Pánek, and Oldřich Tůma (eds.) *A history of the Czech Lands.* Prague: Karolinum, 2009.

362 For more on this see Jaroslav Mlýnský. *Únor 1948 a akční výbory Národní fronty.* [February 1948 and the Action Committees of the National Front]. Prague: Academia, 1948. On developments at the Bar, see Stanislav Balík. *Dějiny advokacie v Čechách, na Moravě a ve Slezsku* [A History of Advocacy in Bohemia, Moravia and Silesia]. Prague: Česká advokátní komora in co-operation with Národní galerie, 2009.

On 31 March 1948 the Regional Action Committee of the National Front in Havlíčkův Brod requested that Resler and judge JUDr. J. Komrs be removed from service. This was in connection with the Stanislav Horčička case (just discussed), in which two journalists had attempted to bring Resler down. In the end, Resler thought he would have done better not to withdraw his suit against them: the Action Committee would have expelled him anyway, but at least a verdict would have been reached.

On 12 April 1948 the Action Committee of the Bohemian Bar Association temporarily excluded JUDr. Kamill Resler from practising as a barrister for six months, with no reason given.[363] Resler appealed against their decision on 22 April 1948. He did not know what to plead, so simply outlined his whole career with emphasis on the proceedings he had conducted and his behaviour.

Although he was not happy with the situation, Resler enjoyed the five months when he was unable to practise. For a change, he did not need to worry about deadlines and hearings, but could immerse himself in legal and historical matters that interested him.[364] His practise was taken over by Dr. Kribel, who Resler reported spent very little on office expenses despite having a very high income – Resler later had to pay out substantial amounts to make up for this.[365]

On 24 May 1948 the Action Committee of the Bar Association in Prague confirmed that the reasons for Resler's dismissal – which were not stated – had not been dishonourable. The committee had acted on request of the publisher of the art magazine *Okénko do dílny umělcovy*, to which Resler had often contributed.

After this, Resler's situation began to improve. On 12 June 1948 the Action Committee of the Bar Association in Prague confirmed that it had no objection to issuing Resler with a certificate of loyalty to the state and nation,[366] which he needed in order to have the transfer of a share in a small rural property from his brother approved. Although the Action Committee rejected Resler's appeal of 5 August, it invited him to submit an application to be re-entered on the register of barristers, which Resler then did on 27 August.

On 5 September 1948 the Action Committee re-registered Resler, and a day later he received formal confirmation that he could once again practise as a barrister. One of his former trainees, JUDr. Krčma, congratulated him on the re-opening of his practice with a quotation from Božena Němcová[367]: "If you walk in the blistering sun, you will cast blistering shadows."[368] In a later

---

363 AHMP 14, Appeal.
364 AHMP 14, Letter to František Krčma on 17 September 1948.
365 NM, Letter to Antonín Švehla on 7 March 1951.
366 NM, Confirmation from the Action Committee of the Bohemian Bar Association.
367 A well-known 19th century Czech writer.
368 AHMP 14, Letter from František Krčma on 14 September 1948.

letter to the Bohemian Bar Association, Resler wrote that he considered the renewal of his membership in the Association "a reparation of the misgivings against me and an expression of trust."

For the new registration, Resler had to pay a registration fee of 1,550 Kčs and take the following oath: "I promise that I will be true to the Czechoslovak Republic and to its people's democratic regime. I promise that I will, always and everywhere, in my professional duties and otherwise, rigorously, diligently and genuinely observe the rights and interests of working people in the spirit of the Košice governmental programme, and will defend and protect those rights and interests. I am aware that there is no place for barristers who betray the Czechoslovak working people in any way." It is debatable what the Bar Association wanted to achieve with this oath, given that eight years earlier barristers had been forced to sign an oath of loyalty to Hitler if they wanted to continue their professional practice.

Resler himself took a realistic and resigned approach to the whole affair of his expulsion. In a letter to his colleague JUDr. Houska he mentioned that when the daughter of one late professor, whom he had defended during the war, had asked him what all the people he had helped during the occupation were doing, he replied to her dryly that they were not so much as lifting a finger; yet he would have been ashamed to appeal to them himself. Similarly, in an application for officers, sergeants and non-commissioned officers in the reserves, which he made in 1948 (this was probably required after the change of regime), he wrote under the question about his activity during the war that he would not provide evidence of having defended dozens of Czechs, because he did not consider it appropriate to appeal to those he had helped.[369]

In some instances, however, his past clients took the initiative themselves to speak up. When Zorka Koníčková-Pátová discovered by chance that Resler had been excluded from the profession, she wrote a letter to the Bar Association in Prague, in which she described his great contribution and help during the war.

Some of the last cases Resler dealt with included the defence of a number of individuals accused of fleeing abroad.[370]

It was not long after that Kamill Resler gave up his legal practice for good, this time on the grounds of ill health. He resigned his membership of the Bar Association on 31 December 1948. He had been overworked for a long time. In 1942 he had fallen down the stairs, which at the time he had put down to his excessive workload. The events of 1945–1947 were extremely stressful for him and he had in his own words "been on the edge of physical and nervous

---

369 AHMP 16, Přihláška pro důstojníky, rotmistry a poddůstojníky aspiranty v záloze [application to serve in the reserves].

370 NM, Letter to Vlastimil Vokolek on 10 November 1948.

exhaustion." He also wrote that "if my health improves such that I am once again able to practise my vocation, which I have enjoyed and which I am not happy to be giving up, I will request registration at the Bar once again." Although the only reasons he ever cited anywhere for having given up practising were those related to his health, it is possible that the fact that he was not sure whether he would be accepted to the Regional Association of Barristers, which came into being from 1 January 1949 with act no. č. 322/1948 Coll. concerning the Bar, may also have played a role. Indeed, his impression was that he would have been unable to practise once again. With the new law, only barristers affiliated with the Regional Associations of Barristers could practise, and these associations were not obliged to accept all registered barristers but could select those who in accordance with section 1 of the act were willing to contribute to the maintenance and strengthening of the democratic people's legal code. Resler did not consider himself one of them.[371]

Resler's health, however, did not improve even after the end of 1948. He began to suffer from Bürger's disease, a rare but serious disease of the blood vessels and nervous system, which caused him pain in his limbs. In 1952 he had a sympathectomy operation, (he was suffering from chronic pain and most likely had the operation to block the sympathetic nerves) which left him with a 17 cm long scar on his abdomen. After that, he began to have more and more difficulty walking.[372]

371 See also Jan Kober. *Advokacie v českých zemích v létech 1848–1994* [Advocacy in the Czech Lands 1848–1994]. Prague: Česká advokátní komora v Praze, 1994, p. 134, and Stanislav Balík. "Advokacie." In M. Bobek, P. Molek, and V. Šimíček (eds.) *Komunistické právo v Československu. Kapitoly z dějin bezpráví*. [Communist Law in Czechoslovakia. Chapters of the History of Injustice]. Brno: Masarykova univerzita, Mezinárodní politologický ústav, , 2009, pp. 892–911. Available at: http://www.komunistickepravo.cz.

372 PNP 47, Letter to Ladislav Přimda on 10 April 1954.

6. ARTIST AND ARTISTS' LAWYER TO THE END

Resler had two passions in his life: legal practice and art, which often became intertwined. He first came into the art world through his involvement in the anarchist movement, to which he was drawn via a rather unlikely and extremely unusual route – chess. In those days, various clubs met regularly at Prague's Union café, including the Mánes Association of Fine Artists, the anarchists, members of Masaryk's Realist Party, the Society of Czech Biblio-philes, and a chess club. At age fifteen, Resler played a mean game of chess and so he started to go to the café to play with his friends, and soon became a regular there.

In the period before the First World War, links between the Slávia and Union cafés were lively – strolling back and forth between the two was a reg-ular Sunday evening pastime. The Union café was established in 1820 and stood on the corner of Ferdinandova (now Národní) avenue and Na Perštýně street. The building it was in was considered for demolition as early as 1923 in order to widen the road, but it was not until 1941 that the café was eventu-ally closed by the Gestapo; in 1949 the road was finally rebuilt and the whole building pulled down.[373]

After eight o'clock in the evening, the promenading would come to an end and guests would settle down in the "Unionka," as they endearingly referred to it, where they would then remain until the small hours. They were always well looked-after by the café's waiter František Patera, who as Resler later recalled, often lent the guests cash to spend on "indulging in revelry," which usually involved cheap turkish tobacco, cigarette papers, matches and most importantly a glass of absinth. Resler would "discuss, or simply daydream, for hours over a glass of water, in which this venomously green liqueur floated about in glowing waves of green, yellow and red, mingling and infusing in a slow, playful swirling motion. (...) And then at midnight we would leave with the self-confident impression, that we had revelled most admirably."[374]

---

373 E. Csémyová, and K. Drössler. *Dvě ztráty v ulici Na Perštýně* [Two losses in Na Perštýně street]. [online]. [accessed 2017-11-28]. Available at: http://wayback.webarchiv.cz/wayback/20130916180 547/http://praguewatch.cz/reports/view/323.

374 Ladislav Tunys. *Noc před popravou. K. H. Frank a jeho obhájce*, Prague 1995, p. 17–18.

At the café, Resler met many notable figures of the times – writer Jaroslav Hašek, Viktor Dyk, Kamilla Neumannová, Karel Toman and others.[375] These encounters were often accompanied by lengthy debates, during which it was not rare for Resler to be asked his opinion on contemporary affairs.

The café outings came to an end when the First World War broke out. Resler would later recall: "After that we rarely heard anything about Mr Patera. Apparently, he was living in southern Bohemian town of Blatná in very modest conditions – if only all those who had owed him money from twenty-five years of 'Unionka' tabs and loans had paid up, he would have become a prosperous gentleman once again."[376]

WORK FOR THE NEUMANN FAMILY[377]

Over the course of his life, Resler represented more than a hundred Czech artists, often for free. Among them poet Stanislav Kostka Neumann, who was a close friend of his, particularly stands out. Resler respected Neumann as a writer and as an anarchist: he had been a leading figure for a generation of anarchist rebels at the end of the 19th century. Resler represented Neumann from 1932 until his death; between 1932 and 1945 this was on the agreement that Neumann would pay Resler for his services only once he was able and willing to do so. The cases involved were a variety of small disputes, from corrections in the press to tax returns and bodily harm.

In 1933 Neumann ran over a young lady named Evženie Hlavešová, née Hejdánková, who claimed for compensation for having suffered concussion, a broken collarbone, internal injuries and various grazes. As a result of the accident, Neumann had his driving licence taken away.[378]

Resler represented Neumann in the case that followed, and the matter was settled peacefully. In Resler's opinion those involved were "very decent people, who (...) do not want to capitalize on your accident and even now, appreciating your financial situation, do not want to cause you difficulties by exacting the money. Nevertheless I would strongly advise you to attempt to pay at least a little contribution." Neumann raised 200 Kčs, as he did not have any money himself. In 1940 Resler attempted to persuade him to pay some more, with no apparent success. When Neumann then died, he left assets in the form of his royalties from copyright, and so in 1950 Resler returned to this

375 Muchka, p. 14.
376 PNP 83, Sporé vzpomínky a vzpomínky na vzpomínky na kavárnu Union [Recollections of the Union Café].
377 PNP, Neumann Stanislav K., Neumann Stanislav – herec, Neumannová Božena.
378 *Národní listy večerník*, no. 110, Friday 21 April 1933, p. 1.

case, traced the lady, who by that time had grown up, and paid her the amount that had been owing.

After his exclusion from the bar and S. K. Neumann's death, Resler sent Neumann's relatives a bill for 6,543.40 Kčs for his work, and also submitted a claim as part of his inheritance proceedings. He did this for two reasons. After the war Neumann's work had become very successful, while Resler's situation had become much worse due to being excluded from the Bar. He concluded his letter to Neumann's relatives with the words: "I am extremely sorry that I can no longer represent your interests, which were always close to my own, since as an enemy of the people I have now had to step down from the profession." He offered to pass their cases on to barrister JUDr. Miroslav Houska, who was the General Secretary of the Central Action Committee. Houska had previously been Resler's trainee, and had worked on some of the Neumann affairs in 1933. Furthermore, he was not only a barrister but also a poet, playwright and translator.

Even so, Resler continued to manage a few matters for the Neumann family, including S. K. Neumann's inheritance; Neumann had decided about this as early as 1934, writing to Resler: "I took a bit of a beating from a minor stroke, just as a warning, and so don't be annoyed with me for remembering that I ought to write my will, and sending you my proposal, which is very clumsy, but carefully considered." Its contents were to remain confidential until his death. He made additions to his will on 18 December 1945 and 11 March 1947. He left his copyright to his three children, a third to each, and named František Hrubín, Ladislav Štoll and Jiří Taufer as the administrators of his literary works. Small household items were left to his partner Lída Špačková, who was to give his literary papers to the named administrators immediately and in particular ensure that Neumann's legal wife Božena Neumannová, with whom he had not lived for twenty years, did not have access to them.

Resler worked on Neumann's inheritance proceedings from the day of his death on 18 June 1947 until sometime in 1953. From 1949, when he had already left the Bar, he did this work for free – and he was not the only one; notary Vladimír Kalda also waived his fee for working on Neumann's affairs in 1950, despite having done a substantial amount. Resler thanked him warmly.

Based on the addendum to his will, Neumann's ashes were to be scattered in the forest by his actress daughter from his second marriage, Soňa Škodová-Neumannová. Resler claimed, however, that Neumann's wishes had later changed and that he wanted the urn containing his ashes to be given to KSČ (the communist party). Hence Resler himself took them from the crematorium, and because there was not yet a suitable place for them at the KSČ, he kept the urn in his own flat for a month and a half before temporarily storing it at the Central secretariat of the KSČ, where it remained, although

Soňa was not happy about this. In 1950 she also reminded Resler to pay her the rental property profits that were her and her siblings' rights from the inheritance. Resler responded to her by letter, reporting the accounts of all the investments that Stanislav Neumann had made in the house, to which Soňa as co-owner had not contributed, and asking her to pay one third of the costs. No response to that letter survives in Resler's archives.

One of the hurdles that Resler had to deal with in the proceedings was the question of Neumann's second wife, Božena Neumannová née Hodačová, from whom he had been separated for 20 years and his "third" but unofficial wife, his partner Lída Špačková. Božena had taken her husband to court in the '30s to demand that he pay maintenance for her and for their daughter and a dowry. She also attempted to deprive him of a voluntary honorary contribution he had received from the Ministry of Education, but Resler managed to prove before the court that as an honorary gift this could not be taken away.

In 1949 Božena sent a letter to Stanislav Neumann the younger, a well-known actor who was Neumann's son from his first marriage to Kamilla Neumannová née Krémová, in which she poignantly demanded money from the inheritance. Stanislav forwarded the letter to Resler, who reckoned that it was capable of "touching even an old cynic," such as himself. Resler responded to Stanislav: "What can we expect from little womanhood, reliant on 'soft cheeks', a seductive bosom and curvy hips – attractive, but passing values, with which it attempts to cover up its subconscious mental inferiority? And on the other side a man who, despite his confidence, fighting spirit, even aggressiveness and childish naivety, is carried away by his emotions and faith – what could that result in? (...) The matter itself is clear (...). I know that you and your sister trust me to handle the matter in a polite manner."

Neumann's second wife was also involved in another incident with which Resler dealt in1951. At that time, Božena was helping to organise a house-move for Mr and Mrs Nedbal, who were moving from Teplice to Austria to be nearer their daughter. A thank you letter they had written to her accidentally reached Kamilla Neumannová, Neumann's first wife, instead. Resler wanted to pass the letter on discreetly to Božena Neumannová, since in it the Nedbals promised to send her 15,000 crowns "for charity," but Božena complained to Resler that his discretion over the letter gave the impression that she was accepting a bribe. Nevertheless, it is clear from the letter, which Resler kept, that the payment was for her services.

Meanwhile, Resler had a better relationship with Neumann's first wife Kamilla. He represented her in a number of suits, in particular related to copyright and book distribution. Kamilla Neumannová ran the publishing house *Knihy dobrých autorů* (KDA, Books by Good Authors), and considered this the only thing she had to pass on to her children. In 1954 Resler published a book about her work entitled *Vydavatelské dílo Kamilly Neumannové* (Kamilla

Neumannová's Publications). When she died in 1956 she left Resler a small painting.

COPYRIGHT DISPUTES

Thanks to his frequent contact with authors, Kamill Resler often worked on matters to do with copyright. He did so both academically – for example, in 1942 he published a short book entitled *Původská práva po Jaroslavu Vrchlickém* (Jaroslav Vrchlický's Copyright) – and in his legal practice. The most famous authors he represented were Stanislav Kostka Neumann and Franz Kafka.

STANISLAV KOSTKA NEUMANN[379]

Resler took care of S. K. Neumann's copyright affairs after his death. During the year and a half immediately preceding his death, Neumann's works had started to bring in significant money, such that Neumann was better off in his sickness and death than he had been during the whole of his life previously, when he had lived a hand-to-mouth existence. Resler did not want anyone except Neumann's relatives to know about his increased royalties in his final year and a half, as this could have led to envy and disputes, and so carefully avoided showing the royalty accounts to anyone but Neumann's heirs. Resler placed S. K. Neumann's interests above everything else.

Unlike other legal services he provided to the Neumann family, though, Resler did not provide copyright administration for free. He charged 5% of the royalties, which was a usual amount at the time; the Československé divadelní a literární jednatelství – Dilia (the Czechoslovak Theatre and Literature Agency) also charged this rate. Initially, Resler represented all three of Neumann's inheritors: Stanislav Neumann and Kamila Značkovská, Neumann's children from his first marriage to Kamilla, and Soňa Škodová-Neumannová, his daughter from his second marriage to Božená. In 1953 Soňa transferred her representation to the Czechoslovak Theatre and Literature Agency – *Dilia*, which provoked several disputes between the copyright administrators. That, however, did not change anything about the way their fathers' rights were managed, since decisions about the rights had to be taken by the majority of inheritors. Resler exchanged many letters with *Dilia* about the Neumanns' copyright matters. He attached a personal appraisal to one of them, which was also a statement of his approach to his profession: "there were times when people represented St. K. Neumann out of friendship and respect for his work, on the agreement that he would pay 'when he could' and

---

379 PNP, Neumann Stanislav K.

'when he felt like it' and at the same time made sure that he was not in need; there were people who represented his family for a lifetime and did not take as much as a haler from them in fees."

The greatest dispute was over the fees for the rights administrators themselves – Resler and *Dilia*. Resler held the view that he, as representative for the majority of the rights holders, carried out all the work and therefore had the right to claim 5% of royalty income from all the rights holders, and not only from the inheritors he directly represented. *Dilia* did not share this view, and wanted Resler to take a share corresponding only to the inheritors he represented.

The positive side of Resler's collaboration with *Dilia* was that despite their many disagreements, they succeeded in working together to publish Neumann's works.

FRANZ KAFKA[380]

In the years after the war, Resler briefly took care of Franz Kafka's literary legacy. Four of Kafka's heirs authorised Resler to negotiate on their behalf. They chose him because one of them – Věra Projsová – had known Resler for many years, and because he was an expert in copyright law. The four heirs in question were the daughters of the original heirs, who had been killed during the Second World War. While working for them, Resler got into a dispute with Dr. Max Brod and his lawyer.[381] Why was this?

Max Brod had a contract with Kafka's previous heirs that gave him the right to "decide in literary matters related to Kafka's works." But this, according to Resler's letter to Brod, did not include the rights to "assign the works for financial gain," that is, to sign contracts for the works to be published. For the heirs, for example, it was unacceptable that Brod had signed a contract with the publisher Schocken Verlag in Tel Aviv in 1940, according to which any Czech publisher wishing to print the works would have to pay Schocken Verlag, as indeed would the heirs should they have wished to publish the works themselves. That contract, according to Resler, had been signed without the then copyright holders' consent, and therefore they were not bound by it. This was one of the reasons why Resler forbade Brod and the Schocken publishing house from publishing Kafka's works at all, which they did not obey. Even so, the main reason why Resler wrote to Brod in the first place was a different, very simple matter – money. Between 1934 and 1940 only 100,000 Kčs in royalties had been collected for the heirs, which seemed to them to be rather little.

---

380   PNP 48; PNP, Kafka Franz, inv. no. 2098–2103.
381   Max Brod was a German speaking Czech (later Israeli) Jewish writer who published Franz Kafka's works.

Max Brod's British lawyer held the opposite view – he believed that Brod had the right to publish the works and manage the profits from doing so, and that Kafka's inheritors had given their agreement in 1936 to the signature of a general contract with the Schocken publishing house.

In a letter to Josef David, Max Brod wrote that Resler's negotiations – on the inheritors' behalf – revealed Kafka's heirs' outrageous ungratefulness to Brod. He also wrote that, to go by what Resler was claiming, Resler's letters (and arguments) did not have any weight. It is not easy to judge who was really in the right. After reading that letter, the heirs assured Brod that they were not ungrateful towards him, and that on the contrary they greatly respected him. However, they were in a difficult financial situation and so were requesting the money that they were entitled to. They also read a copy of Resler's letter after he had sent it, but described his tone as "business-like" and put certain phrases down to the fact that he was a barrister.

Gerta Kaufmannová, one of the heirs, who had just become a British citizen, retracted her authorization for Resler to represent her on 4 March 1947: it was disadvantageous to her to have money from Palestine first of all converted into Czech crowns and later into pounds. At the time, British citizens had to put all their assets into British banks. Through the remainder of the dispute, Gerta supported Schocken Books and Max Brod.

As a result of this development, and because he had retired from the Bar, Resler did not take the case any further, and his representation did not end very well. While many of Neumann's works had been published in Resler's care, his attempts to publish several of Kafka's books while he represented Kafka's heirs, on which he worked together with Václav Petr, Pavel Eisner and Karel Projsa, ended unsuccessfully.

RESLER'S LITERARY ACTIVITY

As we have already seen, Resler was active on the literary scene in many capacities. He wrote and translated articles and books, and collected rare historic documents.

He was extremely strict with himself when it came to his creative writing. Before making an article or book public he had to be completely sure that the text was perfect – he would never have allowed an unfinished work to be published.[382]

---

382 PNP 69, Letter to Selma Etrichová on 10 October 1949.

ARTICLES

From an early age and throughout his life Resler contributed to numerous magazines. Examples of his articles include: *Knihomilství a jeho poslání* (Bibliophilia and its Mission) published in *Literární noviny*; *Z básnických osudů: Kamil Berdych* (Poetic fates: Kamil Berdych) in *Kritický měsíčník* and *Knižní značka dělnické akademie* (The Workers' Academy Book Logo) in the magazine of the Association of Collectors and Friends of Ex Libris in Prague, in which he published frequently during the war and until the 1950s. He also published several articles in the Society of Czech Bibliophiles' bulletin – for example, *K literární prvotině Karolíny Světlé* (On Karolína Světlá's First Work); *Římská vzpomínka na Josefa Horu* (A Roman Recollection of Josef Hora); *Kamila Neumannová, vydavatelka knih dobrých autorů* (Kamila Neumannová, publishing books by fine authors); *In memoriam přítele Jana Žižky* (In Memory of our Friend Jan Žižka) and *O Františku Koblihovi* (On František Kobliha). A complete list of Resler's publications is nowadays available in the National Museum archives.

It is amusing that when Resler himself put together a list of the magazines to which he had contributed, he listed (coincidentally?) the magazine Česká advokacie (Czech Advocacy) straight after *Erotická revue* (Erotic Review), although the list is not in alphabetical order.[383]

Resler did not only write about others' lives, but also gave talks. In addition to many talks on K. H. Frank, which we have already mentioned, Resler enjoyed introducing the public to his favourite literary minds, especially Leo Freimuth and S. K. Neumann. He also spoke about "The late poet Ivan Suk," "Jaroslav Hašek in the builders' apprentices' boarding house" and "A brief history of the secret Czechoslovak socialist press."

BIOGRAPHIES

As we have seen from the titles of the articles he wrote and the talks he gave, Resler enjoyed looking into the lives of key figures in Czech literature. This was not only because he wanted to keep the memory of these important people alive in the nation's mind, but also because he believed they would serve as examples of courageous acts to inspire and inform future generations.

It was in that light, for example, that he narrated the life of Antonín Bouček,[384] who had sold Czech literature for very low prices between 1938 and 1945, including banned literature and books that were supposed to be

---

383   NM, Undated document entitled JUDr. Kamill Resler.
384   Kamill Resler. "Vzdor Antonína Boučka. [Resistance of Antonín Bouček]." *Nový život, měsíčník Svazu čs. spisovatelů*, no. 8 (1954), p. 185–187.

being destroyed. He obtained the books from publishers as well as from other sources. Probably the most interesting book that he got hold of was poet Svatopluk Čech's *Vzpomínky z cest a ze života* (Memoirs of Life and Travels), volume three, which recounted Čech's journeys to Russia. He had taken them during a police inspection in a book warehouse: while the police were inspecting the rear part of the store, these books were in the front part and no-one was watching, so he was able to appropriate them and prevent them from being destroyed.

Resler wanted this story to show how an ordinary person had acted bravely in his everyday life and, like many others, fought his own little resistance fight on a daily basis. Resler had known Bouček well, as he had represented him for several years during the First Republic when he was editor of *Rudé právo*, and had also later worked on his inheritance.

Resler worked on several biographies – he wrote comprehensively on the life of publishers Michael Kácha and Karel Janský, as well as Josef Florian and S. K. Neumann. On the latter he also wrote several articles, and together with Neumann's partner Lída Špačková he developed a short film about Neumann for Československý státní film (Czechoslovak State Film). Not only had Resler been S. K. Neumann's friend, but he was also interested in the fact that he had always remained an honest, virtuous man and Resler had always had great respect for him, seeing him as young-at-heart and something of a rebel.[385]

AS A TRANSLATOR AND PUBLISHER

On occasion, Resler also published his own books. These were largely private print-runs of not more than a few hundred copies, and were often beautifully decorated; he let himself be guided in his publishing activities by what he considered to be beautiful. This meant having artists decorate the books, and often having the books printed on hand made Van Gelder paper, which the Society of Czech Bibliophiles also used. This was, for example, the format in which he published both Karel Hynek Mácha's *Deník mnichův a jiné práce* (A Monk's Diary and other works) and V. H. Brunner's book *Dobrodružství na Sahaře* (An Adventure in the Sahara), from which he intended any profits from the book's sales would go to Brunner's heirs.

In addition to his own writing, Resler also translated. He spent a long time translating E. A. Poe's tale *The Raven*, and also translated several other works, including Rilke's poems and Robert Louis Stevenson's *Treasure Island*, which he translated into Czech as *Ostrov s poklady* (literally: island with treasures).[386] In 1954 he published a text in the Czechoslovak Academy of Sciences' maga-

385 PNP, Neumann Stanislav K., inv. no. 4000–4002.
386 PNP 109, Handwritten translation.

zine Česká literatura (Czech Literature) entitled České a slovenské překlady Internacionály (Czech and Slovak translations of the Internationale).[387]

What Resler's knowledge of languages was really like is not entirely clear. Historian Jiří Kotyk claims that Resler was fluent in Latin, Greek, German, Italian, French, English and Serbo-Croat.[388] And yet in all the materials that survive from Resler there are only Czech and German texts, and Resler himself only makes a mention of the Serbo-Croat in addition to these. His archives and papers do not reveal anything about other languages, and when he received a letter after the war that was written in English he had to have it translated.

NEW YEAR CARDS[389]

Resler regularly made cards to send to his friends wishing them a happy new year, and these were works of art in their own right. As each year drew to a close, Resler would already have an idea of the image that he wanted to draw. He would describe this to one of his artist friends – such as Jan Konůpek or František Bidlo – and get them to produce a drawing. He accompanied the picture with a short text or poem of his own, or something by another author, and the phrase "best of luck in the new year." These cards illustrate Resler's view of events in the Republic from another perspective, and often reflect his circumstances in the given year and events in his life. Resler sent these new year cards almost every year between 1937 and 1955.

Two of the cards he produced – in 1948 and 1954 – deserve particular notice. In 1948 Resler did not produce the card alone, but was assisted by his longstanding friend and colleague JUDr. Jiří Mašek, who wrote a little booklet composed of four poems and entitled *Básně na oslavu právních věcí, které projednával JUDr. Kamill Resler, právní zástupce a obhájce v trestních věcech, zástupce chudých a obhájce z povinnosti atd* (Poems celebrating the legal matters negotiated by JUDr. Kamill Resler, legal representative and counsel in criminal matters, representative of the poor and defence counsel by duty, etc.).[390] The first recalled the Holan-Mánes case, while in the second Jiří Mašek paid tribute to Resler:

---

387 Kamill Resler. "*České a slovenské překlady Internacionály*. [Czech and Slovak translations of the Internationale]." Česká literatura II., no. 2, (1954), pp. 189–192.

388 Jiří Kotyk. *JUDr. Kamil Resler*. [online]. 2005 [accessed 2017-11-28]. Available at: http://archive. is/2013.01.05-210038/http://www.kpp.iipardubice.cz/1123596021-judr-kamil-resler.php.

389 NM, New year cards; PNP 112, New year cards from 1937 and 1941.

390 Kamill Resler (ed.). *Básně na oslavu právních věcí, které projednával JUDr. Kamill Resler, právní zástupce a obhájce v trestních věcech, zástupce chudých a obhájce z povinnosti atd.* [Poems celebrating the legal matters negotiated by JUDr. Kamill Resler, legal representative and counsel in criminal matters, representative of the poor and defence counsel by duty, etc.]. Prague: Kamill Resler, January 1948.

Chorál oslavný	(Festive Hymn)

Personál čistě vymyt	Waiting staff pristinely dressed
ztich, stojí v špalíru.	Stand silently in line.
Geburstag račte Vy mít,	Have a birthday – be our guest!
vsáh' básník na lýru,	A poet strikes his lyre,
k paiánu by ji zladil	The piano joins in with him
ve službách Zderazu.	Rousing Zderaz anew,
Dav klientů tam pádil,	Hoards of clients bustle in,
družičky v svérazu	Like some odd wedding crew.
a nikdo ani nedých,	And no-one catches their breath
když letmo síní mih'	As pale phantoms slip past –
zjev bílý popravených	Those who had gone to their death
úspěšně hájených.	Defended to the last.
Když slávořeči začnou	Speeches now get under way
splétat se ve věnec	Weaving their wreath of cheer.
už s retardací značnou	After quite a long delay,
přišel i slavenec.	The birthday boy is here.
Na dny své značně vzhledný	Rather handsome for his years
(Dantova podoba)	(Dante's re-incarnation)
moh'– nebýt neposedný –	Standing still he disappears
být stavu ozdoba.	'Mid the decoration.
Přátelé v koutku (ví se)	Just a few friends with a frown
zříš jenom neplesat:	Huddle near the whiskey:
„Zda-li pak usadí se	"Do you think he'll settle down
až bude šedesát?"	When he reaches sixty?"
Červ závisti je ztlamil.	The worm of envy got them.
Leč síní burácí:	But now the room resounds:
„Ať žije Resler Kamill	"Long live good Kamill Resler
a všichni junáci!"	And all young partisans!"

This was Mašek's way of remembering the Sedmík and Staatspolizei case. His third and fourth poems were based on Resler's defences before the Extraordinary Courts after the war. In late 1954 Resler organised a big party for his 60th birthday. Aware that it was a special occasion, he decided that rather than organise one large celebration, he would organise two weeks of public events dedicated to his birthday. The celebrations kicked off on 17 December with a ceremonial parade. This was followed by two days of spiritual preparations and a day of rest, so that on Monday 21 the main party could take place, followed by Party no. II on Tuesday and no. III on Wednesday. On that Wednesday 23 December a three-day series of birthdays began – first Kamill Resler's, then foremother Eve's, and finally Jesus'. After a necessary break, Party no. IV took place on Monday 28 December and after one final rest day, the celebrations concluded with Party no. V.

He sent out an invitation for this programme of events in place of his usual new year's card, and accompanied the invitation with the lines:

Děkuji všem	I thank you all,
kdož si vzpomněli i všem,	whether you remembered
kdož si nevzpomněli,	or whether you forgot,
s přáním zdraví a zdaru	and wish you health and success
v novém roce	in the new year.
Kamill Resler.	Kamill Resler

Many of Resler's friends responded to this invitation, or to the announcement of Resler's jubilee in the paper *Literární noviny*, which engendered a similar reaction to that one often experiences today thanks to birthday reminders on Facebook.[391] The messages flooded in from various groups: from people for whom Resler had worked, from writers, bibliophiles and literary organisations, and from other friends. A few of the many messages he received are described here.

Alois Dyk wished that Resler might still live to see greater justice, which would scrutinize and equalize; this was something that Dyk strongly believed in.

Antonie Florianová wished him God's mercy and peace, which the world could not give him.

Jiří Hroz wrote him a few poems, one of which he called *Osud advokáta*, "The fate of a barrister."

Právu kdysi dravě sloužil.	Once he ruthlessly served the law.
Zachraňovat lidi toužil.	His ambition was to save us all.
Přejme mu, že šťasten byl,	We trust though that he now takes pride
sebe sám, že zachránil.	That he himself came out alive.

---

391   PNP 91, Numerous letters and greetings.

After Christmas he received belated birthday wishes from editor Jan Ziegloser, but his was not a traditional greeting: "One step forwards – two steps back, our money's down the d…n – happy holidays".

HIS OWN LIBRARY

Much as he loved all his creative hobbies, Resler's greatest passion lay in yet another – collecting books. Throughout his life he was a passionate collector and gradually built up his library, trying to obtain copies of every edition of each work as far as that was possible. He had complete collections of the first editions and special editions of works by Otokar Březina, Petr Bezruč, the Čapek brothers, Jaroslav Durych, Viktor Dyk, František Gellner, Josef Hora, František Hrubín, Vítězslav Nezval, Jaroslav Seifert and many others. He also owned incomplete collections of Karel Erben, K. H. Mácha, Božena Němcová, R. M. Rilke, E. E. Kisch and others.[392]

Resler spoke of bibliophiles as people who loved reading, "… not books. A bibliophile feels the need to be with books, surrounded by books, build himself a secret world made of books." That is how Resler opened his article in *Literární noviny* entitled *Knihomilství a jeho poslání* (Bibliophilia and its Mission),[393] in which he describes book-lovers and their desires and experiences. He takes as his example a character from the novel *Temno* (Darkness) by Alois Jirásek, who wrote historical novels based on Czech history. When the character found a rare book for sale "in a dirty shed near St. Gallen's church or in a small, dark, Jewish shop, (…) he had to hold himself back several times, while looking at the book he had long been looking for, which made his heart pound and his hands tremble, so as not to give away how much it meant to him." Czech book-lovers were, according to Resler, eager to learn, to give others joy, and to broaden their horizons. Theirs was a "love of books for the artistic pleasure, education and knowledge that they could provide, expressed through collecting books from certain fields or of certain types with a particular emphasis on the books' rarity and on books that were perfectly crafted or illustrated by artists."

Resler particularly appreciated decorated books – special limited editions. He explained that "making them was hard work for the publishers and artists who edited and decorated them, and for the typesetters, printers and bookbinders; they taught them to work precisely and perfectly, and so they had an overall positive influence on the art of book making." However,

---

392 NM, Letter to the Financial board of the District National Committee Prague XII delivered on 8 December 1958.
393 Kamill Resler. "Knihomilství a jeho poslání." *Literární noviny*, no. 1 (1951), also PNP 73.

Resler continued, there were not so many of these "in the current conditions," when book production was supervised by the authorities who preferred large print-runs to educate the masses, and "therefore, collecting books is a meaningful and important activity even in the Socialist state."

Resler had begun to collect books when he was a teenager, and as he grew older, he began to look abroad to complete his collections. He was therefore in correspondence with dozens of second hand bookshops across Europe – from Vienna to Münich and Berlin, from Zürich to Amsterdam and Paris – and in New York.

Even when times became very tough, Resler did not stop ordering books. In October 1938 he was communicating with a bookshop in Paris, and in 1944 bought over 1,000 marks worth of books from a German second-hand bookseller. In June 1948 he was once again writing to a Viennese bookseller about an order. The amount he spent on these books was not insignificant; for example, in 1935 he made a purchase from the Offenbacher bookshop for 1,706 Kčs.[394] Similarly, when his acquaintances were struggling with poverty or debts he would often offer to buy their books from them.[395]

Resler's library was divided into the following collections: General literature, *Biblioteca magica et pneumatica*, The 1938 Czech Autumn, Anarchist Archives, and *Biblioteca erotica et curiosa*. He made these collections freely available to students and others for research.[396]

The collection that Resler considered his most important – and his most treasured – was his library of magic, which was composed of books about the history of superstition, campaigns against superstition, and reactions to superstition in historic laws. He was convinced that there was no match for his collection of books on this topic among any of the private collections in central Europe; for example, Resler claimed that he owned 21 out of the 24 published editions of the book *Malleus maleficiarum*.[397] Another extremely valuable item in his collection was the original court file from the last witch burning in central Europe.

Resler had built up this impressive collection gradually, over many years. Part of it, for example, came from a collection put together by Ema Destinnová, a Czech opera singer who was also interested in literature about sorcery, and had even had her own magical bookplates made.[398]

394 PNP 98, Correspondence with second-hand booksellers.
395 PNP 109, Letter to František Mastík on 8 March 1933.
396 NM, A biography of JUDr. Kamill Resler written by his daughter.
397 NM, Prague Library of Magic.
398 NM, Letter to the Czech Literary Fund on 2 December 1956.

KAREL DYRYNK'S MAGICAL EXPERIENCE IN KAMILL RESLER'S LIBRARY

Some visitors associated Resler's library with magical experiences, and Resler told the story of one of these from Dyrynk's perspective in his 11-page tale *Karel Dyrynk a čarodějnice* (Karel Dyrynk and the Witches):[399] "It was all the fault of Resler's magical library. Its black magic, with all the Sprengers, Molitors, Bodins and God-knows-what all the witches, magicians and sorcerers call their spells, was quite overwhelming. We had a look around the library yesterday – Halas, Picka, doctor Wolf and I. And all at once it enchanted us with its secretive, dark, alluring atmosphere, and captivated us all with its contents and how it pervaded the quiet, medieval, mysterious surroundings.

The room itself was tucked away in a back corner, away from all disturbances, narrow, tall, cramped, its walls hidden behind cabinets and shelves full of old volumes, pictures of dark and mysterious scenes, and cases containing all kinds of magical tools. Between them were two tables, also piled high with mysterious tomes. One of them was evidently a study desk, as the books on it had been pushed to the sides, and in the space that had been cleared between them lay some sort of unfinished manuscript, an old, heavy ink bottle and a quill pen. There were also two bottles of whisky and a few glasses.

Then we gradually began to look at the enigmatic volumes. We became engrossed in the old, yellowed pages of mysterious incunables and early prints of forgotten sciences, browsing and browsing, unable to tear ourselves away. Resler started talking, telling stories, explaining, expounding. He transported us back to the dark, bygone days of the middle ages, when all the spells and statutes in the books were terrifyingly real, helping or hurting the people who believed in them, when people shivered in fright and powerlessness in the face of them, when people were burned because of them and judged according to them. He transported us back to those bygone days, as if he were clearing the dust that had slowly settled on them over the centuries, and brought them back to life as if we were there ourselves. It made an unusual, very deep impression on us.

It was already nearing midnight when we left. I walked home slowly, my head full of deep thoughts following the strange evening. It was a dark night, the sky overcast with thick clouds, with the still, muggy air before a storm. When I reached the square it struck twelve.

No sooner had the clock struck than an abrupt gust of wind blew, swishing through the tops of the trees, shaking them violently, and whistling around the gutters. I looked up, and at that moment spotted high above the houses – quite to my fright – the figure of a woman on a broom. She drove her strange vehicle nimbly, flying in an elegant

---

399 Kamill Resler, (ed.). *Sborník na památku Karla Dyrynka, knihtiskaře, tvůrce písem, knihomila a člověka* [An Anthology in Memory of Karel Dyrynk, Bookprinter, Writer, Bibliophile and Gentleman]. Prague: Československý spisovatel, 1951.

figure of eight around the church tower, and vanished before my stunned eyes just as suddenly as she had appeared. Once I had recovered from my initial shock, I couldn't keep myself from laughing! What things the imagination can produce!"

After Resler ceased to practice as a barrister, his library and the activities of the Society of Czech Bibliophiles occupied a substantial amount of room in his Prague offices. In addition to the private study institute (at the beginning of the 1950s the library recorded 450 visitors in a period of 22 months), the Society of Czech Bibliophiles held daily office hours there, and used the offices as a base for its other activities, including magazine publishing, storage, and correspondence.[400]

During the '50s the authorities repeatedly attempted to empty the three rooms in which these activities took place and return them to residential use. The housing office eventually gave up its attempts, on the orders of the KSČ Central Committee and based on advice from Československý spisovatel, one of the best-known publishing houses in Czechoslovakia at the time. In 1952, there was a plan to move the collections to different premises – which prompted Resler to write to ing. Vlastimil Borek, Deputy Minister of Foreign Affairs to ask him to intervene – but this was eventually called off.[401] In 1955, as part of a move to return certain rooms in residential houses that had been used for administrative purposes to their original residential use, the industrial division of the board of Prague 1's District National Committee decided to terminate the rental contract for Resler's offices at Na Zderaze 11.[402] The daily paper *Mladá fronta* also repeatedly provoked its readers against Resler, criticising the authorities for failing to return his former legal practice to residential use.[403]

Resler, though (and the Society of Czech Bibliophiles) did not want to relinquish the space, and so applied to be allocated appropriate alternative premises. Resler's library had been praised by the assistant Chair of Czech and Slovak literature at Charles University's Philological faculty, thanks to which Resler was in a better position to negotiate. The Ministry of Education and Culture, whose department for the Preservation of State Heritage considered the library to be a collection worthy of preservation for its artistic and historical value, also got involved in the search for suitable alternative premises, and arranged for a shop unit in the New Town to be allocated for the purpose. During his campaign to maintain the status quo, Resler also

---

400 PNP 73, file no. 463/52, Letter to the residential officer of the District National Committee in Prague.

401 PNP 73, Letter to Ing. Vlastimil Borek on 29 July 1952.

402 NM 216/362.

403 "Bibliofil, byt a byrokracie [Bibliophile, Apartment and Bureaucracy]." *Mladá fronta*, 3 July 1956, p. 4, also PNP 91.

wrote to the then Minister of Culture, Ladislav Štoll.[404] As it turned out, the proposed premises were not suitable, and neither were others that were then proposed – they would have needed costly alterations and were damp, therefore unsuitable for documents. In the end, the Prague 2 District National Committee closed the case in spring 1956 on the grounds that it did not have a suitable alternative space. That, of course, did not please editor Vladimír Solecký of *Mladá fronta* in the slightest, and he wrote another article in the paper in response to the decision, although that had no effect on Resler being able to remain in the offices.[405] According to researcher Pavel Muchka, "on 11 March 1956 a dislocation agreement was made, which allocated Resler and the Society of Czech Bibliophiles one room of 70 m² a and part of a neighbouring storeroom belonging to the Ústředí uměleckých řemesel (Centre for artistic crafts) at no. 595/19 Celetná street, in the Old Town [district of Prague]."[406]

After Resler's death, his library was not preserved, primarily due to a lack of space and the family's financial situation.[407] However, while he was still able, Resler had already begun to gradually transfer his books to national institutions. He gave some of his documents to the library of the National Museum in Prague even before the Second World War, and others during the '50s and 60s. Some books also were sold, by Resler himself and later by his heirs, in times of material hardship. For example, in the 1950s, Resler offered many of his collected volumes to museums for purchase, while he gave them others for free.[408] Several institutions were aware that Resler himself owned various old works, and that if he did not himself have those they were interested in, he might well know where they could be obtained. During the '50s, the following institutions all made enquiries with Resler about buying books from him or with his assistance: The Library of the National Museum, The National Museum of Literature, *Karáskova galerie*, The Institute of Czech Literature, The Museum of Decorative Arts, Ústav dějin KSČ (the communist party's historical institute), The Czech Fine Arts Fund, The Theatre Museum, The Jewish Museum, The Brno House of Arts, The Institute of Journalism Studies in Prague, and others. Resler also drew up various special contracts for several of these institutions, and did not charge them a fee for doing so; he considered this his duty as a good Czech bibliophile.

---

404 PNP 91, Letter to Ladislav Štoll on 13 December 1955.
405 "Bibliofil, byt a byrokracie." *Mladá fronta.* 28 April 1956, p. 3, also PNP 73.
406 Muchka, p. 62–63. N. B. This account does not appear to be consistent with the other evidence presented on this matter.
407 VCM, A biography of JUDr. Kamill Resler written by his daughter.
408 PNP 91, file no. 463/52, Letter to the residential officer of the District National Committee in Prague.

Similarly, he took as his honourable duty the supervision of two masters theses at the Journalism department of Charles University's Philosophical Faculty; one of these examined Czech anarchist magazines.[409]

Numerous visitors came to Resler's library, both students and friends. Many of them wrote in Resler's visitors book. One thick book covered the years 1950–1959, more precisely from 20 October 1950 until Christmas 1959, which Resler described with the words: "Ten years of records. So many fortunes / such effort / such work / so many successes / so many disappointments / so many beginnings and endings these simple entries capture. A period when the generation that gave the nation what it had desired for a century – freedom and independence – was dying; a period when the nation was waiting – for its second desire to be met – for a fair social order to be established."[410]

ENCOUNTERS WITH THE REGIME

25 February 1948 is today considered a turning point in Czechoslovak history, as the date on which the totalitarian regime took hold. What were Resler's feelings about the new system? The fact that the Communists had taken power did not have a huge effect on his life, as he wrote in Autumn 1949 in a letter he sent to Venezuela: "I am living quietly through a time of huge societal reshaping, and focusing on my work."[411] Even so, he came into contact a few times with the new regime's security services.

On 3 February 1949, representatives of the *Sbor národní bezpečnosti* (National Security Corps) came to inspect Resler's home. Resler described this experience in his story *Domovní prohlídka / Lidově demokratická povídka* (House Inspection / A People's Democratic Tale),[412] which is briefly summarised below.

Kamill had been working day and night for two days when, at around one o'clock in the morning, the criminal police knocked on his door. They had come because someone had informed them that Resler was keeping a large number of tins of food (which the police presumably considered to be a sign of illegal trading), which they had seen being brought to his flat. Resler and his wife showed the police officers their whole flat, including several hundred tins of food from the American UNRRA support units. When the police failed to find the tens of thousands they had expected, they asked whether

---

409 NM, Letters to Kamil Rösler on 23 February 1959 and to Kamill Resler on 3 March the same year.
410 PNP 91, Note at the end of the visitors book.
411 PNP 69, Letter to Selma Etrichová on 10 October 1949.
412 NM, "Domovní prohlídka" ["House search"] story.

Resler had a car. "I have not yet been able to afford a car, a fur coat or a bowler hat," was his reply.

The uninvited guests were also surprised at how small Resler's wardrobe was, and how few clothes he had. They had probably expected a former barrister to have cupboards full of suits. Some of the last rooms they inspected were the kitchen and larder, where the police failed to notice some tins that were wrapped in paper and two wine bottles containing lard. At the end, while the policemen were somewhat grumpily writing up their report that the information had been false, Resler asked whether they would also like to look inside the piano, where he had taken to hiding flour back in Hitler's day. They ignored this slightly ironic comment, remarking that they were looking for tinned food and not gold, and similarly rejected Resler's offer of a shot of schnapps before their departure. The story ends with the words: "The authorities authoritatively took their leave."

That same year, Resler was contacted once again by the state security services. He described it in another of his unpublished autobiographical stories, which he called simply *Provĕrka* (A Vetting).[413] The vetting referred to in this case took place in several stages. First of all, they vetted him by phone. Next, they posed as telephone repairers in order to ask the concierge of the house where Resler lived about his family. The third vetting took place at the Bar Association, where they copied out the list of barristers whom the Action Committee had excluded from the profession after February 1948. However, they only wrote down the names of those who had been permanently excluded, not those whose exclusion was temporary. Resler concluded his account with the words: "On Monday 3 October 1949 men who threatened the people's democratic system, or who were avoiding work, began to be sent to forced work camps." Resler was not among them.

Historian Jiří Kotyk states in his article *JUDr. Kamill Resler* that Resler was "a victim of the new totalitarian regime. He suffered extreme nervous exhaustion. Only by a hair's breadth did he escape being taken to a forced work camp as a 'work-shy creature', by hiding in a rented flat. In the '50s he made his own translation of A. Koestler's book *Zatmění slunce* about the Moscow Trials of the '30s."[414] Where this information came from, though, is not clear. Based on Resler's description of the events in his story *Provĕrka* (A Vetting) it does not seem likely that he was supposed to be taken to a forced work camp, nor that if he had been, he would have avoided it by temporarily hiding in a different flat. In a later article, Kotyk softened his claims and states instead: "Because he found it hard to find work, he spent many days in a rented flat

---

413   NM, Autobiographical tale 1949, "Provĕrka".
414   Jiří Kotyk,. *JUDr. Kamill Resler.* [online]. 2005 [accessed 2017-11-28]. Available at: http://archive. is/2013.01.05-210038/http://www.kpp.iipardubice.cz/1123596021-judr-kamil-resler.php.

in order to avoid an ID check and not be considered a 'work-shy creature'."[415] That, on the other hand, contradicts Resler's own claim in late 1949 that he was not subject to compulsory work.[116]

Resler did not get involved in any opposition activities, and tried to steer clear of possible provocations. In 1954 he handed some leaflets that he had found pushed under his door in to the police. One of them was the leaflet "Free Europe no. 17," which featured a picture of a tractor harvesting straw and the words: "This year's harvests are the harvests of national self-defence. With everyone's collaboration we will secure the crop, which the greedy regime wants to ruthlessly take away."[417] In 1959 Resler estimated the state's attitude to him as follows: "The current regime behaves very decently towards me and appreciates that my activities are useful, in particular within the literary community. And I am far happier in these activities than in legal practice." Their attitude to Resler also changed after it had come to light that Resler had defended communists free of charge during the First Republic and in particular under the Germans.[418] Hence after that Resler's problems were largely only financial.

Resler with his friend, writer Jaroslav Seifert, Nobel laureate for literature. (NM)

As a Bibliophile, at the end of the 195s. (NM)

415 Jiří Kotyk. *JUDr. Kamill Resler (1893–1961), oběť šikany komunistického režimu.* [JUDr. Kamill Resler (1893–1961), Bullied by the Communist Regime]. [online]. 2011 [accessed 2017-11-28]. Available at: http://www.kraj.kppardubicka.cz/stranky/cti-prispevky.php?id=JUDr._Kamill_Resler_ (1893%961961),_obet_sikany_komunistickeho_rezimu.

416 VCM, CV for Orbis.

417 See e.g.: *Žatec ve třetím odboji. Odbojová skupina Praha–Žatec.* [Žatec in the third resistance. The Prague–Žatec Resistance Group]. [online]. [accessed 2017-11-28], p. 8. Available at: http://www.ustrcr.cz/data/pdf/vystavy/zatec-3odboj/panely.pdf.

418 NM, Letter to Zdeněk Kratochvíl on 18 January 1959.

Both Resler's children were members of the Communist Party, as were his brother and his son, and almost a fifth of the Czechoslovak population. Resler himself was never a member of any political party, as he notes in the story *Provĕrka* (A Vetting). He was nevertheless strongly critical of card-carrying communists, in particular his son-in-law.

With his wife Libuše. (heirs)

In 1958. (AHMP)

EMPLOYMENT AND RESLER'S FINANCIAL SITUATION

Resler ceased practice as a barrister for good at the end of 1948. Although he was not obliged to work after that, he himself wrote that he wanted to continue working, and that he needed a job largely for financial reasons. In a private letter, he wrote "at the age of 56 I left the Bar and became a writer, and have found myself at the outset of a career for the second time in my life, with bare hands and no pension or income, muddling along as best I can. So far I have managed not to lose my good cheer." In another letter he describes it thus: "I never get away from life's struggles. No sooner have I got over one hurdle than another comes along, but so far I have just about managed to stay on my feet."[419]

---

419 NM, Letter to Kristian Fanta and Vlastimil Vokolek.

In 1949 he tried to get a job in the rare and antiquated prints department at *Orbis* publishers, since that field was familiar to him as a bibliophile.[420] He did not get the job there, but did get many other jobs after leaving the legal profession; these were often temporary and not particularly well paid.

In later years Resler sometimes even had difficulty providing for his own household financially. And so from the time that Resler left the Bar, his wife Libuše's brothers began to help them out financially. In order to repay his debts to Libuše and her family, Resler left his library to her in his will.[421]

To begin with, Resler's income largely came from collecting old debts from his legal clients, which his debtors often paid in instalments over many years. A few examples follow. Writer Ferdinand Schlögl-Merzina owed Resler almost 24,000 Kčs, which he paid in instalments in the early 1950s.[422] At that time Resler was also receiving payments from Major Jaroslav Beneš from Červené Janovice, who had borrowed 5,500 Kčs. Resler sent Beneš a request for the remaining fifth of the loan and asked him to really pay it this time – at least in instalments – because he was in financial difficulty.[423]

Even so, despite his difficult situation, Resler was very benevolent about people paying off their debts to him. He constantly conceded to new "non-extendable" deadlines for his creditors, and gave them plenty of time to find the money. He wrote to writer Běla Vičarová that he wanted to come to a compromise with her, and that it would be enough for him if she sent him even a very small instalment, or at least a letter, so that he could see that she was trying. However, when she failed even to make contact he had no choice but to demand that she pay the full amount of 2,400 Kčs – although he did not want to take her to court.[424]

Bigger problems occurred when some of Resler's former clients moved abroad. For example, in 1950 he reminded Marianna Steinerová, who was by then in London, that she owed him 15,734 Kčs for legal services he had provided in 1948. She refused to pay the debt on the grounds that he had begun to ask for them too late – two years after the case had closed.

The Czechoslovak National Bank, on the other hand, would not leave Resler alone, and continually reminded him from 1950 until 1962, to collect his outstanding receivables. If he had not made proper attempts to recover these amounts, as he was required to do by section 7 para. 1 of exchange act no. 92/1946 Coll., he could have been tried for threatening the exchange economy, under section 145 of criminal act no. 86/1950 Coll., or at the very least for an exchange offence under section 64 of administrative criminal act no. 88/1950

420 KNM 1, CV for Orbis.
421 NM, Letter to Libuše Reslerová from her husband.
422 PNP, inv. no. 5303–5345.
423 PNP 118, Letter to Jaroslav Beneš on 26 October 1954.
424 PNP 46, Letter to Běla Vičarová on 12 August 1948.

Coll. The authorities' reminders stopped only after his death, when Kamill Resler's heirs informed them that the paperwork relative to the amounts he was owed had not been preserved.[425]

In 1951 Resler was briefly employed to organise the library at the Central Association of Barristers (previously the Bohemian Bar Association in Prague). However, he was not properly paid for this job according to the laws in place at the time, and so he also had to make a claim against the Central Association of Barristers to obtain fair pay for his work.[426] For the remainder of the year he prepared the book *Sborník na památku Karla Dyrynka* (An Anthology in Memory of Karel Dyrynk)[427] for publication, and received 15,000 Kčs as an advance on the sales of the book.[428]

During Resler's legal career, the Reslers set aside plenty of savings for their retirement. However, the 1953 currency reform deprived them of these, and so they instead had to begin to sell off their property, including the piano.[429] In 1953 Resler's total income was 5,629 Kčs, which was not sufficient to live off.

This meant that Resler also had to sell off some of his collections. In early 1955 he successfully offered the Museum of Decorative Arts in Prague his collection of emergency money. This consisted of German, Austrian and Czech currency made of various materials – including paper, but also canvas, silk, leather, wood, clay, glass and metal. Examples of so-called emergency tender are emergency banknotes issued on pink paper by the village of Velká Hamra at the beginning of the First World War due to a lack of coins; money made of yellow metal with the words "Supplement 20 halers," issued by the *Elektrické dráhy hl. města Prahy* (the electrical rail transport company in Prague) in 1918; wooden money from the village of Hadersfeld in the Vienna Woods from 1920 and vouchers for 25 pfennigs made in Berlín in 1921. For Czechs, the 100-mark banknotes issued by the city of Constanz in 1922 were particularly interesting; they bore the image of a head and the title "John Huss"[430] with a text in German stating: "O Hus, you would not have been burned for your teachings today – the despicable usury nowadays means that firewood is too expensive." Meanwhile, the banknote for five hundred marks has two images on it: Hus having his ecclesiastical title removed, and Hus being taken to the

---

425 PNP 69, Application to write off amounts owed from abroad on 17 April 1962.
426 NM, Letter to the Central Association of Barristers on 24 April 1953.
427 Kamill Resler,. *Sborník na památku Karla Dyrynka*. [An Anthology in Memory of Karel Dyrynk]. Prague: Československý spisovatel, 1951.
428 PNP 66, Letter to Československý spisovatel on 3 August 1951.
429 NM, On K. Resler, by Blanka Brunnerová, 1998.
430 Hus was a Czech protestant reformer of the early 15th Century who was burned at the stake in Constance in 1415.

stake. Resler asked for 900 Kčs for his collection, which contained 438 items, and this was granted.[431]

On the basis of his many activities for the good of Czech literature, which we shall discuss further, Resler requested a monthly grant of 1,000 Kčs from the Czech Literary Fund in 1955.[432] He explained in his application that he was in receipt of an army pension of 30 Kčs per month and that his son received a disability pension of 500 Kčs, out of which he paid maintenance for his daughter Eliška of 270 Kčs. He requested this grant every year until 1960 and was always successful, which was a great help to him.

In 1958 the Reslers spent some time in the spa town of Teplice in Bohemia, where they received warm greetings from their friends the Seiferts, whom they had met on many occasions both at the Seiferts' home and in Resler's office.[433] Because of the services that Resler had provided free of charge to Seifert during the war, in relation to a case concerning housekeeping wages, Seifert had offered to repay Resler if he needed it. In 1954 Seifert sent Resler 2,000 Kčs "for past services, for which you forgot to charge me" which he had made from his book *Nad listy M. Švabinského* (On M. Švabinský's letters), and for which Resler was extremely grateful.[434] He had considered the matter long forgotten, since Seifert had no obligation to pay him anything – Resler had represented over a hundred people for free in the same way, and did not consider that the services he had provided free of charge should later be paid for, nor did he expect anything of the sort. Nevertheless, he desperately needed the money at the time, and the contribution Seifert sent him enabled him to breathe easier.[435]

In 1959 Resler was granted a pension of 270 Kčs per month, which reflected 12 years of social security contributions; the years during which he had practised at the Bar were not counted.

Even though he had been a member of the Association of Czechoslovak Invalids since 7 June 1952, Resler found himself a new job again for financial reasons in 1960, at the age of 67.[436] This was at the Regional Culture House for the Prague region, where he was involved in cataloguing the libraries of national castles and palaces. He began at the castle in Hořovice; here, Resler had the impression that everything was haunted by the ghost of a foreign nobleman. Even his very first day there was strange: he reported that one visitor, a German lady, who looked very kind and deeply compassionate, mistook him

431 PNP 109, Kamill Resler: Emergency tender collections and letter to the Museum of Decorative Arts on 2 January 1955.
432 NM, Letter to the Czech Literary Fund on 2 April 1955.
433 NM, e.g. letter from Seifert on 28 October 1954.
434 NM, Letter from the Society of Czech Bibliophiles on 28 December 1954.
435 NM, Letter to Jaroslav Seifert on 2 January 1955.
436 NM 216/301, Membership card for the Association of Czechoslovak Invalids.

for a German duke who was living out his miserable old age in an unfriendly country and hostile class, and bowed to him. Resler bowed in return. The second day, some electricians from Strašnice made the same mistake.[437]

As always, Resler did his best to be paid as he should be according to the law. While he was working in the castle libraries, he believed he was not being paid correctly for his travel and meal allowances.[438] He also had a few other small problems – he had to ask for a new lamp, he tried to get his secretary to work harder, and he wanted to have improvements made to the flat he had been assigned.[439] After finishing in Hořovice he continued his work at the castle in Křivoklát, but he did not manage to finish his work there.

A few days before his death he announced: "It is bad when an old man has to work, but it is brutal when an old and ill man has to work!"[440] His wife wrote: "It was all utter torture and to no avail, we still didn't get anything, we lost everything, all his life's work for nothing."[441]

KAMILL RESLER'S DEATH AND WILL

Kamill Resler died in 1960 – but this was not JUDr. Kamill Resler, only his namesake. At least nine of Resler's acquaintances went to the funeral, and when Resler found out, he thanked them all and told them he hoped they would be able to attend his funeral once again.

At the end of June 1961, Kamill Resler was admitted to hospital in Vinohrady. He did not have much appetite and the only thing he enjoyed were two portions of ice cream. While he was in hospital his cousin died, but he was not told on account of his own frail condition. On Tuesday 11 July he read a letter from his grandchildren in Nasavrky, telling him what had been happening there: that their teeth hurt, that they were going to pick cherries, how they missed him, and how much they were looking forward to seeing him. After reading the letter Resler lay down, fell asleep, and never woke up again. A sudden spasm had caused insufficient blood flow to his brain, and death.

That day, Resler's son had phoned the hospital and the doctor had told him that his father was doing well, which he had immediately written in

---

437 Resler on himself: Hořovice; Křivoklát, AHMP 16. Muchka writes that Resler worked for the Castle Libraries department of the National Museum Libraries, but that does not correspond to what Resler wrote himself. Nevertheless, Muchka provides a more detailed account of Resler's library work: Muchka, p. 67.

438 NM, Odvolání proti rozhodnutí s j. č. 649/61 [appeal].

439 NM, Letter to the Local National Committee council and the accommodation commitee of the Křivoklát National Council, delivered on 17 July 1961.

440 AHMP 17, JUDr Kamill Resler, b. 23. 12. 1893 died 11. 7. 1961.

441 AHMP 16, Handwritten note by Libuše Reslerová.

a letter to his mother, Resler's wife. The hospital was quicker to inform her of his death, which it did by telegram, inviting her to begin making funeral arrangements.[442]

A short notice announced Resler's death in the papers, and a longer article was also published in the newsletter of the *Spolek sběratelů a přátel ex libris* (Association of Collectors and Friends of Ex Libris) in Prague.[443] The urn containing his ashes is – together with those of his wife and son – kept at the Czechoslovak Hussite Church's church in Vinohrady, which is next to a park named after a person close to his heart – poet Petr Bezruč. Poet J. Zhor captured his character well in the lines: "He never trod the beaten track, and never bowed his head to anyone. Such a man was Kamill Resler."[444]

After Resler's death, his relatives received hundreds of letters of condolence. Those who wrote focused particularly on his work as a writer, and included numerous personal memories of Kamill Resler as a barrister, artist and friend. One lady wrote about his life as follows: "He filled his life with compassion for human suffering, and the fight against evil; may the knowledge of that comfort you in your grief." The Kiesewetter family was also among those who had not forgotten Resler.

His funeral did not take place entirely as he had wished. In 1941 he wrote that he wanted to be cremated in a coffin made of rough planks of ordinary unpainted wood, covered in a square black flag with a crimson ribbon in the corner, without flowers or other decorations. He wanted his sabre, which was scorched from a grenade explosion in Russia in September 1915, to be laid at the foot of his coffin. The music was to be sprightly and upbeat, not funereal. In reality, the anarchist coffin decoration he had wished for was replaced with a traditional wreath, but Suk's *V nový život* (New Life) march was played, as Resler had specified in his will. As a bequest, the sum of 1,111 Kčs was to be paid to a young proletarian poet, to be selected by Josef Hora, František Halas and others.

Over the course of his life, Resler changed his testament and the provisions he had made in case of his death, and in fact his simplest will was his last. In a version of his will that he wrote on 20 September 1944, Resler left everything to his wife, who was in turn to pay obligatory shares to their children – Kamill Jiří and Blanka – and reasonably reward the employees at his legal practice. However, he later disinherited his daughter Blanka, because on the very same day, for no apparent reason, she refused to help look after her brother Kamill who was suffering from an attack of nervous anxiety, and would not let him into her flat in the late evening. That will was then replaced

---

442 AHMP 17, Telegram to Libuše Reslerová received 12 July 1961.
443 AHMP 17, News of the Association of Collectors and Friends of Ex Libris in Prague.
444 Tomáš Pasák. "Bouřlivák Kamill Resler. [Rebel Kamill Resler]." *Lidové noviny*, 30 April 1994, p. IV.

by a new will that Resler wrote on 18 February 1945, from which Blanka was still excluded. As a result of the disinheritance, Blanka was to lose out on 100,000 crowns, as well as property and other items left to her in the previous will of June 1938. In the new will, Resler left his properties to his son – that is, the houses in Hlásná Třebaň and Nasavrky and land in Hlásná Třebaň and Radotín. In the section on his library, Resler specified that his heirs must look after the library and make use of it "for personal freedom and the freedom of all people," but only on condition that they remain true Czechs. He then bequeathed "endurance" and "the fight" to all his descendants. In other matters he was very generous – he left substantial amounts of money to several of his friends and 1,000 Kčs to each of his employees, per year they had worked for him. His wishes for his funeral remained similar to those he had expressed in 1941, but the grant for the young poet was now seven times higher.

Resler's last will, written in August 1953, was extremely short. In it he established his wife Libuše Reslerová as his sole heir, without mentioning any others; they would have received shares as stipulated by the law.[445]

After Resler's death, his wife was granted only a basic pension – at first 189 Kčs, and after her appeal 197 Kčs per month.[446] This was later raised, but only after Resler was accepted posthumously as a member of the *Svaz protifašistických bojovníků* (Union of Antifascist Fighters), which he had deliberately refrained from applying for after the war, out of selflessness. The deputy Prime Minister of the time was František Krajčír, who was a bibliophile and so knew Resler and showed great understanding.[447] On 31 May 1969 Resler was also posthumously recognised as having been part of the National Fight for Freedom.[448]

The Czech Literary Fund sent Resler's widow a one-off contribution of 2,000 Kčs to help her in her difficult situation, even without her asking.[449]

Resler's son Kamill Jiří Resler died on 24 July 1970 by jumping from a third floor window. Up until then, he had worked as a university librarian and as a translator.[450] He suffered from many illnesses, both psychological and physical, as a result of which he was not able to study medicine. According to MUDr. Sobotka from the Ústav soudního lékařství (Institute of Forensic Medicine), his body was as worn out as a sixty-year-old's, although he was only 43.[451] During checks in 1970 his membership of the communist party

---

445   NM, Will, and Blanka Brunnerová's comments on it.
446   AHMP 16, Pension statement.
447   Note by Blanka Brunnerová, AHMP 16.
448   VCM, Certificate of participation in the fight for freedom.
449   PNP 91, Letter from the Czech Literary Fund on 17 July 1961.
450   PNP 112, Thanks from the family for words of comfort following the death of Kamil Jiří Resler.
451   NM, Letter from Blanka Brunnerová on 22 May 1987.

(KSČ) had been cancelled, which had affected him deeply, as he had long had a very good position in the party – for example, while at university he had taken on the role of campaign secretary.[452]

Resler's daughter Blanka married radio clerk Jiří Brunner, son of V. H. Brunner, a writer about whom Resler had published a book, and whom he had supported. The Brunners and their three children spent a year in Moscow in 1956.[453] Jiří became the manager of a publishing house and of the magazine *Svět Sovětů* ('World of Soviets') and was a member of the board of the *Svaz československo-sovětského přátelství* (Union of Czechoslovak-Soviet Friendship).[454] It was Blanka who took care of many of Resler's papers, sorting them and giving or selling them to various archives, and helping to ensure Resler's wishes were met. Among other things, she also contributed to the development of the screenplay for the film *Ex offo*.

Blanka lived to see the 100th anniversary of Resler's birth, for which an exhibition was held at the National Museum in 1994. The Museum of Czech Literature in Prague and the J. A. Comenius Pedagogical Museum in Prague also jointly organised an afternoon in Resler's memory.[455]

Blanka Brunnerová died on 21 September 2001.

---

452 NM, Campaign secretary's notebook.
453 PNP 69, Letter to Salma Etrichová on 8 October 1956.
454 VCM, Literary works by Kamill Resler, final page.
455 VCM, Invitation to memorial afternoon.

AFTERWORD

Kamill Resler's life is inspirational in at least two ways. First, it may influence the way we see the defence lawyer's position within a fair trial. Kamill Resler demonstrates how the defence should behave, both from a legal and from a humane perspective. Second, he offers us a view of something greater – he points out that each of us should live justly and should do our best to resist evil., Finally, Resler's life is proof that it is possible to live correctly regardless of the times, even under a Nazi or communist dictatorship.

When Kamill Resler defended K. H. Frank, he set the standard of defence extremely high. For today's lawyers his situation is more or less unimaginable. He defended a man he detested, and who had been personally responsible for his own relatives' and friends' deaths. He was given one week to prepare for the trial. Although the trial took up several entire weeks of his time, he was not paid for it, and as a result of his absence from the office he lost several other clients to his competitors. The media, and society more generally, were firmly against him. He knew full well that the judges were also not favourable towards his client.

Despite all of these obstacles, Kamill Resler made a successful defence. Success in defence does not mean the client's acquittal, but ensuring that the trial proceeds fairly. In this case, K. H. Frank was sentenced according to the law and as the result of a fair trial. The arguments that Resler raised during the proceedings were related to all possible procedural and material flaws. After all, Resler realized that if Frank's conviction was to be seen as the result of a fair trial and not as an act of revenge, he needed to use all the tools the law made available to him.

Indeed, Kamill Resler went further than the law required of him. He discussed Nazi crimes with Frank and spent the last three hours before the execution with him. He understood that the defence lawyer is granted to the condemned as the last person in the world who must stand by him – including during the moments before his execution. During those moments he tried to cheer Frank up, to distract him from his impending execution and to shield him from outside pressures, especially from journalists. He attempted to help him not only on a legal level but also as a fellow human.

The result of Resler's defence was that all those present could see that the trial was fair. Neither the public nor Frank himself could consider it a simple act of revenge. Indeed, Resler claimed that Frank eventually abandoned Nazism: evidently, his influence as defence lawyer was very great. The question remains as to whether a defence lawyer should, or could, play a role in the accused acknowledging guilt for certain actions. As Karl Jaspers wrote in the Question of German Guilt in 1946, being pronounced guilty does not help us in the more crucial matter of admitting our guilt and changing our ways.[456]

Over the course of his career, then, Resler experienced times when he knew that the procedures would be fair, and times when it was clear a fair result could not be expected, both during the Nazi period and at the beginning of communist government in Czechoslovakia. When the legal side of things failed, for example when Czechs were wrongly convicted during the war, he at least tried to deal kindly with their relatives and loved-ones, arranging for them to visit the prison during the trial, or just before the execution, or translating last letters home. There is a clear dichotomy between Resler's dealings with his clients as a lawyer and those as a fellow human, although the two approches came together in his relations with certain clients, in particular the close artist friends whom he represented for free.

What inspiration can a barrister take from Kamill Resler's life? To be meticulous and to fight properly for one's clients using various legal tools. While doing so, Resler never crossed the ethical boundaries appropriate to a barrister, nor did he behave dishonourably. It is therefore possible to take from him the lesson that it is possible to achieve legal victories even when acting honourably – which sometimes does not seem easy today. And that a barrister should never stop being a human, and recognizing that he is dealing with other people – and not with objects.

The Frank defence was the outcome of a life in which Resker dealt with various less challenging defences and situations; he did not become who he was overnight. While defending Kiesewetter he discovered what it is like to lose one's friends as a result of defending an "enemy of the nation." During the war, he discovered what it is to defend people who are to be executed and know that there is little you can do to change that outcome. Over the course of his career he defended many clients for no financial reward and discovered that it was worthwhile. He spoke perfect German and was, for Kiesewetter for example, capable of conducting litigation in German. He did not avoid stressfu situations or cases, especially if he believed that their aim was good. His earlier cases thus gave him a taste of all the individual aspects that eventually came together in the Frank trial.

---

456 For an elaborated discussion on this topic see Jakub Drápal. "Význam přístupu obhájce k pachateli na případu K. H. Franka [The significance of the defence counsel's approach to the accused in the K. H. Frank case]." In R. Svatoš, J. Kříha (eds.) *II. Kriminologické dny*. České Budějovice: VŠERS, 2014, pp. 14–45.

The second inspiring message of Resler's life is that it is possible to live correctly anywhere and at any time. At the beginning of the 1950s, at the peak of the communist reprisals, Kamill Resler wrote in a letter to a friend, "one can live anywhere." He was honest and brave in demonstrating how difficult situations could be overcome. Resler was born in Austria-Hungary, and fought for four years during the First World War and a further two years in the newly independent Czechoslovak Republic. Under the First Republic he spent a happy twenty years, at the end of which he stood up for justice even against several of his friends and part of the nation. During the Second Republic he worked to protect his Jewish colleagues, and during the Second World War was active in the resistance and defended dozens of Czechs (most of whom were executed) and helped their families. For three years after the war he intensively defended individuals against whom he had himself long fought; this was extremely difficult for him to come to terms with personally. He survived the harshest of the communist repression by staying out of the limelight, hardly scraping together a living. His important role only began to be recognised by society in the second half of the 1950s.

Throughout all of the periods mentioned, Resler's behaviour demonstrated that it is possible to live an honourable and just life anywhere – each period required him to adapt to external circumstances to some extent, but at the same time, Resler never crossed his own strong moral boundaries. This was clear when he refused to shoot insurgents during the First World War (although only theoretically), objected to people being judged according to a criminal code that contravened human rights during the Second World War, and, after the war raised questions about the legitimacy of the Czechoslovak legislation. Like many others, Resler frequently found his personal values and views to be in conflict with the requirements of the political regime at the time; in these conflicts he displayed greater resourcefulness and bravery than many others. At times, he stood up to the external pressures directly; at other times he skilfully avoided their hardest blows. A good example is that when a compulsory meeting of lawyers was organised to mourn Heydrich's death, Resler did attend and sign his name, but then slipped out by the back door so that he would not have to sit through the meeting itself, which went against his conscience. Nevertheless he was often willing to object more publicly, such as during his efforts to protect his Jewish colleagues during the Second Republic, or through his activities for the resistance movement. The question of when one should stand up to the regime and when one should be willing to come to a compromise has been central to Czech history throughout the 20th Century, and there is no simple answer. Resler's life offers us one solution which, though not simple, is as a whole inspiring, effective, and impressive for its integrity and courage.

Taking such a courageous and honourable approach to life was never easy under any regime, although it was harder under some than others. It was always necessary to fight and to stand up for justice, while knowing how to relax and not destroy oneself. With his declaration that "one can live any-where" Resler efficiently summarised his entire story, and the ethos by which he had lived his life. His example reminds us though, that it is also a question of quality of life.

REFERENCES

AGNEW, Hugh. *The Czechs and the Lands of the Bohemian Crown.* Stanford: Hoover Press, 2004.

BALÍK, Stanislav. *Dějiny advokacie v Čechách, na Moravě a ve Slezsku* [A History of Advocacy in Bohemia, Moravia and Silesia]. Prague: Česká advokátní komora in co-operation with Národní galerie, 2009.

BALÍK, Stanislav. "Advokacie [Advocacy]." In *Komunistické právo v Československu. Kapitoly z dějin bezpráví* [Communist Law in Czechoslovakia. Chapters of the History of Injustice], edited by Michal Bobek, Pavel Molek, and Vojtěch Šimíček, pp. 892–911, Brno: Masarykova univerzita, Mezinárodní politologický institut, 2009. Available at http://www.komunistickepravo.cz.

BORÁK, Mečislav. *Spravedlnost podle dekretu* [Justice by decree]. Ostrava: Tilia, 1998.

BRYANT, Chad. *Prague in Black. Nazi Rule and Czech Nationalism.* Cambridge: Harvard University Press, 2007.

CORNWALL, Mark. "'A Leap into Ice-Cold Water': The Manoeuvres of the Henlein Movement in Czechoslovakia, 1933-8." In *Czechoslovakia in a Nationalist and Fascist Europe, 1918-1948*, edited by Mark Cornwall, and Robert John Weston Evans, Oxford: Oxford University Press and British Academy, 2007.

CSÉMYOVÁ, Eva, and Karolína DRÖSSLER. *Dvě ztráty v ulici Na Perštýně* [Two losses in Na Perštýně street]. [online]. [accessed 2017-11-28]. Available at: http://wayback.webarchiv.cz/wayback/20130916180547/http://praguewatch.cz/reports/view/323.

DRÁPAL, Jakub. "Význam přístupu obhájce k pachateli na případu K. H. Franka [The significance of the defence counsel's approach to the accused in the K. H. Frank case]." In (eds.) *II. Kriminologické dny*, edited by R. Svatoš, and J. Kříha, České Budějovice: VŠERS, 2014, p. 14-45.

DRÁPAL, Jakub. "Postup advokacie proti židovským advokátům [The Bar's Move Against Jewish Barristers]." In *Rozpad židovského života: 167 dní druhé republiky* [The Disintegration of Jewish Life: 167 Days of the Second Republic], edited by Marcela Zoufalá, Jiří Holý, and Pavel Sládek. Prague: Academia, 2016.

DIMOND, Mark. "The Sokol and Czech Nationalism, 1918-48." In *Czechoslovakia in a Nationalist and Fascist Europe, 1918-1948*, edited by Mark Cornwall, and Robert John Weston Evans. Oxford: Oxford University Press and British Academy, 2007.

DŽAMBO, Jozo. *Advokat koji je volio knjige. Život češkoga pravnika i bibliofila Kamila Reslera (1893-1961).* A lecture delivered in Česká Beseda, Sarajevo, 28 April 2016.

Ex offo, [film]. Directed by Jaromír Polišanský. Czech Republic, Česká televize, 1997.

FROMMER, Benjamin. *National Cleansing: Retribution against Nazi Collaborators in Postwar Czechoslovakia.* New York: Cambridge University Press, 2005.

GEBHART, Jan, and Jan KUKLÍK. *Velké dějiny zemí Koruny české: Svazek XV. a 1938-1945* [The Great History of the Lands of the Czech Crown: volume XV.a 1938–1945]. Prague: Paseka, 2007.

GEBHART, Jan, and Jan KUKLÍK. *Velké dějiny zemí Koruny české: Svazek XV.b 1938-1945* [The Great History of the Lands of the Czech Crown: volume XV.b 1938–1945]. Prague: Paseka, 2007.

HRUBÝ, Jan. *Aféry první republiky* [Affairs of the first Republic]. Prague: Práce, 1984.

CHODĚJOVSKÝ, Jan. *Miloslav Hýsek.* [online]. 2012 [accessed 2017-11-28]. Available from: http://abicko.avcr.cz/archiv/2007/3/07/.

K. H. Frank - vrah Českého národa před soudem lidu, proces a rozsudek nad K. H. Frankem [K. H. Frank, murderer of the Czech people before the People's Court, the Trial and judgement of K. H. Frank], Pravda 1946/7, Žilina.

KLINE, Mary C. "Benedict Roezl – Famous Orchid Collectors." *Amer. Orch. Soc. Bull.* 32, no. 8 (1963).

KOBER, Jan. *Advokacie v českých zemích v létech 1848–1994* [Advocacy in the Czech Lands 1848–1994]. Prague: Česká advokátní komora v Praze, 1994.

KOSATÍK, Pavel. *Advokát, který měl rád knížky* [A barrister who liked books]. Český rozhlas Vltava, broadcast 18.06.1995 at 20:00.

KOSTA, Oskar. "Hledání a bloudění Franze Kafky [Franz Kafka's Searching and Wandering]." *Nový život, měsíčník pro literaturu a umění*, no. 10 (1958).

KOTYK, Jiří. *JUDr. Kamill Resler.* [online]. [accessed 2017-11-28]. Available at: http://archive.is/2013.01.05-210038/http://www.kpp.iipardubice.cz/1123596021-judr-kamil-resler.php.

KOTYK, Jiří. *JUDr. Kamill Resler (1893–1961), oběť šikany komunistického režimu* [JUDr. Kamill Resler (1893–1961), bullied by the communist regime]. [online]. 10.08.2011 [accessed 2017-11-28]. Available at: http://www.kraj.kppardubicka.cz/stranky/cti-prispevky.php?id=JUDr._Kamill_Resler_(1893%961961),_obet_sikany_komunistickeho_rezimu.

Kreditanstalt der Deutschen. [online]. [accessed 2017-11-28]. Available at: http://www.cnb.cz/cs/o_cnb/archiv_cnb/fondy/kredit_deutschen.html.

KROUPA, Drahoslav. "Poslední dny a chvíle K. H. Franka [K. H. Frank's last days and final moments]." In *Almanach VIII. B, maturitního ročníku 1942 reálného gymnázia v Třebíči* [Class VIII B final year almanach, 1942, *Reálné gymnazium* in Třebíč], 1997.

KUKLÍK, Jan. *Czech law in historical contexts.* Prague: Karolinum, 2015.

KÜPPER, René. *Karl Hermann Frank (1898–1946): Politická biografie sudetoněmeckého nacionálního socialisty* [A political biography of the Sudeten German National Socialists]. Prague: Argo, 2012.

KÜPPER, René. *Karl Hermann Frank (1898–1946): Politische Biographie eines sudetendeutschen Nationalsozialisten.* Munich: Oldenbourg Wissensch., 2010.

KUTHAN, Pavel Jaroslav. *V těžkých dobách (2/20): První dobrovolníci* [In hard times (2/20): The first volunteers]. [online]. [accessed 2013-09-15]. Available at: http://www.valka.cz/clanek_11043.html.

LÁNÍČEK, Jan. *Czech, Slovaks and the Jews 1938–48: Beyond Idealisation and Condemnation.* Basingstoke, UK: Palgrave Macmillan, 2013.

MASTNÝ, Vojtěch. *The Czech Under Nazi Rule: The Failure of National Resistance 1939–1942*, Columbia University Press, 1971.

MELŠOVÁ, Jitka. *Ústecké kalendárium – květen 2011.* [online]. [accessed 2017-11-28]. Available at: http://www.zpravodaj.probit.cz/2011/UOkalend_5_11.htm.

MLÝNSKÝ, Jaroslav. *Únor 1948 a akční výbory Národní fronty* [February 1948 and the Action Committees of the National Front]. Prague: Academia, 1978.

MUCHKA, Pavel. *Kamill Resler, právník a bibliofil* [Kamill Resler, lawyer and bibliophile]. Bachelor dissertation. Hradec Králové: Univerzita Hradec Králové, Filozofická fakulta, 2009.

NAKONEČNÝ, Milan. *Vlajka* [Flag]. Prague: Chvojkovo nakladatelství, 2001.

NĚMEC, Mirek. *Erziehung zum Staatsbürger? Deutsche Sekundarschulen in der Tschechoslowakei 1918–1938.* Essen: Klartext Verlag, 2010.

Odpověď ministra spravedlnosti na interpelaci poslanců Paška, Pešáka, V. Davida a Koštejna (tisk 485) ve věci protiprávního postupu krajského soudu v Kutné Hoře [Response from the Minister of Justice to the questions by Deputies Pašek, Pešák, V. David and Koštejn (print 485) relating to unlawful action by the Regional Court in Kutná Hora]. [online]. [accessed 2017-11-28]. Available at: http://www.psp.cz/eknih/1946uns/tisky/t0634_00.htm.

PACNER, Karel. *Československo ve zvláštních službách: Pohledy do historie československých výzvědných služeb 1914–1989, díl II 1939–1945* [Czechoslovakia in the special services: Perspectives on the history of Czechoslovak intelligence services 1914–1989, part II 1939–1945]. Prague: Themis, 2002.

PÁNEK, Jaroslav, and Oldřich TŮMA (eds.) *A History of the Czech Lands.* Prague: Karolinum, 2009.

PEJČOCH, Ivo. *Osud generála, který se v osudných chvílích přidal na špatnou stranu* [The fate of a general who in fateful moments took the wrong side]. [online]. 2012 [accessed 2017-11-28]. Avail-

able at: http://www.vhu.cz/osud-generala-ktery-se-v-osudnych-chvilich-pridal-na-spatnou
-stranu/.

PERNES, Jiří. "Establishment and First Crisis of the Communist Regime in Czechoslovakia
(1948–1958)." In *A History of the Czech Lands*, edited by Jaroslav Pánek, and Oldřich Tůma.
Prague: Karolinum, 2009.

PETRŮV, Helena. *Zákonné bezpráví* [Legal Injustice]. Prague: Auditorium, 2011.

RADVANOVSKÝ, Zdeněk. "The Transfer of Czechoslovakia's Germans and its Impact in the Border Region after the Second World War." In *Czechoslovakia in a Nationalist and Fascist Europe,
1918–1948*, edited by Mark Cornwall, and Robert John Weston Evans, Oxford: Oxford University Press and British Academy, 2007.

ROTHKIRCHEN, Livia. *The Jews of Bohemia and Moravia: Facing the Holocaust*. Lincoln: University of Nebraska Press, 2006.

ŘEHULOVÁ, Lenka. *Profesionální etika advokáta a kárné řízení jako důsledek porušení povinností
advokáta v podmínkách právní úpravy České republiky* [Barristers' Professional Ethics and Disciplinary Proceedings as the Result of Breaching One's Duties as a Barrister in the Law of the
Czech Republic]. Dissertation. PF MU. Brno, 2012/2013.

Richard Bienert. [online]. [accessed 2017-11-28]. Available at: http://www.vlada.cz/cz/clenove
-vlady/historie-minulych-vlad/rejstrik-predsedu-vlad/richard-bienert-440/.

SLÁDEK, Milan. *Němci v Čechách. Německá menšina v Českých zemích a Československu 1848–1946*
[Germans in the Czech lands. The German minority in the Czech lands and Czechoslovakia
1848–1946]. Prague: PRAGMA, 2002.

SLAVÍK, Ivan. "Kdo byl Chrysostom Mastík? [Who was Chrysostom Mastík?]," *Box 3* (1993),
pp. 130–131.

Statistická příručka království Českého. [A Statistical Handbook to the Bohemian Kingdom]. 2. ed.
Prague: Zemská statistická kancelář království Českého, 1913.

SUK, Ivan. *Reportáž o Norimberku: 1945–1946* [A report about Nuremberg: 1945–1946]. Prague:
Nová osvěta, 1946.

TOMÁŠEK, Dušan, and Robert KVAČEK. *Obžalována je vláda* [The government is prosecuted].
Ed. 1, Prague: Themis, 1999.

TÓTH, Andrej, Lukáš NOVOTNÝ, and Michal STEHLÍK. *Národnostní menšiny v Československu
1918–1938: od státu národního ke státu národnostnímu* [National minorities in Czechoslovakia
1918–1938: From a national state to an ethnic state]. Prague: Univerzita Karlova v Praze, Filozofická fakulta, and TOCGA, 2012.

TUNYS, Ladislav. *Noc před popravou. K. H. Frank a jeho obhájce* [The night before the execution.
K. H. Frank and his defence counsel]. Prague: Nakladatelství J&J, 1995.

VESELÁ, Renata. *Rodinné právo v době protektorátu* [Family law in the protectorate]. [online].
2010 [accessed 2017-11-28]. Available at: http://www.law.muni.cz/sborniky/dny_prava_2010
/files/prispevky/08_promeny/Vesela_Renata_(4462).pdf.

VESELÝ, Pravoslav. A. *Omladina a pokrokové hnutí: trochu historie a trochu vzpomínek* [The Youth
and Progressive Movements: a little history and a few memories]. Prague, 1902.

VYKOUPIL, Libor. *Jiří Stříbrný: portrét politika* [Jiří Stříbrný: Portrait of a politician]. 1st. ed.
Brno: Masarykova univerzita, 2003, p. 220 ff. Available online at: http://digilib.phil.muni.cz
/handle/11222.digilib/103757.

VÝKUSA, Karel. *Zpověď K. H. Franka* [K. H. Frank's confession]. Prague: Cíl, March 1946.

ZAJÍČEK, Karel (ed.) .*Český národ soudí K. H. Franka* [The Czech nation tries K. H. Frank]. Prague:
Ministerstvo informací, 1947.

ŽAMBERSKÁ, Jana. *Retribuční soudnictví – Mimořádný lidový soud v Plzni* [Retributional justice –
The extraordinary people's court in Pilsen]. Pilsen, 2010, Dissertation. Západočeská univerzita v Plzni. Fakulta filozofická.

Žatec ve třetím odboji. Odbojová skupina Praha Žatec [Žatec in the third resistance. The Prague–
Žatec Resistance Group]. [online]. [accessed 2017-11-28], p. 8. Available at: http://www
.ustrcr.cz/data/pdf/vystavy/zatec-30dboj/panely.pdf.

NEWSPAPERS AND MAGAZINES

České slovo, 25 March 1936
Dikobraz, 17 April 1946
Dikobraz, 30 April 1946
Dnešek, vol. II, no. 9
Expres, 15 April 1936
Jiskra, 22 February 1946
Lidové noviny, 30 April 1994
Mladá fronta, 28 April 1956
Mladá fronta, 3 July 1956
My, 21 June 1947
Národní listy Večerník, 11 January 1932
Národní listy Večerník, 21 April 1933
Národní listy, 24 March 1936
Národní osvobození, 13 March 1936
Národní politika, 13 March 1936
Pondělní ranní noviny, 24 October 1938
Právo lidu, 10 October 1938
Právo lidu, 25 December 1946
Právo lidu, 25 December 1947
Práce, 23 March 1946
Rakovnické listy, vol. II, nos. 43, 44, 45
Rudé právo, 18 January 1946
Rudé právo, 19 January 1946
Rudé právo, 22 January 1946
Rudé právo, 16 March 1947
Rudé právo, 12 October 1954
Svět práce, 8 May 1946
Svobodné slovo, 16 January 1946
Svobodné slovo, 17 January 1947
Svobodné slovo, 19 April 1947
Svobodné noviny, 22 January 1946
Telegram, 16 March 1936
Telegraf, 26 June 1936
Večerní České slovo, 24 June 1936

ARCHIVES AND FONDS

The abbreviations used to refer to these archival sources in the footnotes to the text are given in brackets.

Archiv České advokátní komory, fond JUDr. Kamill Resler [Archives of the Czech Bar Association, fonds: JUDr. Kamill Resler] (ČAK)
Archiv Hlavního Města Praha, fond Resler Kamil JUDr., Archivní soubor 1702,
nezpracovaný [Prague City Archives, fonds: Resler Kamil JUDr., Archivní soubor 1702, unprocessed] (AHMP)
Archiv Národního muzea, fond Resler Kamill [Archives of the National Museum, fonds: Resler Kamill] (NM)
Archiv Univerzity Karlovy, Akademický senát, inv. č. 3406, „Výhody pro studenty-vojáky,"
sign. 86, č. kartonu 233 [Archive of Charles University] (AUK)
Literární archiv Památníku národního písemnictví, fond Resler Kamil [Literary Archive of the Museum of Czech Literature, fonds: Resler Kamil] (PNP)

Národní muzeum – Knihovna Národního muzea, fond Nakladatelství Kamil Resler [National
Museum – Library of the National Museum, fonds: Nakladatelství Kamil Resler] (KNM)
Vojenský ústřední archiv, Vojenský historický archiv, fond Kamill Resler, kmenový list,
kvalifikační listina [Central Military Archive, Military History Archive, fonds: Kamill Resler,
kmenový list, kvalifikační listina] (VHA)
Východočeské muzeum v Pardubicích, fond Pardubický Slavín II./61 [East Bohemian Museum
in Pardubice, fonds: Pardubický Slavín II./61] (VCM)

RESLER'S MAJOR PUBLICATIONS[457]

RESLER, Kamill. *Codex mejdanensis. Pravidla, zákony a řády rytířského mejdánu v březnu 1920 Pánu
herny ku poctě dobře sesazené*, Prague: Rytířstvo mejdánské, 1931.
RESLER, Kamill. *Hlas v hluku zalehlý. 1936–1938.* Prague: Karel Dyrynk, 1938.
RESLER, Kamill (ed.). *Zemříti pod praporem! Zpěvy ze září 1938.* Prague: J. Picka, 1938.
RESLER, Kamill. *Grafik Rajon, říjen 1905, + červen 1940.* Prague: Mirro Pegrassi, 1940.
RESLER, Kamill, and Karel JÁNSKÝ. *Padesát let Karla Janského.* Prague: Klub nakladatelů Kmen,
1941.
RESLER, Kamill. *Michael Kácha, průkopník krásné české knihy.* Prague: Tiskárna Protektorátu Čechy a Morava, 1941.
RESLER, Kamill. *Původská práva po Jaroslavu Vrchlickém. 1912–1942.* Prague: Typus, 1942.
RESLER, Kamill. "Josef Florian zemřel před rokem (29. 12. 1941): Jan Konůpek pro Starou Říši
a o Staré Říši." In: Marginálie, vol. 16 (1942).
RESLER, Kamill. "Obnova lidového soudnictví v Českých zemích." *Právní prakse,* vol. XII (1948),
p. 55–66.
RESLER, Kamill. "Usnášení Mimořádných lidových soudů v Českých zemích." *Právní prakse,*
vol. XII (1948), p. 144–149.
RESLER, Kamill (ed.). *Básně na oslavu právních věcí, které projednával JUDr. Kamill Resler, právní
zástupce a obhájce v trestních věcech, zástupce chudých a obhájce z povinnosti atd.* Prague: Kamill
Resler, January 1948.
RESLER, Kamill. *Sborník na památku Karla Dyrynka, knihtiskaře, tvůrce písem, knihomila a člověka.*
Prague: Československý spisovatel, 1951.
RESLER, Kamill. "Knihomilství a jeho poslání." *Literární noviny,* no. 1 (1951), also PNP 73.
RESLER, Kamill, *Buřiči. Stříbrný vítr.* Published in the edition of Křižovatky díla Fráni Šrámka,
Prague: Československý spisovatel, 1952.
RESLER Kamill. "Vzdor Antonína Boučka." *Nový život, měsíčník Svazu čs. spisovatelů,* no. 8 (1954),
p. 185–187.
RESLER, Kamill. "České a slovenské překlady Internacionály." Česká literatura II., no. 2, 1954,
p. 189–192.
RESLER, Kamill, and Karel Čechák, *Kytičky na hrob malé paní: k uctění památky Erny Jánské
k 1. výročí její smrti.* Prague: 1954.
RESLER, Kamill, and Jaroslav Picka,. *Spolek českých bibliofilů Methodu Kalábovi k 70. narozeninám,* Prague: Československý spisovatel, 1955.
RESLER, Kamill, and Jan ČERVENKA. *Stará zvonice.* Prague: J. Picka, 1958.
RESLER, Kamill. "Vzpomínky na vzpomínky na kavárnu Union." In *Kavárna Union,* edited by
Adolf Hoffmeister, Prague: Nakladatelství československých výtvarných umělců, 1958.

457 A complete list of Resler's publications is available in the National Museum archives.

MAGAZINES AND ANTHOLOGIES TO WHICH RESLER CONTRIBUTED[458]

Zprávy Spolku Českých Bibliofilů
Bibliofil
Marginálie
Okénko do dílny umělcovy
Knižní značka
Ročenka českých knihtiskařů
Vitrinka
Český bibliofil
Právní prakse
Typografie
Literární noviny
Kritický měsíčník
Nejmenší revue
Erotická revue
Česká advokacie
Rakovnické listy
Řád
Česká literatura
Kostnické Jiskry

---

458 The magazines are listed in order of the approximate number of articles that Resler published in each.

INDEX OF NAMES